POLITICS
WITHOUT
POWER

The Atherton Press Political Science Series

POLITICS WITHOUT POWER

The National Party Committees

Cornelius P. Cotter and Bernard C. Hennessy

ATHERTON PRESS

A Division of Prentice-Hall, Inc.

70 Fifth Avenue

New York 10011   1964

POLITICS WITHOUT POWER
The National Party Committees

Cornelius P. Cotter and Bernard C. Hennessy

Preface

A 1946 pamphlet issued by the Republican National Committee is titled "Your Staff at Republican Headquarters." On the cover is a lithograph of the building at 1337 Connecticut Avenue, N.W., which then housed the committee. The twenty-one pages of the pamphlet contain photographs, biographies, and job descriptions for the major staff members and positions. The organization of the committee would be familiar to those who know the present organization with its campaign, finance, labor, publicity, and women's divisions. But what chiefly strikes one about the pamphlet is its institutional look. It creates the impression of a durable institution with a past, a future, and some substance—a national party headquarters for a *national* party. But, despite its well-established and permanent look, as a party headquarters the Republican National Committee is incomprehensible to the foreign visitors who sometimes find their way to it. And, as we point out in Chapter 1, it is very much off the beaten path for the American tourist.

The national committees are bundles of paradoxes. They are our chief symbols of party government, our nearest approximation to party responsibility, the conservators of a national heritage of peaceful change in national politics and adminis- tration, substitutes for (rather than carriers of) party ideologies, and yet, withal, pretty much headless, drifting organizations. We repeat in the text the adage about the committees being the umbilical cords between national conventions. The very vagueness and lack of direction of their activities between presidential elections is one of the main sources of staff frustration. And, given a presidential nominee, the likelihood is, as we point out, that, unless he is the incumbent seeking re-election, he will bypass the resources available to him at the national committees in favor of his own campaign organization.

The picture is not pleasing to the responsible party government or the presidential-party advocates of reform. The fault is as much in the *ad hoc* nature of the American interest in politics as in anything else. That, and the prospect that any notable can make a lateral entry into the parties using the decentralized electoral machinery to create public support and win delegates in the primaries, makes it very difficult in- deed for national committee staffers of the party out of power to pre- dict who their next boss will be. The weakness of the position of titular head of the party worsens this condition.

Yet national committees of the two parties may become more than they are today. We hope that this study will help to focus attention on the national party committees and that they may in time become more useful instruments for responsibility in American politics.

The origins of this book are to be traced to our service as National Committee faculty fellows at the two national committees. Hennessy served with Chairman Paul Butler at the Democratic National Com- mittee in 1959, and Cotter with Chairmen Meade Alcorn and Thruston B. Morton at the Republican National Committee in 1959 and part of 1960. In the years that followed we have tried to keep close to de- velopments at the national committees.

Our purpose is simple: to tell who and what the national commit- tees are, where they are located in relation to other politically oriented organizations, what they do, and what modest steps might be taken to make better use of them. The purpose is simple, but the phenomena to be scrutinized are complex, embedded in history, evanescent, and al- ways on the verge of becoming something different. And this, perhaps, is the best reason for seeking to exert some small influence on their future development.

Academicians should read all of this book. Those from the political world might want to start with Chapter 3, although we are presumptuous enough to think that the first two chapters, admittedly somewhat duller than the rest, would not hurt even the old pros.

The distinguished newspaperwoman and author, Helen Hill Miller, deserves great credit and no blame for the development of this study. Acting as executive secretary to the Stern Family Fund, Mrs. Miller introduced the study prospect to the trustees of the Fund, headed by Mrs. Edgar Stern, Sr., who graciously provided support for it.

We hope that in our objectivity or our captiousness we have not offended our many friends at the two national committees. To the chairmen and staffs and to the National Committee faculty fellows who preceded and succeeded us, we are uniquely indebted, as we are to Rhoten Smith, director, and the trustees of the predecessor institution to the National Center for Education in Politics (NCEP), the Citizenship Clearing House, co-sponsor, with the national committees, of the fellowships.

Special thanks are due Ralph Goldman for giving us access to his excellent study of the national party chairmen and American politics and to Robert J. Huckshorn for his critical review of the manuscript at the penultimate stage of its preparation.

Particular and personal debts of gratitude are owed to a few persons who were especially helpful to us. These are Roger Davidson, Maureen Drummy, Roosevelt Ferguson, George Heneghan, Erna Hennessy, and Katherine O'Neil.

The following aided us in gathering data on national committee members: O. Webster Adams, Jr., Charles Backstrom, Donald Balmer, James Browne, John Calpin, Joseph Cerrell, H. Dicken Cherry, Morris W. H. Collins, Dorothy Cline, Wilder Crane, Manning Dauer, John De Grove, Paul Dolan, Alvin Dozeman, William Dunfey, William Farber, Robert Gilmour, Ralph Goldman, George Goodwin, Jean Graham, John Grumm, Royce Hanson, Donald Hayhurst, Donald Herzberg, Robert Horwitz, Mary Evelyn Huey, William Irwin, Dennis Jensen, Malcolm Jewell, Harold Jinks, Donald Johnson, Charles Jones, Conrad Joyner, Wendell Kay, Joseph Kelly, John Kessel, Karl Lamb, Louis Masotti, Nicholas Masters, Donald Matthews, Richard Murphy,

Robert McNeill, Karl O'Lessker, Arthur Peterson, James Robinson, Robert Salisbury, John Saloma, Olive Shadgett, William Shear, Edward Sherman, R. J. Snow, Frank Sorauf, Gerald Sorte, Robert Spencer, Donald Strong, Ralph Wade, John Wahlke, Philip Wilder, W. T. Wilkins, J. D. Williams, Richard Wires, and Sidney Wise.

Linda and Robert Crew, Rose Isom, and Pat Mewhinney were of particular help in the final stages of preparing the manuscript for publication.

Cornelius P. Cotter
Bernard C. Hennessy

Contents

1

What Are the National Party Committees?

When visitors come to Washington and see the Capitol, they step into Statuary Hall and queue to the right or left according to their choice of House or Senate galleries. They regard the Capitol, more than the White House or the Supreme Court, as the seat of American national government. The Capitol guides will carefully point out that the seats on the floor of the House are divided into two sections and that, when a representative on one side refers to "my honored and distinguished friend on the other side of the aisle," he is referring to a member of the other party. Party government is what we are said to enjoy in the United States. Every little boy or girl is born either a Democrat or a Republican. According to popular understanding, at any given time either the Republicans or the Democrats rule.

But it is doubtful that we enjoy a political system in which the people give elected office holders clear-cut mandates. In the forty-eight congresses between 1868 and 1962, only 69 per cent of the time has there even been a *possibility* of party government—that is,

1

times when the presidency and the Congress were controlled by the same party. Nevertheless, even in the remaining 31 per cent of the time, when we have had a president of one party and a majority of the other party in the House or Senate, we find it meaningful as well as convenient to say that in the United States there is something which can be termed party government. We find it meaningful because to some extent—if only in organizing the Congress—the parties influence the officers and shape the institutions within which national policies are made. And if responsible party government can be but an aspiration, it is, as such, a desirable one.

THE PEOPLE OF THE NATIONAL PARTY COMMITTEES

In September, 1959, a group of thirty political scientists gathered at a conference on American political parties. Some of the participants had been selected for their reputations as established experts on politics and parties; others were there because of special studies they had made of party organization or processes; the rest were bright young Ph.D.'s who had read almost all the literature about United States political parties.

One session of the conference was given to a discussion of the national party committees. Two of the four panelists had been members of the staff of the Democratic National Committee, and the other two had been members of the Republican National Committee staff.

After an hour and a half of learned discussion, a member of the group surprised himself and the others by blurting out, "This is all well and good and interesting, but you're not talking about the national committees!"

He was right. These experts were not talking about the national committees. They were talking about the chairmen and the staffs of the national committees, not about the national committee members as a collectivity. Indeed, very little has ever been said about the national committees as committees.

There are two kinds of written materials which are described as being about the national party committees. One is the inside dopester chronicle of the greats and the staffs of the greats: Michelson's *The Ghost Talks* and Redding's *Inside the Democratic Party* are the prototypes here.[1] The other kind of publicly available material on the com-

[1] Charles Michelson, *The Ghost Talks* (New York: G. P. Putnam's Sons, 1944); and Jack Redding, *Inside the Democratic Party* (Indianapolis: Bobbs

mittees is scholarly or journalistic. The scholarly output is very small in numbers of works: four chapters in one book,[2] three doctoral dissertations,[3] and a few papers presented at meetings of the American Political Science Association, plus some obscure articles in learned journals. An additional source of information about the national committees consists of popular articles by political columnists and newsmen.

The literature which purports to be about the national committees is mainly about the chairmen and the national staffs of the committees. It could hardly be otherwise, for the national committees themselves are large groups of people variously selected, representing different amounts and kinds of local political interests, who come together now and then to vote on matters of undifferentiated triviality or importance, about which they are largely uninformed and in which they are often uninterested.

This may appear to be a harsh or smart-aleck description of the national committees of the major American political parties. It is neither. There are many good reasons that the committees, as groups of committeemen and committeewomen, cannot be more significant bodies at this stage in the evolution of the American party system. The committee chairmen and national bureaucracy may be, and often are, people who have considerable personal and institutional influence. But the committees, as committees, are important mainly for what they will acquiesce in, rather than what they will propose or decide.

Professor Bone is quite straightforward in making the point: "The committee members themselves are hardly able to exercise any significant control over the chairman or the general headquarters staff." In a perceptive analogy, he compares the committee-staff relationship with that often obtained in large trade or professional groups.

> This situation is little different from that of the large
> interest groups whose houses of delegates or boards are

Merrill, 1958). Those who choose to may speculate why no ghost has talked from inside the Republican National Committee staff.

[2] Hugh A. Bone, *Party Committees and National Politics* (Seattle: University of Washington Press, 1958).

[3] Ralph M. Goldman, "Party Chairmen and Party Faction 1789–1900" (University of Chicago, 1951); Marie Chatham, "The Role of the National Party Chairmen from Hanna to Farley" (University of Maryland, 1953); and Bancroft C. Henderson, "The Democratic National Committee" (University of Minnesota, 1958).

also unable to oversee the details in the national office
bureaucracy.[4]

The national party committees are obscure, changeable, pragmatic, and hard to define, yet surprisingly permanent. Their character
can be attributed to the fitful nature of the interest which Americans
show in politics and to the extreme decentralization of American government and politics which drains power and resources from the center
to the periphery.

The national committees have been described as umbilical cords
between national conventions. They tie together the conventions in the
simple sense that they are elected by one convention and serve until
new members are elected by the next. We say they are elected. However, so diffuse is political power in the United States and so divergent
are the practices from one state to another that national committeemen
and -women are actually chosen under state law, sometimes in primary
elections, sometimes in state convention, and their "election" at the
national conventions constitutes no more than a ratification of earlier
choices.

The national committees consist of a national committeeman and
a national committeewoman from each state, the District of Columbia,
Puerto Rico, the Virgin Islands, and (in the Democratic Party) the
Canal Zone. In addition, since 1952 the chairman of the Republican
state central committee may, under certain conditions, be a member
of his national committee.

The members of the national committee assemble one to three
times a year in various cities around the country, Washington and Chicago being among the favorites, and on these occasions, in theory at
least, frame national committee policy and program. Also in theory the
national committees elect the national chairman, although in the presidential election years the candidate will select the chairman. When the
party has the presidency, the president will designate the chairman, but
under other circumstances it is more usual for the chairman's designation to result from a process of consent and compromise by party
leaders than for the choice to be made through open election by the
national committeemen and committeewomen. In other words, the
national committee plays more of a ratifying than a selecting role in
the choice of chairman, as in all other critical decisions.

At the national committee headquarters are to be found staffs

[4] Bone, *op. cit.*, p. 8.

which will vary greatly in size from time to time, according to the proximity of an off-year or a presidential election or according to budgetary considerations. The chairman of the national committee is not only a leader of a kind of party legislature, but also is the head of a small bureaucracy. Indeed, national committee policy and program will tend to be formulated by the staff and then proposed to and defended before the national chairman who will present it, as modified by him, to the executive committee of the national committee, or to his close advisers, and the full committee for ratification. Thus there is a good deal of realism in the tendency, when speaking of the national committee, to be thinking of the national committee chairman and staff. This is not to underestimate the importance and the influence of individual national committeemen and committeewomen, some of whom are very high-ranking leaders in their states, but it is to suggest that the national chairman and his staff are, or may be, visible nationally when the members are not.

THE HEADQUARTERS OF THE COMMITTEES

Tourists rarely find time to visit the headquarters of the parties which provide us with such party government as we have. Were they to do so, they would find the Republican National Committee in the Cafritz Building, 1625 I (the letter "I," often spelled "eye") Street, N.W. Unheralded by so much as a plaque outside the building, the national committee occupies the second floor and shares space in the building with security brokers, insurance offices, lawyers, and office furniture firms.

The offices of the Democratic National Committee, located sufficiently nearby that staffers from both committees frequent the same luncheon and watering spots, are generally similar to those of the Republicans. The Democrats, too, are renters in a city where many lesser political groups have their own grand and imposing buildings.

The Democratic National Committee once owned a building, and the story of this property-holding is worth a summary telling, if only because it dramatizes a certain unreal quality about the national party committees. In early 1950 some friends of Chairman William Boyle, including Richard C. Patterson, a former ambassador and party contributor, and Turney Gratz, assistant to the chairman, proposed the purchase of a four-story building at 1733–35 De Sales Street as a permanent headquarters for the committee. Because the committee as a committee had no identifiable legal status—being merely a group of people with some rules and officers—it was thought wise to have the deed in Patterson's name. Accordingly, an elaborate system of notes and loans and bank arrangements was worked out to raise the purchase price of $100,000. Chairman Boyle's comments, when he asked the committee to approve his actions, illustrate the complexity and unwieldiness of the national committees in the legal sense:

> As you well know, such a transaction is very involved legally. We cannot, of course, hold and operate anything for profit, so the thing comes to this: We have to do something about the building. If, under the law, we could find that we could lease it and hold it until such time as we could obtain the materials, then it would be the idea that we might fix it up and move. It is right across from the Mayflower, a very good location.[5]

The building needed extensive repair and remodeling. Materials were not available because of Korean War shortages and restrictions. The building was sold in 1952, and the proceeds were less than the outstanding obligations. Aside from some fringe fees to lawyers and bankers, the Democratic Committee's own-your-own-home campaign was a flop for everyone. Turney Gratz later became a realtor; his experience with the De Sales Street purchase no doubt gave him some hints about what not to do in that business.

The Republican National Committee has never owned its own building, although in 1950 serious consideration was given to the purchase of a house at Sixteenth Street and Scott Circle, N.W., which at the time was occupied by the Republican Club. The argument was made that the "three national committees"—the Congressional and the Senatorial Campaign Committee and the RNC—should be housed under one roof.

For many years the offices of the Democratic National Committee moved back and forth between Washington and New York as the convenience of the chairman, its tasks, or its finances required. Chairmen John Raskob, James A. Farley, and Edward J. Flynn had interests in New York which made it easy for national committee

---

[5] *Official Report of the Proceedings of the Democratic National Convention, Chicago, Ill., July 21 to July 26, inclusive, 1952* (Washington, D.C.: Democratic National Committee, 1952), p. 619. Hereafter convention proceedings will be cited as *Democratic* (or *Republican*) *Proceedings* and year.

people and activities to be transferred from Washington to New York's Biltmore Hotel or Empire State Building.[6]

Since the middle 1930's, the Democratic National Committee, in its contracted stage during the latency period of the four-year cycle, has maintained its sole offices in Washington. The DNC has been located at various times in the National Press Building, the Mayflower Hotel, and office buildings on Eighteenth Street and on Connecticut Avenue. It is now to be found in the Riddell Building, 1730 K Street, N.W.

When the RNC's longest-term staff member first came to the committee in 1928, its offices were in the Barr Building on Seventeenth Street, N.W. During this period the Research Division of the national committee was located at 718 Jackson Place (adjacent to the Brookings Institution). Subsequently the full committee staff joined the Research Division, taking over the entire building above the first floor. With the advent of John Hamilton as chairman in 1936, the staff expanded to the point that a fifth floor was added to the building. Thereafter, 718 Jackson was sold to the American Federation of Labor (which, with the merged Congress of Industrial Organizations, today occupies an imposing edifice diagonally across Lafayette Park from 718), and the RNC staff moved into an old house on Connecticut Avenue. From there the committee, in its wanderings, took itself to Fifteenth Street near K, thence to the Washington Hotel, where most of the staff were accommodated during the 1952 campaign. Finally, with the affluence which accompanies a presidential victory—its first in twenty-four years—the committee took offices on the second floor of the Cafritz Building, 1625 I Street, N.W. Like the Democratic National Committee, its peregrinations over the years have been many but have never taken it more than a few blocks distance from the White House.

This brief account of the homelessness of the two national party committees dramatizes the fact that the committees are not felt to have much permanence, stability, or institutional importance. If we

[6] Raskob had a large financial interest in the Empire State Building, and one infers from Michelson's account that much unrented space was cheaply or freely available to the DNC during the early years of that architectural wonder. Michelson, *op. cit.* The Biltmore Hotel was for many years *the* Democratic hotel in New York, site of the New York city and state committee headquarters and from time to time (most lately in 1948) general headquarters for the presidential campaign.

regarded our parties with anything like the respect and seriousness
the British show for theirs, it is difficult to believe that the two national committees would be renters in obscure buildings amid the
splendid structures which house the lobbying activities of labor and
industry.

CORE FUNCTIONS OF THE NATIONAL COMMITTEES

A major purpose of the national committee is to survive. This
may seem to be a trite and flippant statement, and the purpose un-
worthy, but consider that, at election time in the United States,
groups and individuals come together in association almost as acci-
dentally and irrationally as molecules of gas come together in a chamber. The results of the multilayered local, state, and national elections
are determined in large part by the effectiveness of the ephemeral relationships which are built up by hundreds of thousands of separate
and discrete campaign organizations. In surviving between the four-
year presidential elections, the national committee, perhaps especially
the staff, provides a vehicle for continuity and for funding experience
to ensure that it will not be necessary to start from the beginning in
every presidential election. The national committee staffs constitute
nuclei around which or from which full-fledged campaign organizations can be built.

In this sense, it is a function of the national committees to survive in the years between presidential elections. In a presidential year,
it is a function of the national committees to stage impressive conventions and to provide—if the candidate and his advisers will accept
it—some management for the campaign. In off-year congressional
elections it has increasingly become a function of the national committees, with the Congressional Campaign Committees and the Senatorial Campaign Committees, to maximize the number of party victories in the House and Senate contests.

A real question can be raised whether the national committee
offices constitute the national headquarters for the two parties. In
thinking of the national committee as the national headquarters for
the party, we must keep in mind the fact that the Congressional
Campaign Committee is the national campaign organization for each
of the parties in the House and that the Senatorial Campaign Committee for each party serves a like function in the Senate. Hence it is
not accurate to suggest that the national committees provide the *only*
national headquarters for the party; the Hill party committees are

free, independent, and, at least for some purposes, equal. These committees, tracing their origins to the post-Civil War conflict between the presidential and congressional factions of the Republican Party, are exclusively concerned with electing their partisans to the Senate and the House.

Although we shall refer to relationships between the national committees and the Hill committees in various contexts, our focus is the former. The Hill committees are separately treated in Hugh Bone's *Party Committees and National Politics*[7] and are the subject of comment in the recent study by Charles L. Clapp, *The Congressman: His Work as He Sees It.*[8] All who have been close to the scene agree that a latent hostility exists between the denizens of Capitol Hill and those of the downtown national committees. This is confirmed by Bone and Clapp.

Much responsibility for this conflict can be attributed to misunderstanding and inadequate communication between the party committees of each party. The varying nature of the constituencies of the Hill and the downtown committees produces inevitable competition and some hostility. The campaign committees on the Hill are very cognizant of being constantly up against the gun. There is always an election that has just passed or is just coming. The national committees' concern with quadrennial conventions and presidential elections enables their staffs (in the eyes of many congressmen and congressional staffers) to live in comfortable isolation from the realities of politics. Concerned with national public relations, party image-making, and presidential politics, the national committees, again in the eyes of those on the Hill, eat up party funds which could better be employed in congressional elections and eat them up with no discernible electoral profit to the party.

Such generalizations are dangerous, however. The Republican Congressional Campaign Committee, being the best heeled, most amply staffed of the four Senate and House campaign committees, performs services for Republicans for which Democrats must look to their national committee. In each party, the three committees are becoming more and more cooperative in fund-raising and allocation of funds among the committees. On the Republican side a succession of chairmen drafted from Congress and the movement of some Congressional Committee staff to the Republican National Committee have helped

[7] *Op. cit.,* chaps. 5 and 6.
[8] (Washington, D.C.: Brookings Institution, 1963), pp. 354–366.

open the avenues of communication and create a sense of mutual benefit between these groups. Finally, each national committee is participating in special and mid-term congressional elections to an increasing
extent, a practice which gives promise of welding the congressional
and presidential party apparatus more closely together.

But, although the three committees cooperate with each other—
sometimes sporadically and reluctantly—the national committees stage
the national conventions and supposedly manage the presidential campaign. It is therefore not wholly misleading to call the national committees the national party headquarters, bearing in mind that the
three committees collectively comprise the permanent "standing" national party apparatus. At the Republican National Committee it has
recently become popular to refer to "the three national committees,"
suggesting coordinate status. A succession of national chairmen selected
from the Senate and House may have influenced this trend.

Just as the national committees do not comprise single and simple
national headquarters, so, too, the national committees may not be the
headquarters for parties that are national. This is a way of pointing
out that a total of over six thousand county committees, together with
more than one hundred state and territorial committees (and a few
active congressional district committees), share with the national committees the responsibility of winning elections. It is only as these thousands of party groups perform with energy and zeal and as the hundreds of thousands of precinct organizations which are the platoon
strength of the two parties get people registered and turned out to
vote that local, state, and national electoral victories can be recorded.
It is because of the constituency orientation of American politicians
and because of the extremely local and frequently parochial nature of
the constituency that students of American politics are inclined to
suggest that we do not have two national parties but rather a myriad
of state, local, and national parties which occasionally find it convenient, and all too frequently find it inconvenient, to come together
under the umbrella of the national party whose designation they regularly employ.

Aside from the questions of whether they constitute national headquarters for national parties, it is also true that the national committees of the two major parties are not real agencies like the House of
Representatives, the Bureau of the Budget, or a county highway department. Unlike most of the other governmental units and agencies
which social scientists set themselves to describe or explain, the national

party committees have little identifiable and definable being. They are not embedded in the law. They do not display those patterned and regular interactions among persons and roles which sociologists find in groups such as the family, organizations like the YMCA, or associations like the AFL-CIO. The national party committees are, in some ways, "non-things."

The national committees are quasi-public groups, part of the political system, but not easily or usefully analyzed as discrete units.[9] The national party system, as a subsystem of the American political system, is, to use an anatomical analogy, rather like the lymphatic apparatus as contrasted with the more wholly self-contained parts such as the heart, the muscles, or the lungs. The entire body politic would suffer—indeed, die—without some processes for doing the work of political parties. Yet the forms and devices by which this work is accomplished defy generalization and regularity.

To inquire meaningfully about the national party committees demands a consideration of what the committees do (in addition to what their organization looks like inside and outside) in the political party system, which is the energizing subsystem of the total political system. We need something akin to the organism-in-the-environment approach. It is a group-in-the-systems approach. We try to view widely the formal and informal interactions of committee officers, members, and staff with other politically important individuals and groups, successively focusing, after some preliminary stage-setting, on the members, the officers (mainly the chairmen), and the staffs. We then consider the activities of the national committee (members, officers, and staff) and finally indulge in some speculation about likely and/or desirable developments.

[9] Fenno found that the president's cabinet is another "non-thing" like the national committees, an amorphous collection of customary and *ad hoc* arrangements with "a great multiplicity of external relationships which are not in the first instance matters of its internal characteristics," but which "so heavily condition cabinet behavior that ultimately the cabinet must be understood as part of what might be called the entire governmental process." Richard F. Fenno, Jr., *The President's Cabinet* (New York: Vintage Books, 1958), p. 6.

2

Development and Organization of the National Party Committees

The first permanent national committee was created by the 1848 Democratic presidential nominating convention in Baltimore. Before the convention of 1848 there had been a few interstate presidential campaign committees of uncertain membership, brief duration, and unknown effectiveness. Even earlier, committees of correspondence, a preorganizational device presumably as old as written politics, had been used to bind together in loose networks of communication and encouragement the scattered partisans of candidate or faction.[1]

[1] Some imaginative historians have traced the origin of the national committees as far back as 1804. See *Democratic Proceedings 1948* (Washington: Judd & Detweiler, Inc., n.d.), p. 516; and Henry Minor, *The Story of the Democratic Party* (New York: Macmillan Co., 1928), p. 47. The use of a nationwide coordinating committee in 1812 was noted in Gordon S. P. Kleeberg, *The Formation of the Republican Party* (New York: Moods Publishing Co., 1911), p. 192. See also Frank R. Kent, *The Democratic Party: A History* (New York: Century Co., 1928), p. 112; and Paul T. David, Ralph M. Goldman, and Richard C. Bain, *The Politics of National Party Conventions* (Washington, D.C.: Brookings Institution, 1959), p. 18.

The development of a national party system between 1820 and 1860 required among other things the growth of agencies which could claim to be representative of the whole country. The national committees of the parties were created to perform three national tasks— the organization and direction of the presidential campaign, the promulgation of the Call for the next convention, and the arrangement of the physical details of the convention.[2]

The 1848 Democratic National Convention adopted the following motion and thereby established several lasting precedents:

> Ordered, That a committee of one from each state, to be named by the respective delegations, be appointed to promote the Democratic cause, with power to fill vacancies, and to be designated "The Democratic National Committee."[3]

The most notable precedent is that of equal state representation. State control over the appointment of committee members recognized the federal nature of party organization. "To promote the Democratic cause" makes the committee primarily a campaign committee. Because the convention creates the national committee by naming its members, the terms of office for members of the national committee are set at four years or until the next convention. The clause, "with power to fill vacancies," gives authority to replace members who resign or die between conventions; if one of the convention nominees resigned or died before the election, this clause might have been used by the committee to fill that vacancy, but this interpretation seems not to have been intended.

The national committee created by the 1848 convention sent out the Call for the convention of 1852, thus establishing its status as the link between conventions. Since 1848 each convention has created a new committee. The Democratic National Committee has therefore been in continuous existence for 116 years.

Republicans, when they organized their party, had several prece-

---

[2] "Prior to the organization of the National Committee, conventions were called by the Democratic members of the New Hampshire Legislature." *Cannon's Manual 1960*, p. 3. (The proper title is *Democratic Manual for the Democratic National Convention*, published every four years by the Democratic National Committee, but it is always called *Cannon's Manual* because it was compiled by Rep. Clarence Cannon.)

[3] Quoted in *Democratic Proceedings 1948, op. cit.*, p. 518. See also Chatham, *op. cit.*, p. 17.

dents to guide them. The use and value of committees of correspondence, central committees, and the national committees of the Democratic and Whig parties were clearly recognized.

Before the creation of the Republican Party, the Whigs had used committees of correspondence and *ad hoc* campaign committees in the elections of 1844, 1848, and 1852.[4] The Whigs and the Know Nothings, like the Anti-Masons before them, were experienced in the use of those devices for promoting intraparty equality and harmony.[5]

The convention method of nomination and the federal nature of the electoral system forced national campaigners to use interstate committees. Nomination by caucus had allowed the selection of the nominee far in advance of the election. The Tennessee legislature, for example, had "nominated" Andrew Jackson in October, 1825, giving him and his supporters three years to campaign for the race in 1828. But the conventions, after the first few of both parties, were uniformly held in the year of the elections. Partisans of the nominee were thus required quickly to create (or to have in being) campaign machinery as representative as possible of all factions of their party. They could no longer, as in leisurely preconvention days, develop their campaign over two or three years before the election. In 1856 the new Republican Party, seeking immediate national victory, could not revert to antique and unpopular methods, but had to adopt the organizational structure of the established party.

Ripon, Wisconsin, is generally considered to be the birthplace of the Republican Party. It was at Ripon that the first recorded meeting of "Republicans" was held by Free Soilers, Whigs, and Democrats in a Congregational church on February 28, 1854. Similar clubs or associations were being organized throughout the North. A convention at Jackson, Michigan, which was held on July 6, 1854, adopted a platform and nominated a party ticket for the state.[6]

The immediate precursor of the Republican National Committee was an *ad hoc* group set up not to elect the candidate of an existing party, but to complete the task of bringing the new party into existence. Meeting in Pittsburgh in February, 1856, a "committee on national

---

[4] In their last national convention as a party (1852), the Whigs created a national committee with Samuel Vinton as chairman. *Ibid.*, p. 4.

[5] For the Know Nothings' Council in the 1850's, see Jesse Macy, *Political Parties in the United States 1846–1861* (New York: Macmillan Co., 1900), p. 225.

[6] *The History of the Republican Party 1854–1962* (Washington, D.C.: Republican National Committee, 1962), pp. 7–9.

organization" recommended the appointment of a "national executive committee" to consist of one member from each state.[7] Edwin D. Morgan, a wealthy New York merchant, became chairman of the Executive Committee. The committee was authorized to add a member from each state not represented at the Pittsburgh convention and to fill vacancies. Meeting at the Willard Hotel in Washington on March 27, 1856, it issued a formal Call for the first Republican national nominating convention to be held in Philadelphia on June 17, 1856. The Call and some arrangements for the Philadelphia convention were the only formal acts of the group.

The predecessor of the present Republican National Committee was finally created on the second day of the Philadelphia nominating convention. Edwin D. Morgan of New York, previous chairman of the Executive Committee, who called the convention to order, was elected chairman of the first Republican National Committee. The committee was given authority to decide where the next national convention would be held.[8] This committee served for four years.

THE NATIONAL COMMITTEES AND THE LAW

Political parties are wholly without constitutional basis, products of slow evolution, trial and error, tradition, and use. Even now, after more than one hundred and sixty years of experience, the party system is nearly untouched by federal laws. As a people we have come to terms with the existence of parties, but we resist the temptation to national regulation of their operations. At the state level there are many laws governing political party activity, but many gaps and much inconsistency exist.

The national committees were created not to institutionalize a theory or from any impulse of good or evil, but simply to do a job. At first mere *ad hoc* arrangements, they are still to a large degree creations of unclear dimensions and uncertain traditions. As some of the activities of the national committees became more regularized, often in the context of the major political battles of the past hundred years, the forms of organization also became more regularized—but not through federal statutes. Even today committee action and the behavior of chairman and staff are free from any except bothersome legal regulation. The so-called Corrupt Practices Acts and other legislation relating to party financing—notably the acts of 1907, 1935, and 1943

[7] Kleeberg, *op. cit.,* p. 195.
[8] *Republican Proceedings 1856, 1860, 1864,* p. 42.

barring banks, other corporations, and labor unions from contributing to party committees and/or candidates for certain offices—are the only items of federal legislation which bear directly on the operations of the national committees. In practice, these statutes are not regulations but harassments; they complicate much but prevent nothing. They not only allow, but almost compel, good men to violate them daily.

The national committees of the American political parties are not mentioned by name in the statutes of the United States government. Ample constitutional basis exists for extensive regulation of national party activity. Articles I and II of the United States Constitution abound with pegs on which even the most strict-constructionist federal judge would allow regulatory laws to be hung. It is as true today as it was in 1920 that

> . . . Congress might provide for federal supervision of all elections, primary, general, and special, relating to nomination and election to office under the Constitution and laws of the United States, and provide for enforcement thereof by mandamus, or any other suitable remedy, but it has not done so.[9]

Federal statutes purporting to prevent "corrupt practices" apply to any political committee which "accepts contributions and makes expenditures for the purpose of influencing or attempting to influence the election of candidates for presidential or vice-presidential electors."[10] Every such political committee is required to have a chairman and a treasurer, the treasurer being charged with keeping certain records pertaining to the acceptance of contributions and the disbursement of funds. Of the implications of these acts (1910, 1925, 1939, and 1940) for the financial operations of the national committees, more will be said subsequently. Here we need only note that, in addition to financial regulation, these acts forbid the publication and distribution of anonymous campaign literature. The sum of federal regulation of political parties comes, then, to this: a few badly drawn and ineffective laws relating to political financing and one simple statute forbidding anonymous literature.

Many state statutes are of indirect importance to the national committees. The selection of committee members—technically, the nomination of members—is in some states regulated by law, as it is in

[9] *In re Higdon* (D. C. Mo. 1920) 269 F. 152.
[10] U.S. Code, Title 2, chap. 8, § 241.

Oregon, Florida, and Alaska, where members are chosen in primary elections. Other state statutes relating to campaign practices, for example, or the certification of delegates to the national conventions may from time to time have an important bearing on national committee functions. But by and large the national committees are free to conduct their business quite unhampered by state regulations.

Moreover, there is some precedent for the view that the national committees may safely ignore state law when there is sufficient incentive to do so. Consider the Call to the 1928 convention issued by the Republican National Committee on December 7, 1927. It declared that

> . . . no State law shall be observed which hinders, abridges or denies to any citizen of the United States eligible under the United States Constitution to the office of President or Vice-President the right or privilege of being a candidate under such state law for the nomination for President or Vice-President: or which authorizes the election of a number of Delegates or Alternates from any State to the National Convention different from that fixed in this call.[11]

As the Republican convention—and the Republican National Committee when acting under convention mandate—will not be bound by state laws contrary to its own rules, neither will it be bound by state party rules and practices. National supremacy was established early and well. In 1860 the convention rejected the contention of the Maryland delegation that its state convention had bound it to the use of the unit rule.[12] Again in 1876 the issue arose over the state instructions to the Pennsylvania delegation to vote as a unit. The question, boldly put by one delegate, was

> . . . whether the state of Pennsylvania shall make rules and laws for this convention, or whether this convention is supreme and shall make its own laws. This convention is a supreme body. No state, no caucus, has a right to make its laws and bring them in here and say that they shall bind this convention. We are supreme; we are original; we stand here representing the great Republican party of this nation, and neither Pennsylvania, nor New York, nor any state,

---

[11] *Republican Proceedings 1928,* p. 11.
[12] *Republican Proceedings 1860,* pp. 150–151.

can come in here and bind us down with their caucus resolutions.[13]

Historically the Democrats have been more willing to bind their
conventions and their national committees to state party regulations.
Since 1860 Democratic conventions have tolerated the unit rule under
which, as Cannon forthrightly puts it, "a majority of the delegates
from a state may cast the entire vote of the state regardless of the
preference of the minority."[14]

When the state party organ (convention or committee) mandates
the unit rule, the Democratic National Convention not only binds itself to such a ruling, but in at least one case it has also refused to allow
a delegation to abandon the unit rule.

> The Michigan delegation, bound in 1952 by a unit rule
> through a routine and little-noticed action at the end of
> its state convention, attempted repeatedly to secure rulings
> permitting it to discard the rule, which had little support
> in the delegation itself.[15]

As with state party rulings, the Democratic Committee and convention seem more willing than their Republican counterparts to bind
themselves to state laws. In 1912, while the Republican convention
refused to accept a California law contrary to national party practice,
the Democratic convention, by a close vote, acquiesced in an Ohio law
although it could have enforced a conflicting Ohio state party convention ruling.[16]

In recent years each party convention and party committee has
accepted responsibility for carrying out state laws and state party
mandates which are relatively unambiguous and which bring with
them no great national party divisions. Where the national organs find
it necessary to interpret ambiguous situations of law and fact in the
context of rival state factions and factional claims, they reserve the
right to make final determination.

There is, presently, in both parties at the national level a presumption in favor of acknowledging and enforcing state law when appli-
cable and state party rules in the absence of state law. When conflicts

[13] *Republican Proceedings 1876,* pp. 97–98.
[14] *Cannon's Manual 1960,* p. 49.
[15] David, Goldman, and Bain, *op. cit.,* p. 202. The authors of this volume
note that Michigan abandoned the unit rule before the 1956 convention.
[16] *Democratic Proceedings 1912,* pp. 59–76.

arise, however, a national supremacy is claimed and exercised, the national body choosing which of the conflicting arguments of law and party rules to accept and apply.[17] As long as the laws and courts of the United States resist the regulation of party activities and groups, the national committees will be free to exercise this discretion and this ultimate national supremacy.

REPRESENTATION ON THE NATIONAL COMMITTEES

As the convention system of presidential nomination demanded a ready campaign organization capable of quickly launching the electioneering machinery, so federalism and the electoral system required equality of membership for the national committees. One member from each state was simple, certain, and practical. After the act of 1845 established a uniform date for the selection of presidential electors in each state, the campaigns had to be conducted simultaneously almost everywhere. The friends of the candidates could no longer travel from state to state campaigning among the electorate or bargaining with state legislatures. The campaigns had to be conducted in each state by the regular party leaders of the state.

It was presumably this element of simultaneous campaigning, plus a Western fear that the older states would have undue influence on the national committee, that induced Sen. Jesse D. Bright of Indiana, in the convention of 1848, to insist on an amendment establishing a Democratic national committee of one member from each state instead of the original motion for fifteen chosen by the chair. In 1856 the Republicans adopted the equal representation rule without considering any other possibilities. In 1920 the Democrats, and in 1924 the Republicans, expanded representation on their national (and other) committees, to include women—a logical concession to the Nineteenth Amendment—but they retained the principle of equal representation. The Republicans, for whom the South had become a rotten borough in presidential nominating conventions, had successive difficulties bred of the manipulation of the Southern delegations but did nothing to-

---

[17] Note, for example, the 1952 Republican convention fight over rival Georgia delegations. The minority argument in the Credentials Committee was nominally based on the view that a lower state court ruling in favor of the minority's rivals should not be binding as long as it was on appeal. In the end the acceptance of the minority report had little to do with the laws or courts of Georgia; it was the key test vote of the convention by which the Eisenhower majority of convention delegates overturned the Taft majority of national committee members. *Republican Proceedings 1952*, pp. 164–195.

ward moderating the principle of equal representation until after the nomination of Eisenhower at the 1952 convention.

At the 1952 convention the Eisenhower forces won in spite of the committee's equal representation rule. They took advantage of their majority to change the balance of power in the national committee by adding to it the state chairman of sure Republican states and most marginal states. The core paragraph of the rule selectively adding state chairmen reads as follows:

> (b) The State Chairman of each State that casts its electoral votes for the Republican candidate for President at the preceding Presidential election, or in which State a majority of the Representatives in Congress and members of the United States Senate (in computing the majority the total membership of the House of Representatives from such State shall be added to the membership in the United States Senate of such State) are Republicans or in which State there is a Republican Governor, shall be a member of the Republican National Committee by virtue of his office as State Chairman. The Territory Chairman of each Territory having a Republican delegate to Congress shall be a member of the National Committee by virtue of his office.[18]

The rule and its probable effects seem to have been discussed only perfunctorily in the meeting of the Rules Committee, with only a bare majority attending; the change created little comment among delegates generally. In the excitement over the Taft-Eisenhower struggle, the implication of the change seemed to have been ignored by many delegates. The national committeewomen and Southern committeemen, however, recognized that the change would almost certainly decrease their influence in national party affairs. Floor debate was led by national committeewomen and was candidly placed on loss of Southern power and unfairness to women.

With the addition of the state chairmen under Rule 22, the Southern representation on the Republican National Committee was immediately reduced from 24.3 per cent to 18.7 per cent. By 1956, as a result of the Eisenhower victory in Texas, Virginia, and elsewhere, Southern representation on the committee had increased to 20.3 per cent. By 1960 only eight of the fifty state chairmen were not members

[18] *Republican Proceedings 1952*, p. 281.

of the national committee, and two of the eight were not Southern. Thus, eight years after the rule went into effect, seven of thirteen Southern chairmen had qualified, and Southern representation on the committee (22.3 per cent) was only two percentage points reduced from the period before state chairmen were members.

QUALIFICATIONS AND SELECTION

Members of the national committees must meet simple requirements as to sex, residence, and nomination procedures. The Democratic National Committee consists of an equal number of men and women, one of each sex for each state and territory. On the Republican side, the male-female balance was destroyed in 1952 by the addition of certain state chairmen to the national committee. Since women state chairmen are very rare (although possible in many states), the 1952 rule is not likely to result in additional women members of the Republican Committee.

Cannon's Manual states that Democratic national "committeemen and committeewomen must be residents of the State, Territory, or District from which elected."[19] The residence requirement is sometimes loosely construed in the case of territorial members, but by and large there is nothing surprising or onerous about a rule which requires a committee member to live in the jurisdiction he represents. There seem to be few cases of resignation of committeemen because of removal from the state, but committeewomen more frequently give up their posts for this reason, presumably to move with their husbands to new jobs. The mores of the patriarchal society work against the political woman in this way as in many others; she cannot so easily tie her family to her political career as is possible for—as, indeed, is the common practice of—the male. This is, however, a general sociological disability of the woman in politics and needs no extensive comment here.

For the Democrats in the 1960's, beyond the sex and residence requirements, "no further qualifications are prescribed for membership on the National Committee."[20] Although this may be generally true, in the past fifteen years considerable uncertainty has existed over the so-called loyalty oath which required national committee members to agree to support the nominees of the convention.[21] In August, 1949,

[19] *Cannon's Manual 1960,* p. 4.

[20] Since the effect of territorial membership on the national committees is probably not great, we forgo detailed discussion of the development of the practice of such representation.

[21] For the story of this episode in the history of North-South relations in the

and again in October, 1952, the names of several national committee-men and -women were "expunged from the rolls" of the Democratic National Committee for supporting Dixiecrat or Republican presidential candidates. In the intense feelings then prevailing, no non-Southern opposition to these ousters was recorded, but no new authority existed for the action. The Democratic Committee did not then have a convention-approved rule, such as the Republican Committee has had for many years, for unseating members. There was precedent and a presumption that the Democratic National Committee could remove members for cause, but not until 1960 did the convention adopt a resolution:

> It is the duty of every member of the Democratic National Committee to declare affirmatively for the nominees of the Convention, and that his or her failure to do so shall be cause for the Democratic National Committee or its duly authorized subcommittee to declare his or her seat vacant after notice and opportunity for hearing.[22]

Accordingly, the new Democratic Committee which met on July 16, just after the 1960 convention, required all members to put in writing their support for Kennedy and Johnson. All but one of the committee members signed the pledge in a "surprising display" of "peace, harmony and good will," and promised to support the ticket "actively."[23] Judge Tom P. Brady, Mississippi national committeeman, promised to sign when he received authorization from the Mississippi Democratic State Executive Committee. Mrs. J. Alton Phillips, the Mississippi Democratic national committeewoman, signed the pledge. The presence of vice-presidential nominee Lyndon B. Johnson on the ticket was the probable cause for the Southern forces' giving up a battle which they had earlier promised to fight.[24] After the election it was discovered that Judge Brady had not signed the pledge, but he remained a member of the DNC in good standing.

The power of the Republican Committee to expel members for cause is unambiguous and long-standing. Since 1912 a rule approved

Democratic Party, see Abraham Holtzman, *The Loyalty Pledge Controversy in the Democratic Party* ("Eagleton Institute Cases in Practical Politics" [New York: McGraw-Hill, 1960]).

[22] Resolution A, approved by the Democratic National Committee, September 16, 1959, and approved by the Democratic National Convention of 1960.
[23] *New York Times,* July 17, 1960.
[24] *Loc. cit.*

by the convention (Rule 27 in 1960) has given to the national committee the "power to declare vacant the seat of any member who refuses to support the nominees of the Convention which elected such National Committee, and to fill such vacancy."[25]

In the absence of contest, the nominations put forward by states' delegations at the conventions are, in Cannon's words, "invariably ratified by the Convention." Both committees have been given authority to decide in cases of rival claims to committee membership. The Democratic procedure, according to Cannon, calls for the appointment of a subcommittee to hear evidence, consider briefs, and make a report to the committee chairman; "the findings of the subcommittee when approved by the Chairman are final."[26] The Republicans have no general rule or similar procedure to be followed by the national committee, but precedent exists back to 1880 for the Republican National Committee to decide contests.[27]

Unless contests occur at the state level, the national committee will not go behind the act of state party certification to question the qualifications or *bona fides* of the nominees put forward. In 1884 the Republican convention declared that no person who was not eligible to be a member of the electoral college could be a member of the national committee, thus barring from the committee congressmen and senators and, in the words of the United States Constitution, all persons "holding an office of trust or profit under the United States." The alleged reason for this innovation was to prevent a possible conflict between the new federal Civil Service act and a committeeman's responsibilities to the national committee.[28] The committee members were expected to solicit contributions from federal employees, and it was thought at first that the Pendleton Act of 1883 would make this difficult or impossible for members of Congress or patronage appointees. It was soon discovered, however, that the 1883 act would not, in fact, prevent partisan fund-raising in the bureaucracy. Thus reassured,

25 *Republican Proceedings 1960*, p. 172.

26 *Cannon's Manual 1960*, p. 4.

27 When the Dakota territorial delegation presented two names to the convention, the problem was "referred to the new National Committee, with power to designate who shall fill the place." *Republican Proceedings 1880*, p. 173. In 1912, when the Oklahoma delegation nominated two persons, the question was referred to the "new National Committee." *Republican Proceedings 1912*, pp. 408–409.

28 The restriction was recommended by the national committee. Kleeberg, *op. cit.*, p. 145. See also *Republican Proceedings 1884*, pp. 80–81; and *New York Times*, June 6, 1884.

members of Congress and executive officers continued as national committee members. In 1888 the rule was abandoned.[29]

In the early years of the committees, the members were almost invariably selected by the convention delegates or by state conventions at which the delegates themselves were selected. In the last decade of the nineteenth century and the first decade of the twentieth, some states began to choose committee members in primary elections. At the height of Progressive fervor, largely through William Jennings Bryan's influence, it was said,[30] the Democratic convention of 1912 actually resolved as part of its platform that

> . . . committeemen who are hereafter to constitute the membership of the Democratic National Committee, and whose election is not provided for by law, shall be chosen in each State at primary elections. . . .[31]

This, as might be expected, proved to be a fatuous declaration, but the primary election is today the method of selecting committee members in four states and the District of Columbia.[32]

One might suppose that election by state-wide primary would ensure a more durable base and greater influence for the committee members so chosen. On the other hand, it might result in exacerbated intraparty conflict with a possible reduction in the influence of committee members. Scattered and impressionistic evidence indicates that neither result is common.

Election of national committeemen and -women (especially the women) in some states is a source of comic relief and an object of

[29] The Committee on Rules and Order of Business did not include the rule in its report. In the debate following the report, no objections were raised to the deletion of the provision. *Republican Proceedings 1888,* pp. 45–55. It has never been adopted by any other convention nor "raised in connection with the National Committee." Kleeberg, *op. cit.,* p. 198.

[30] James Albert Woodburn, *Political Parties and Party Problems in the United States* (New York: G. P. Putnam's Sons, 1914), p. 299.
solved as part of its platform that

[31] *Democratic Proceedings 1912,* p. 368.

[32] *Cannon's Manual* says national committeemen and -women are chosen by primary elections in six states. Delaware seems to be erroneously included in Cannon's list; there the national committee members are chosen at state meetings (called "little conventions") in April of the quadrennium. The national committee members of both parties tend to have high influence and long tenure in Delaware (letter from Prof. Paul Dolan, University of Delaware, June 26, 1962). Since 1959, when *Cannon's Manual* was revised for 1960, Democratic Committee members in Arkansas have been chosen by the state committee rather than in a primary election.

mirth for political insiders. A long-time observer of Florida politics writes:

> We have been electing the Democratic committeeman and committeewoman in Florida for about 40 years. Republican National Committee members are also elected. The posts have not been regarded as of sufficient importance to cause prominent office holders or party people to run for them. I cannot remember a Governor, or Senator, or member of the House running for this post.
>
> Our average practice . . . is when the second primary is held, there are about 12 candidates for each national committee office; somebody whose name begins with the top of the bracket alphabetically, is elected. For example, Mrs. Alford was for many years the national committeewoman. In 1960 it happened that there were a series of local candidates in many counties named Robert Johnson. At the same time, a complete unknown filed for kicks. He was Robert Johnson of Duval County, who had never been active in anything. He was elected. So, on the average, we either elect somebody whose name begins with A, or a common name, and then nobody ever hears of the people again.[33]

In Oregon, where Populist legislation and constitutional provisions have deeply marked all political life, the election of national committeemen seems to have had important consequences for the influence patterns of the state's partisan politics. In recent years the contests for committeemen, especially in the Democratic Party, have had overtones of the urban-rural conflict between Multnomah County (Portland) and the rest of the state, but more frequently the contests have been an ideological struggle between New Deal liberals and conservative Democrats or a battle of personalities. The state chairman in Oregon is chosen by the state central committee (on which Multnomah County, with one-third of the state population, has one thirty-sixth of the votes), and the national committeeman tends to be in conflict with, or in control of, the chairman. Thus in Truman's second term, Monroe Sweetland, national committeeman, obtained a federal judgeship for

[33] Letter from Prof. Manning Dauer, July 6, 1962.

his nominee over William Josslin, the state chairman, who wanted the position for himself.

Only in Oregon must the national committeemen campaign state-wide: Robert Mautz, a GOP national committee candidate in 1956, used billboards and the whole paraphernalia of campaigning in a successful race which cost him a reported $16,642.14. C. Girard "Jebby" Davidson, a New Deal lawyer and former assistant secretary of the interior, reported campaign expenditures of $8,196.68 in his successful 1956 race for Democratic national committeeman. Voting is likewise heavy; Davidson received 135,025 votes in 1960, and his two opponents together obtained nearly as many.

The election of national committeewomen in Oregon is more like that of both men and women in Florida. The women's races usually hinge on name familiarity or on attractiveness of candidate (a cocktail waitress was elected Democratic national committeewoman in 1956).

Professor Balmer sums up the effect of popular election of national committee members in Oregon:

> The role of national committeemen and national committee-women depends heavily on the personalities involved and the patterns of power relations between office holders; it usually takes money to be elected NCM and a vigorous campaign too; the Democratic experience with the national committeewoman position is that someone without money might win but could not afford the expenses of the office (which are considerable, and the state party has nothing), hence becomes a cipher nationally; there is inherent tension built into the system; when either the state chairman or the national committeeman dominates, all is well, but when they are equal in actual influence, severe damage may result to the party.[34]

The generalization, if any can be made at all, is that primary elections for national committee positions exist in weak party states and that one index of weakness is the failure of major candidates or party factions to fight for control of the committee posts. The candi-

[34] Letter from Prof. Donald Balmer, June 30, 1962. See also his "Intraparty Relations in Oregon," *Western Political Quarterly,* XI (September 1958), 10–11.

dates and factions are not interested in the national committee memberships because the jobs themselves carry no power or influence. The prestige which they bear is not, in itself, worth risking the expense and uncertainty of a state-wide campaign. In the District of Columbia, with a numerically and geographically small electorate, the national committee races have lately been quite spirited, but this may occur only when there is a contest over pledged slates of convention delegates, who are chosen at the same time the national committeemen and -women are elected.

In many states the national committeemen and -women are still chosen as they were in the early years of national committee existence. Frequently party custom has been sanctioned by law. Figure 1 shows the methods of selection used by the various states.

The most common method of selecting national committee members is by state party convention. The typical procedure is for delegates to be elected to the state conventions by county or district conventions and for the state conventions, by vote, to elect the national committeemen and -women. In some states—Maine, Michigan, and Minnesota (since 1956)—the state conventions elect the national convention delegates who in turn select the national committee members, but the more usual method, when conventions are used, is to elect the national committee members directly.

As Figure 1 shows, the convention method of direct selection of national committee members is favored in weak party states (especially in the Midwest and Rocky Mountains). Of the nineteen states employing this method of selection, only Rhode Island and Virginia can be said to have been among the stronger organization states in recent years. In strong party states the regular leaders are assured over time of convention control; in the others, the dominant factions or coalitions take shape through the agreements and tests of strength of the pre-convention and convention periods. In Colorado, for example, where the conservative and liberal wings of the Republican Party are evenly matched, the liberals elected Jean Tool state chairman in 1959, with the result that in 1960 Arthur Sheeley, a conservative national committeeman who had supported Tool's opponent, was replaced by William T. Power of the liberal wing.

The selection of national committee members by the national convention delegation is the second most common method. The Democrats employ this method in thirteen states, and the Republicans in sixteen. In states with stronger parties, such as Connecticut, Delaware,

Illinois, and New York, whatever factional conflicts exist tend to be resolved or temporarily bridged by the end of the delegate selection process—even so in New York, where a large number of delegates are elected.[35] In some states there is the tendency to produce delegations which are representative of either voter feeling—as in California and New Hampshire (and Minnesota in 1952 and 1956), where delegates are selected by presidential primaries[36]—or of the temporarily successful party factional leader or coalition.[37]

In fifteen states the national committee members of one or both parties are chosen by the state committees. Some of these are relatively powerful committees, having influence over county committees and local officeholders; these states—Pennsylvania, Indiana, New Jersey —have been controlled by a few elected party or government leaders, such as Mayor Frank Hague of Jersey City, Gov. David Lawrence of Pennsylvania, Rep. William Green of Philadelphia, National Chairman Frank McKinney and National Committeeman Frank McHale of Indiana, or, in even earlier days, Sen. Boies Penrose or Joseph R. Grundy of Pennsylvania.

Weak party states appear also on the list of those in which national committee members are chosen by the state committees. In some such states large, loose committees are comparable to state party conventions. In Arizona, for example, the state committees of three hundred to five hundred members are constituted in September of the even-numbered years; in the late spring of the presidential year, they meet to choose convention delegates and select national committee members. In Washington, however, the opposite seems true; there an unrepresentative Democratic state committee of seventy-eight members has "taken advantage of the law which permits a party to 'make its

---

[35] See Bert E. Swanson, "The Presidential Convention as a Stage in the Struggle for Political Leadership: The New York Democratic Delegation," in Paul Tillett (ed.), *Inside Politics: The National Convention, 1960* (Dobbs Ferry, N.Y.: Oceana Publications, 1962), pp. 193–215.

[36] Thus James Roosevelt and Mrs. Edward Heller, 1948 Truman supporters, were replaced in 1952 as California national committee members by John Anson Ford and Mrs. Clara Shirpser, Kefauver supporters; Emmett Kelley was likewise replaced as national committeeman from New Hampshire when, in 1952, as he declares, "I stuck with Truman too long."

[37] As in Georgia, where the governor himself sometimes takes the Democratic national committeeman job, and in Massachusetts and Ohio, where the McCormack, Kennedy, Lodge, Taft, Lausche, and DiSalle factions have all at one time or another controlled delegations and thus national committee memberships.

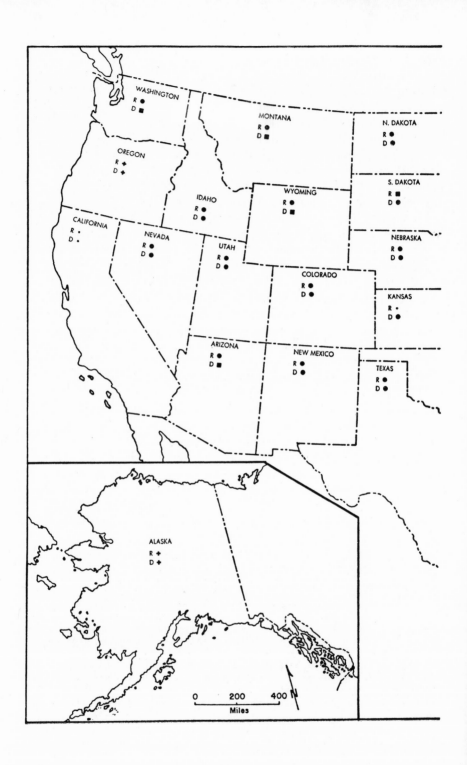

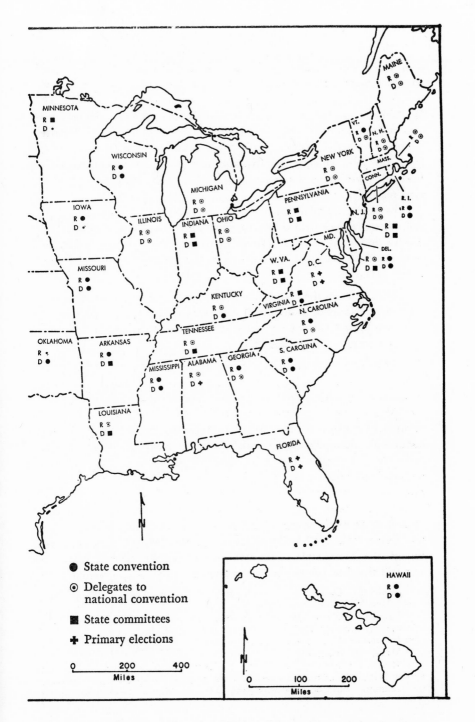

Figure 1. Methods for Choosing National Committeemen and -Women

own rules and regulations' to provide a state executive committee which is more representative."[38] It is presumably this executive committee which agrees on national committeemen and -women. The Washington parties are poor, dedicated to what Wilson calls the amateur style in politics,[39] and cannot undertake to pay national committee members' expenses; consequently there seems to be no rush of applicants for jobs which are costly and not especially prestigious. Once selected, Washington national committeemen and -women tend to have long tenure.

Between national conventions vacancies on the national party committees may be filled by the state party agency having such authority under the laws or customs of the state. This practice was first recognized by formal resolution in the Republican convention of 1884 which declared

> . . . that in the case of a vacancy occurring in the Republican National Committee, such vacancy may be filled by the State Central Committee of the State, Territory, or District thus left unrepresented.[40]

The Democratic convention sanctioned the filling of vacancies by the state committees in 1896. In both cases intense and bitter differences between party factions led to the rule changes.[41]

Although there is some disagreement about who shall decide when vacancies exist in case of disputed ousters or resignations, both national committees claim this right—and have made good their claim. Vacancies exist if a member has resigned and if the national committee (or national chairman alone) has accepted the resignation. Wright Morrow, Texas Democratic national committeeman, was among the 1952 "Shivercrat" defections to Eisenhower; Stephen Mitchell, the national chairman, chose to interpret a letter from Morrow as a resignation, and the Democratic National Committee ratified Mitchell's action even though the Texas state committee persisted in the view that Morrow was still the duly elected and accredited national committeeman.[42]

[38] Daniel M. Ogden, Jr., and Hugh A. Bone, *Washington Politics* (New York: New York University Press, 1960), p. 27.

[39] James Q. Wilson, *The Amateur Democrat: Club Politics in Three Cities* (Chicago: University of Chicago Press, 1962), pp. 2–13.

[40] *Republican Proceedings 1884*, p. 165.

[41] Macy, *op. cit.*, p. 80.

[42] Morrow's name does not thereafter appear on lists or records of the Democratic National Committee, except for the account of his attempt to speak at the committee meeting in Washington, D.C., on May 5, 1954, when he was

Likewise the national committees reserve the right, if they please, to continue to recognize as bona fide members of the committees those whom state party agencies have purported to have removed from office; the national committees' argument is that, once accepted as a member by the convention (or the committee, in case of contest), only the national committee itself is the final judge of a member's right to continue to serve until the next convention. When Camille Gravel, Jr., was "removed" from his Democratic national committeeman post by the state committee of Louisiana for being insufficiently segregationist, Chairman Butler and the DNC refused to consider Gravel removed or his state-endorsed successor elected. Butler's response to a question on the C.B.S. television show, "Face the Nation," illustrates the strong position a chairman may take if he can mobilize the sentiment of the committee majority and of the party leaders, generally, against a state committee:

> RALPH MCGILL (*Atlanta Constitution*): What is the status in Louisiana now, where the State has removed a man and the Committee—you say the Committee only can do it, the National Committee?

> PAUL BUTLER: Well, the status is that Mr. Gravel, of Louisiana, is still the national committeeman, . . . and until the Democratic National Committee has taken any action on any formal charges which may be filed by the State Committee, or someone for the State Committee of Louisiana, against Mr. Gravel, and until the National Committee votes by a two-thirds vote to remove him, he will remain representative of the Democratic Party in Louisiana, and we will not recognize the action taken by the State Committee, and that is according to the rules.[43]

OFFICERS AND MEETINGS

The committees are given great latitude by the conventions for

coldly told by Mitchell, "You are not a member of this committee. In what role do you address me?" *Democratic Proceedings 1956*, p. 552. No Texas national committeeman was recognized until November 17, 1955, when Lieut. Gov. Ben Ramsey was seated with the endorsement of Lyndon Johnson, Sam Rayburn, and Paul Butler.

[43] Columbia Broadcasting System, "Face the Nation" transcript, November 2, 1958, p. 18.

the selection of staff and the day-to-day operations between conventions.

Few officers are required. Practice and federal law provide for a chairman and treasurer. Custom also provides for vice-chairmen and assistant chairmen (or assistants *to* the chairmen) who are typically deserving and more-or-less influential state party leaders or friends of the chairmen, one of whom has been, since 1920, a woman with high title and honors (if not always high influence).

The current Republican usage is similar to that of the Democrats, though spelled out in somewhat greater detail:

> The Officers of the National Committee shall consist of a Chairman; four (4) Vice Chairmen, who shall be two (2) men and two (2) women; a Secretary, a Treasurer, and such other officers as the Committee shall deem necessary, all to be elected by the National Committee. The Chairman shall appoint a General Counsel for the Committee and an Assistant Chairman, who shall be a woman and who shall be director of women's activities.[44]

The Democrats empower their national committee by means of a separate resolution, rather than, as in the Republican case, with a section of the general report of the convention rules committee. The 1956 Democratic resolution on national committee officers is illustrative of recent years:

> *Resolved,* That said National Committee be and it is hereby authorized to elect a Chairman, not more than six Vice Chairmen, a Secretary, and a Treasurer, and that the Chairman so elected be and he is hereby authorized to appoint such assistants and committees as may be considered necessary for the efficient conduct of the business and affairs of the said Committee.[45]

Both national chairmen are authorized to fill all minor posts, and their recommendations (or those of presidents transmitted through them) with regard to such major officers as treasurer and vice-chairmen are almost always adopted. The Democratic chairman is empowered to fill by temporary appointment, subject to approval of the

[44] *Republican Proceedings 1960,* p. 171.
[45] *Democratic Proceedings 1956,* p. 112.

Executive Committee, vacancies in any office other than that of chairman.[46] Such temporary appointments must be confirmed at the next meeting of the full committee.

On occasion conflict may exist between or among major officers, as in the period 1956–1960 when Matthew McCloskey, the Democratic treasurer, and Chairman Paul Butler were in frequent disagreement. In such cases the chairman may be required by the nature of the political balance to keep the officer with whom he is at odds—as the congressional party leadership and the big state leaders, led by Governor Lawrence of Pennsylvania, supported McCloskey against Butler.

The normal state of affairs is that of the chairman's control of his own shop. Election of vice-chairmen may be wholly honorary and reflect an effort to give representation to the various segments of the party (members of Congress, governors, big contributors, and so on). Some vice-chairmen have been influential, but the majority have probably played a relatively unimportant role in the deliberations and policy-making of the committees.

The Democrats have in recent years tended to use the vice-chairmen posts to strengthen the often thin bond between the presidential and congressional wings of the party. At the beginning of Butler's tenure, three new vice-chairmen were added: Sen. Mike Mansfield of Montana to represent Democratic senators, Rep. Hale Boggs of Louisiana (Speaker Rayburn's nominee) to represent the members of the House, and Gov. Robert Meyner of New Jersey to represent the Democratic chief executives of the states.[47]

The distribution of vice-chairmen posts in the Democratic National Committee was codified in the official rules created in 1957. These rules, as approved by the 1960 convention, provide for the female vice-chairman, whose position has become traditional since Charle Williams was first elected to the post by the national committee after the convention of 1920, and five other vice-chairmen who are identified as

> . . . the Chairman of the Minorities Division, the Chairman of the Nationalities Division, a Democratic Governor, a Democratic United States Senator, and a Democratic United States Representative.

[46] Article IX, paragraph 5, Rules of the Democratic National Committee.
[47] *Democratic Proceedings 1956*, pp. 715–716.

Like the chairman, the vice-chairmen do not have to be members;
they serve for four years and are removable for cause by the majority
vote of the full membership of the committee. The chairman may fill
vacancies in the ranks of the vice-chairmen subject to confirmation by
the next meeting of the national committee.

Republican vice-chairmen (two men and two women) have, for
many years, come from the committee membership itself. This difference in practice between the Democratic and Republican committees
reflects in part both the smaller gap, organizationally and ideologically,
between the congressional and presidential parties and—perhaps just
another way of saying the same thing—the dominance that the congressional party has had in Republican Party affairs since the Willkie
trauma of 1940.

The full national committees meet more often than they used to.
Thirty years ago—even fifteen years ago—the national committees met
not more than three or four times in the quadrennium. It is now common for both committees to meet twice a year and more often if necessary.[48] To those who believe that the national committees ought to
grow in influence and authority, it is comforting to think that more
frequent meetings mean increased importance.

This may not be the case. Other reasons could be offered for
more frequent meetings—it is simply easier to meet in the jet age than
it was in the rail (or prop) age, and the chairmen are therefore more
willing to call a meeting for the transaction of less important business
or, which is perhaps even more plausible, the publicity mileage of committee meetings (especially if advisory groups can make "issues news"
in connection with the meetings) provides in itself a sufficient reason
for gathering. The relation between more frequent meetings and the
importance of the committees is yet to be seen. All we know for certain
is that the committees are meeting more frequently.

Agendas, rules of order, and meeting style are flexible, depending
on what needs to be done, which dignitaries may be in attendance, the
opposition expected (if any), and the personal desires and ego needs
of the chairman. The Democrats publish the verbatim record of all

---

[48] Article VII, paragraph 2, of the Rules of the Democratic National Committee (as revised February 12, 1958) requires "at least two meetings . . .
each year upon call of the Chairman . . . unless any such meeting is dispensed
with by prior vote of a majority of the full membership of the National Committee."

regular meetings and even include verbatim accounts of executive sessions sometimes.[49]

The Democratic National Committee observes Robert's *Rules of Order,* rather than the rules of the House of Representatives, which are followed by the Democratic conventions and the Republican National Committee. The authorization of Robert's *Rules* in the general rules of the Democratic National Committee, as drawn by the Butler-inspired special committee in 1957, may have been an attempt to generalize and make amateur the proceedings of the committee and, to this extent, make the procedures less dependent on knowledge and skill of congressional procedure.

Both national committees employ executive committees to facilitate the business of the committees between the semiannual meetings and to give counsel—and protection—to the chairman. The Executive Committee of the Republican National Committee, since its establishment by the convention of 1888,[50] has apparently been somewhat more active than its Democratic counterpart.

At present, the RNC Executive Committee consists of fifteen people, all currently drawn from the membership of the whole committee although this is not required by the rules, plus the major RNC officers serving ex officio. The Executive Committee members are appointed by the chairman, due regard being taken for factional, ideological, and geographic representation and for ability and seniority as well. The Executive Committee meets infrequently, at the times of the whole committee meetings and perhaps once or twice more per year, but closer contact is maintained by mail and telephone with some who serve as advisers and trouble shooters for the chairman. The Republican Executive Committee, like its Democratic counterpart, is useful mainly as a device for protection for the chairman, communication, and legitimation.

Informal groups of advisers and fellow committee members have surrounded Democratic chairmen since the committee was first established. For many years the Democratic National Committee has had blanket authorization for such "committees as may be considered necessary for the efficient conduct of the business." Despite this authority, the Democrats did not create a permanently organized executive com-

---

[49] See, for example, the record of the committee meeting of December 4, 1954, *Democratic Procedings 1956,* pp. 573 ff.

[50] *Republican Proceedings 1888,* p. 79.

mittee until 1951. Michelson says that Raskob and Shouse sometimes issued orders and statements in the name of the "executive committee," but the term was a mere device of legitimation, and he "never saw even a pretended list of its members."[51]

In 1951, when Frank McKinney became chairman of the Democratic National Committee as part of a Truman-inspired effort to prepare for the convention and campaign of 1952, a genuine executive committee was established. A committee of eleven was set up on October 31, 1951. Its members come from the national committee and are chosen by regional groups.

Despite the recent stabilization of the Executive Committee of the Democratic National Committee, the evidence to date indicates that the Executive Committee is not much used by the chairmen, not often called together, and not often called separately. Here, as in all such arrangements, the requirements of geographical representation almost ensure that the membership of the Executive Committee will have neither the physical closeness which allows consultation among mere acquaintances nor the personal friendships which move individuals to consult by letter and phone over longer distances.

[51] Michelson, *op. cit.*, p. 51.

3

National Committee Members: Who and Why

If the study of politics is, as it is widely agreed to be, the study of influence and the influential, it may be worthwhile to discover, if we can, how influential the members of the two national party committees are and how they bring to bear their influence.

Collectively the national committee is not much more than a categorical group. In Chapter 1 we suggested that the national party committees have few of the characteristics which sociologists find in human groups and organizations. The national committee members have very little collective identity, little patterned interaction, and only rudimentary common values and goals.

Except for occasional meetings—largely for show and news-making purposes—the national committees may be thought of not so much as groups, but as lists of people who have obtained their national committee memberships through organizational processes wholly separate in each state. The national committee members get whatever power they have as other American political leaders get their power: from local and state laws, offices, elections, and assorted credits of good will and favor.

It cannot be too often stressed that political power in America is drastically decentralized, focused in the cities and counties. American politics is feudal in nature. The state committees may have some important power bases in the statutes and state elective offices. The national committees as collective agencies have only that fleeting coalescence of power which comes with the mobilization of presidential campaigns and the integrative influence of an incumbent president.

Weak as the national committees are, the individual members might be, to continue the analogy with European feudalism, local notables, meeting intermittently for a display of the symbols of unity and the legitimation of the chief of state. They could be important leaders of the provinces, lords of the state party organizations, bosses of the county and city machines. Alternatively, the committee members could be the agents of the local princes; they could be ambassadors, chargés d'affaires, or perhaps mere secretaries and couriers.

In this chapter we report on some of the politically relevant facts in the lives of 682 members of the two national committees from 1948 to 1963. We submit some statistics about their social characteristics. We then deal, both quantitatively and qualitatively as our data allow, with the question of their influence and importance as state or local political leaders.

On the importance of the members of the national party committees, several differing views may be found. One has it that the members—at least the committee*men*—are ordinarily the real leaders of powerful state and local party machines. This view seems to have arisen in the 1920's and early 1930's, when political scientists were first systematically gathering field data about politics and when city and state bosses were first being appreciated as something more than objects of muckraking horror.

The late Professor Sait declared in 1939, "The members of the [national] committee are almost always crack politicians, men whose acuteness of observation has been sharpened by experience and whose character gives them an ascendancy among state politicians."[1]

Likewise, J. T. Salter declared that

. . . the national committee, like the United States Senate, is composed of the most powerful politicians in the country

[1] Edward McChesney Sait, *American Parties and Elections* (2nd ed.; New York: Appleton-Century, 1939), p. 375. Prof. Howard Penniman, editor of the fourth edition of Sait's text (1948), added, "State and city bosses are . . . likely to be named to the committees."

or their representatives. This committee is at the apex of the party structure, and is so powerful that it has been called the "President Maker."[2]

Other commentators are less confident of the power of individual committee members. P. Orman Ray, writing in 1924, made a more equivocal assessment. National committee members, he said, "are usually keen observers of the trend of political sentiment in their respective states, and often they find themselves in a position to smooth over dissensions within the party, and thus to promote harmony."[3] V. O. Key says

. . . national committeemen tend to be men of both substance and political stature in their states. Most of them are either lawyers or businessmen; many mix law, business, and politics. The national committeeman may be the real chief of his state party organization or his national power may be rooted in the leadership of a metropolitan center. He may be a lieutenant of the real leader of his state party, or his membership on the national committee may be a recognition by the state organization for financial support or an accolade for an elder statesman.[4]

The author of the most complete study heretofore made of the national party committees finds simple generalizations impossible. Bone says that "national committeemen often do not participate in party decisions at the local level," although some (he calls them "conspicuous exceptions") "have power within their states and are in a position to influence the decisions made there."[5]

In theory the committeemen and committeewomen provide the channel through which the national headquarters deals with state and local groups. . . . In practice there is little pattern or consistency of operation. . . . National committeemen are not infrequently bypassed by the White

[2] J. T. Salter, *Boss Rule: Portraits in City Politics* (New York: Whittlesey House, 1935), p. 5.
[3] P. Orman Ray, *An Introduction to Political Parties and Practical Politics* (New York: Charles Scribner's Sons, 1924), p. 170.
[4] V. O. Key, Jr., *Politics, Parties, and Pressure Groups* (4th ed.; New York: Thomas Y. Crowell, 1958), p. 348.
[5] Bone, *op. cit.*, pp. 13–14.

House or the national chairman on matters dealing with candidates, finance, and other considerations.[6]

Despite the existence of many locally powerful committee members, the implication of Bone's commentary is that members of the national committees are generally not among the most influential state party leaders.

One approach to the question of the importance of the national committee members is to ask what kinds of people the national committee members are. With one exception no data have ever been published on the social backgrounds of members of the national committees. More than thirty years ago an investigation of the then-incumbent national committeemen (no data were available on women members) disclosed that they were older than most public officials, generally had long political experience, and were overwhelmingly businessmen, with banking, insurance, and utilities being most represented; only nineteen of 108 gained their livelihood solely in the law, although forty-four claimed to be lawyers.[7]

Quantitative studies of the biographical data of political decision-makers tell us some things of value about the systems and processes of politics. As Matthews puts it, "The social and psychological characteristics of the individual officials acting within a political institutional framework must be considered before an adequate understanding of politics and government is possible."[8] Accordingly, we offer some data in tabular form to illuminate a few of the social characteristics of contemporary and recent members of the Republican and Democratic national committees.

We are equally aware that mere quantification is a bootless task. Important questions "cannot be answered by the assiduous collection of facts alone. Facts do not speak for themselves. Some kind of theorizing is essential to the development of knowledge."[9] Two forms of theorizing have a place in political analysis. One is a common-sense, hunch kind of generalization. Ordinarily thought to be the stock in

[6] *Ibid.*, pp. 17–18.

[7] Wallace S. Sayre, "Personnel of Republican and Democratic National Committees," *American Political Science Review*, XXVI (April 1932), 360–362. In addition to Sayre's article (more accurately, a research note), some data on Democratic National Committee members are available in Henderson, *op. cit.*

[8] Donald R. Matthews, *The Social Background of Political Decision Makers* (New York: Doubleday & Co., 1954), p. 2.

[9] *Ibid.*, p. 6.

trade of the successful political activist, common-sense generalization is also much used by social scientists in the analysis of who gets what, when, and how. The other kind of theorizing is more scientific and presupposes a procedure in which tentative generalizations called hypotheses are tested in an environment of controlled and/or measurable forces. Our consideration of members of the two national party committees involves rather more of the first, than of the second, kind of theorizing.

We gathered information on all members of both national committees from 1948 to 1963. Our intention was to obtain data on age, education, religion, occupation, party or governmental positions held before, during, and after service on the committee, and some nonfactual judgments about the reasons they were selected committee members and the party influence possessed by the members when on the committees. Some, but not in every case all, of the above information and judgments were obtained for 682 of the 686 people who served on the committees from the national conventions of 1948 to the end of calendar 1962. The four members not included were Democrats representing the Canal Zone, excluded because the Republicans do not have Canal Zone representation on their committee. Information was obtained principally from three sources: the files and staffs of the national committees, such standard reference works as *Who's Who*, and political and academic reporters in the states.

At the two national headquarters there are lists giving members back to about World War I on the Democratic side and to about 1900 on the Republican. For most former members there is no other information; frequently there is confusion, overlapping, and gaps in the information relating to period of service by individual members. Some effort is made to keep biographical information on current members of the committees. In 1956 and again in 1961 the Democratic national chairmen wrote each member of the committee asking for a biography and a picture; about half the members failed to acknowledge or answer the letter. Aside from these requests from the chairman, no attempt has ever been made to collect data from Democratic members. At the Republican headquarters somewhat better records are kept, but little is known about many members who served as recently as the 1930's and early 1940's.

Despite the thinness of biographical data at the two national headquarters, we were able to get from staff members reasonably full information about many committeemen and -women. Some of the committee members are personally well known to national staffers, many others are written to and talked about; the grapevine among political activists is quite effective, though largely oral. Our access to national committees' written and unwritten information about present and recent past members was good.

Standard reference books were also helpful, more for the committeemen and Republican state chairmen than for the committeewomen. Regional *Who's Who's* and *Who's Who among American Women* were also useful.

Equally important in our search for information about the 682 national committee members since 1948 was our use of two-way correspondence and conversation with knowledgeable political observers and participants in the states. Many of our academic colleagues were relied on. Nearly four hundred one-page data sheets were distributed to political and other social scientists, to newsmen, and to political leaders, asking for personal information and judgments on committee members state by state. These state reporters and informants contributed to this task more than they are aware, giving information which, quite truthfully, could not have been amassed otherwise, short of 682 separate interviews.[10]

The composite picture of national party committee members from 1948 to 1963 is one of moderate to high social status, income, party influence; of middle age (forty to sixty years old) ; and of a group representative of the sections and states from which they come. Not surprising. A number of surprises and trends, however, get submerged in the composite. A brief look at the data by categories of social, economic, and political factors will bring out the more detailed patterns of the composite picture.

NUMBERS AND TURNOVER

Since 1948 376 people have served on the Republican National Committee. Of this total, 133 were committeemen, 123 were committeewomen, and 120 were state chairmen eligible under the rules since 1952. The relatively greater instability of the office of Republican state chairmen is demonstrated by these figures; nearly as many state chairmen as national committeemen have served on the committee despite

---

[10] The use of knowledgeable informants as sources of specific information and for judgments of qualitative factors in politics is too little used by social scientists. As students of government become increasingly comfortable with field techniques (especially participant observation), the possibilities mount for valid, comparative, and cumulative data on political forces and behavior.

the shorter period of chairmen's service (ten rather than fourteen years) and the fact that only about forty of the fifty state chairmen are eligible. These statistics indicate that state chairmen have greater vulnerability than national committeemen.[11]

The number of Democratic National Committee members during the 1948–1963 period, 306, is made up of 159 committeemen and 147 committeewomen. The somewhat greater turnover of men than women in both parties appears to result not from the slightly older age at which committeemen tend to take office, but from the greater number of resignations because of intraparty competition for the job and competing pressures for time and energy. The record for the longest service on either national committee was held by West Virginia Republican Committeeman Walter S. Hallanan, who was a member of the GOP national body for thirty-four years, from 1928 until his death in January, 1963. The senior member of the Democratic National Committee is Mrs. Emma Guffy Miller of Pennsylvania, who has served continuously since 1932, never misses a meeting, and delights in calling herself "the old grey mare."

Seniority alone is not important on the committees, although it may have been in early years when chairmen were chosen exclusively from committee members.[12] As would be expected, members with longer service are often better known to chairmen and fellow members and therefore tend to be singled out for duty on special committees or to be more readily recognized at meetings. But these advantages are merely those which familiarity brings to personal relations. If he happens to be as well known as older members, a new member will receive all the recognition his merit or his supposed influence will support. Unlike the House of Representatives, and other legislative bodies, on the national committees length of service has no special importance which is reflected in institutional arrangement or tradition.

Tenure and turnover by state membership ranges from the long incumbencies of Pennsylvania Democrats Mrs. Miller and Gov. David Lawrence (1940 to date) to the revolving door of the North Carolina Democracy, which was represented by nine committeemen and three committeewomen in the fourteen years under investigation here. On

---

[11] We surmise that state chairmen are thought to be more influential and therefore more vulnerable. They are worth being gunned for by intraparty rivals; national committeemen are not, to the same extent. Our intuition, rather than our data, leads us to this surmise.

[12] Chatham, *op. cit.*, p. 11.

the Republican Committee both Delaware and Idaho were represented
by eleven people during the 1948–1963 period, but each has had a
three-member delegation since 1952.

AGE

It is sometimes said that the post of national committeeman, especially, is given to elder statesmen of the state party. As we shall see,
there is some evidence for this in the reasons given by our state correspondents for individuals being selected as national committee members.

The information we have on committee members' ages also tends
to bear out the statement that in some cases loyal party leaders are
"put out to pasture" in the national committee. As Table 1 shows, 38
per cent of the 131 Republican national committeemen whose ages are
known were over fifty-five when they took office, as compared with
15 per cent of the ninety-six state chairmen members of the committee (whose ages are known). The number of cases is quite small,
but the difference between the distributions is significant (by the chi-
square test) to the .01 level.[13]

One explanation for the greater age of national committeemen
than of state chairmen is that the committee posts are sometimes given
to senior party leaders as rewards for their years of work. We believe
this to be the case. We might also suggest a more general explanation,
one that is consistent with our finding that there is greater turnover
among state chairmen than among national committeemen. In his
study of age of achievement in many fields of human activity, Lehman
finds that groups showing less conflict and greater stability have older
leaders and that groups having greater conflict and unrest tend to
choose younger leaders.[14] This is, in a sense, another manifestation of
the young radicals versus the old conservatives, but Lehman's concern,
like ours, is with the ages of leaders, not merely of rank-and-file fol-
lowers of movements. The contrast, as it appears in our data, is that,
on the one hand, of younger state chairmen more embattled in party

---

[13] In 1957 the forty-one Democratic national committeemen who answered
Henderson's questionnaire averaged fifty-five years of age, and the forty-two
Democratic state chairmen averaged fifty-two years of age. Henderson, *op. cit.*,
pp. 159–160.

[14] Harvey C. Lehman, *Age and Achievement* (Princeton: Princeton University Press, 1953), p. 283. For a good summary of data from studies of age
and leaders in America, see Wendell Bell, Richard J. Hill, and Charles R.
Wright, *Public Leadership* (San Francisco: Chandler Publishing Co., 1961),
pp. 56–73.

fights at home, under conditions of higher risk, with less prospect for long tenure; with older national committeemen, on the other hand, whose office is more stable and less conflict-ridden (at least in part because they have less opportunity to advance or hinder the personal satisfactions which other, potentially rival, party leaders receive from political life).

TABLE 1

AGE OF COMMITTEEMEN AND -WOMEN WHEN THEY TOOK OFFICE

Age	Democrats		Republicans		
	Men	Women	Men	Women	State chairmen
	(N=159)	(N=147)	(N=133)	(N=123)	(N=120)
25 – 35	7.5%	6.1%	3.8%	8.9%	4.1%
36 – 45	20.1	23.8	15.8	21.9	27.5
46 – 55	38.4	32.7	41.3	35.0	36.7
56 – 65	22.0	18.4	28.6	20.3	7.5
Over 65	10.1	7.5	9.0	4.1	4.2
Unknown	1.9	11.5	1.5	9.8	20.0

EDUCATION

In every study of the formal educational levels of Democratic and Republican Party activists, the Republicans turn out to be better educated. Our findings are not exceptional. Table 2 indicates that only 10 per cent of the Republican committee members about whom we have information had no college work; 18 per cent of the Democratic members completed their formal schooling with twelfth-grade graduation or before. Sixty per cent of the Democrats about whom we have information had at least one college degree; 67 per cent of the Republicans made the same claim.

Sayre found that 36 per cent of the 1932 national committeemen of both parties had a college degree.[15] In our sample, 64 per cent of the national committee members about whom we have schooling data (N = 610) claimed to have at least one college degree. Here is another

[15] Of forty-two Democratic committeemen who responded to Henderson's 1957 questionnaire, thirty-three (79 per cent) claimed to have at least one college degree. When Democratic national committeewomen are added, the number in Henderson's sample becomes seventy-two, of whom 67 per cent had one or more college degrees. *Op. cit.,* pp. 161–162.

statistic—the literature of social science is full of them—testifying to
the educational revolution of the twentieth century.

TABLE 2

EDUCATION OF COMMITTEE MEMBERS

	Grammar school	High school	Some college	College degree	Unknown	N
Democrats	.7%	15.0%	19.6%	53.3%	11.4%	306
Republicans	0	9.3	20.5	60.4	9.8	376

RELIGION

As with education and occupation, our findings on the religious
affiliations of national committee members were unexceptional. We
expected that more Democrats would be Roman Catholic and low-
church Protestant, that more Republicans would be high-church Protestant. Our only surprise was in the small number of Jewish members
(we expected that more Democrats than Republicans would be Jews).
Out of 636 political leaders whose religion was identified, only eleven
were Jewish; this percentage is below the national average and well
below what one would expect for the elite group with which we are
concerned here. No explanation is offered.

The large number of people identified as simply Protestant represents in many cases the lack of more specific information on the part
of our informants, and we think it also represents in many cases the
official autobiographical response of politicians who are not so candid
as the one Democrat who admitted to having no religion at all.

Our findings on religious affiliations of national committee members from 1948 to 1963 differ little from the figures of Sayre in 1932 and
of Henderson in 1957. The only surprising difference is Sayre's report of
a larger number of Republican low-church Protestants (sixteen low
and eleven high) and a smaller number of Democratic low-church
Protestants (fifteen high and six low); these differences may be attributed to chance in Sayre's small sample (thirty Republicans and
thirty-three Democrats).

We find that the Democratic National Committee members are
a more-or-less accurate reflection of the religious distribution of the
population at large (see Table 3). According to a Census Bureau sur-

vey of 1958, 66.2 per cent of the American people are Protestant; 25.7 per cent, Catholic; and 3.2 per cent, Jewish. On the Republican National Committee, Protestants have been heavily overrepresented, Catholics and Jews underrepresented.

TABLE 3

RELIGIOUS AFFILIATION (OR PREFERENCE)

OF NATIONAL COMMITTEE MEMBERS

	Democrats		*Republicans*	
	Number	Per cent	Number	Per cent
Protestant				
(sect not known)	85	27.8	168	44.7
Protestant (sect given)				
Episcopalian	27	8.8	46	12.2
Presbyterian	26	8.5	43	11.4
Methodist	26	8.5	25	6.6
Baptist	16	5.2	11	2.9
Congregationalist	2	*	16	4.3
Lutheran	7	2.3	10	2.7
Christian Church	7	2.3	2	*
Disciple of Christ				
Church	1	*		
Other small sects	1	*	2	*
		64.7		85.9
Roman Catholic	85	27.8	28	7.4
Mormon	4	1.3	8	2.1
Jewish	7	2.3	4	1.1
Christian Scientist	2	*	4	1.1
Unitarian	2	*	2	*
Quaker			1	*
None	1	*		
	299		370	
Unknown	7	2.3	6	1.6
Totals	306		376	

* Less than 1%

The religious distribution of all national committee members from 1948 to 1963 is similar to that found by Matthews for United States senators who served from 1947 to 1957. Protestants are generally overrepresented (when compared with the national average) and the high-prestige sects, especially Episcopalians and Presbyterians, overrepresented among Protestant members.[16] Our findings on the religion of national party committee members tend to confirm the general proposition, drawn from many recent studies, that Protestants (especially high-church Protestants) are overrepresented in all fields of national social and political leadership in America.[17]

OCCUPATION

Table 4 again confirms the importance of the legal profession among the leaders in American politics. Twenty-eight per cent of all members of the two national party committees from 1948 to 1963 were lawyers. Only four of the national committeewomen were lawyers. Hence, when the male committee members alone are considered, the percentage of lawyers is 41.5. Many of the lawyers appear not to be in regular practice; many have other interests.

Sayre and Henderson both found the national committees to be dominated by lawyers, especially lawyer-businessmen (of Sayre's forty-four lawyers, only nineteen were engaged exclusively in practice). In 1932, 40.7 per cent of the committeemen of both parties were lawyers. Henderson's review of *Who's Who* in 1944 found 51 per cent of the listed Democratic national committeemen to be lawyers; of his 1957 sample of Democratic committeemen, 54 per cent were lawyers.[18] From these studies it seems reasonable to conclude that the proportion of lawyers among national committeemen has remained relatively constant, at 40 to 45 per cent, from 1932 to 1963. One hundred twenty-seven of the male committee members listed more than one occupation in their official biographies; lawyers, corporation executives, and bankers were common among the multiple listings (we made a judgment about each member's principal occupation and listed only that).

In his investigation of the members of the 1932 Democratic and Republican national committees, Sayre found that almost none represented the interests of the skilled and unskilled working classes. He seems to have been surprised and to have felt, as did many of the political scientists at that time, that unrepresentative elites constituted

[16] D. R. Matthews, *U.S. Senators and Their World* (Chapel Hill: University of North Carolina Press, 1960), p. 23.
[17] Bell *et al., op. cit.,* p. 95.
[18] Henderson, *op. cit.,* p. 169.

a flaw in the practice of democracy. We are no longer surprised to find that few members of the lower socioeconomic groups become high-level political leaders—probably fewer, in fact, than in earlier days. Nor is our view of the relation between representativeness and representation so simple; lawyers and even corporation executives may represent the policy interests of the lower socioeconomic groups as well as individuals from those groups.

One might think, however, that leaders of groups which traditionally champion the interests of workers, especially leaders of trade unions, would be found among the national party committee members. We did, in fact, find one—but only one—labor leader among the Democratic national committeemen; but one labor leader does not make a category any more than one swallow makes a summer, and we put him in our somewhat catch-all clerical and quasi-professional grouping. Our speculation is that labor leaders, although active in the local and state party organizations (mainly the Democratic, of course), do not want, or are not given, a national committee seat until they are too old or too identified as something else to retain their title of labor leader. It may be, in part, a reflection of what appears to be a lack of connection, or a too indirect connection, between the matters with which the national committees deal and the bread-and-butter politics with which the labor unions identify at the state and local levels.

Some of the categories may require comment. Professionals other than lawyers are primarily doctors and teachers. We found enough newspaper people (mainly publishers and editors), radio and television broadcasters, and assorted writers to warrant, we thought, the category of communications industry. Bankers, too, we thought, could be separated from other businessmen. The line between small-business and corporation executives is fuzzy, and our judgments are no doubt less accurate in many cases than we would have wished them to be. Holders of public office are almost all partisanly elected officials— members of Congress, governors, mayors—but in some cases they are political appointees. Over-all, the patterns are clear, and we believe our categorization to be reasonably accurate, although there seems to be no way to classify properly a committeewoman who was said to be an "unemployed professional society woman" or a committeeman described as a "self-made bachelor."

TABLE 4

OCCUPATIONS OF NATIONAL COMMITTEE MEMBERS, 1948–1963

Occupation	Democrat Number	Democrat Per cent	Republican Number	Republican Per cent	Total Number	Total Per cent
Lawyer	72	27.2	103	29.3	175	28.4
Corporation executive	32	12.1	57	16.2	89	14.4
Housewife	32	12.1	32	9.1	64	10.4
Holder of public office	34	12.8	20	5.7	54	8.8
Clerical and quasi-professional worker	23	8.7	29	8.2	52	8.4
Professional other than lawyer	14	5.2	22	6.3	36	5.8
Insurance, investment, real estate man	16	6.0	21	6.0	36	5.8
Farmers and ranchers	10	3.8	25	7.1	35	5.7
Communications industry member	13	4.9	15	4.3	28	4.5
Small businessman	10	3.8	18	5.1	28	4.5
Banker	9	3.4	10	2.8	19	3.1
	265	100	352	100.1	617	99.8
Unknown*	41		24		65	

* Of sixty-five people whose occupations are unknown, three were identified as "retired"; forty-five were women, mainly housewives it may be assumed.

PATHS TO NATIONAL COMMITTEE MEMBERSHIP

How does a person get to be a member of his national party committee? In Chapter 2 we described the various ways in which nominations are made to the national committee and the way in which the national conventions approve the state nominations by *pro forma* action. Here we deal with reasons for membership, not processes of selection.

There is a custom in politics—given lip service even by the most ambitious—that one should be a reluctant candidate. In accordance with this old custom, many members of the national party committees say they neither sought nor wanted the job. We will not detain ourselves with speculation over how many genuine drafts there have been in filling the office of national committeeman or -woman. Some may not want the job for any positive reasons of power or prestige, but many such people, we suspect, nevertheless *do* want the job to prevent its falling to a rival individual or faction in state politics. We assume that in almost all cases there are potential takers for the job (although it was reported that thirteen people became national committee members because "no one else wanted the job"). We assume, in short, that among political leaders and activists there is a demand for national committee positions.

The inquiry then becomes one of determining the major reasons that national committee members get chosen in the various political environments of the state parties and whether some general recruitment and selection guides can be extracted from the heterogeneity of our 682 cases.

The manner in which members are selected ordinarily has much to do with the national and state influence they can exert once on the national committee. Although we separate these two aspects of our inquiry for the sake of orderly presentation of data, it is clear that there is an important reciprocity: many members are selected because they are already important in the state party. Although some increase their influence in the state party after becoming national committee members, there are no clear cases of this occurring as a result of national committee membership alone. Here again is evidence that influence flows from the states, through individuals, to the national agencies, rather than the other way around.

As might be expected, we found it difficult in some instances to assess the reason or reasons that particular people were chosen as national committeemen and -women. In most cases reasons were obvious to our state reporters and to us as we gained familiarity with the intra-party dynamics of the states.

One other preliminary point: we do not discuss here the 120 state chairmen who have served on the Republican National Committee since 1952. They are members of the committee by rule, because they are state chairmen; no other reason is necessary or even relevant.

To them that have shall be given. The most common reason for selection as national committee member is simply the fact that the individual is already a successful and visible party or governmental leader in the state. More than any other way, national committeemen and -women get the job because they are governors or mayors or congressmen or state legislators or party committee chairmen (state or local) and vice-chairmen. In the overwhelming number of instances, successful candidates for national committee membership already have power bases in the state party organization; these power bases are of two kinds, resting on office and money. From what our informants say about the committeemen and -women in their states and from what we know, it is clear that office is more important than money.

Of the 498 members about whom we have adequate knowledge on this point (subtracting the 120 Republican state chairmen and another sixty-four people inadequately known by us), 89 per cent (443) held party or governmental jobs in their state and/or community before their selection to the national committee. Eleven were governors or ex-governors when they became national committeemen; fifteen were members of Congress or former members of Congress; seventy-nine were or had been members of their state legislatures; several had been state party chairmen before becoming national committeemen (in a few cases, both offices were held concurrently).

It is even more common for national committeewomen to have been state or county vice-chairmen before or at the time of their selection to the national body. The general disabilities of women in politics, plus the typical state laws which require a parallel structure of female vice-chairmen for party committees, have important but obvious consequences for the selection of national committeewomen. Women are less likely to hold state or local governmental office, but the relative opportunities are greater for women than for men to hold party office, because there are fewer women than men activists (at least at the middle and upper levels of county and state party organization).

The second most common reason given for national committee membership was "money and time to take on the job." Money and time are obviously related; a committee member must be able to spend his own money for trips to meetings, conventions, and party functions (in a few states the party central committee pays part or all of the expenses to national committee meetings) and also must be able to take time from his regular business. More than travel and communication (postage and telephone) expenses are involved in the national committee job, for members are expected to contribute to such state and national money-raising events as dinners and rallies and to campaign funds.

Our hunch is that the national committee members are less important now as sources of party contributions than was the case fifty years ago. More money is now needed at all levels of party activity, and more broadly based financing has been developed in the past several decades. Nevertheless, the ability to make donations—sometimes large donations—is one of the factors in availability for national committee members. It is hardly a typical case, but in the late 1950's, the Republican state chairman in Texas, it is said, received a $1,000 check from his national committeewoman and sent it back with this note: "When you send me a check worth endorsing, I'll endorse it." The story is that she thought this quite clever and returned a check for $50,000, which he endorsed.

The third most common reason for membership, as given by our state reporters, was related to personal friendships between successful candidates for public office and successful aspirants to national committee membership. Democratic governors, especially in the South, often have traditional right to name the national committee members for their states. Elsewhere, U.S. senators may have such traditional rights.

More times than might be expected, members were said to have been chosen by chance—because they had the same name as a popular candidate for public office, because they were alphabetically first on a ballot, or because of convention or caucus vagaries.

In many cases, too, members were chosen to balance representation of geographical areas, of factions in the state party, of religion or ethnic background, of liberals and conservatives. Sometimes the choice fell on a person merely because he or she was "inoffensive." One person, it was reported, was chosen as "a sop to the eggheads."

IMPORTANCE OF NATIONAL COMMITTEE MEMBERS
IN THEIR STATES

We may discover some career facts of national committee members. We may attempt to relate, as we have, some socioeconomic variables to those career facts. We may gather some histories of how and why members became members. All these exercises are unquestionably useful to improve our understanding of the ingredients and dynamics of political party activity in America. But we want to know, if we can, more than these facts. We want to know how influential in their own states the members of the national committees are. The measure of influence, broadly speaking, is a question of judgment, for no index of behavioral characteristics can be constructed which will provide more than some clues to an assessment of general influence.

We asked our correspondents in the states to rate the national committee members they knew. In many cases the final judgment of the importance of the member was made from more than one rating, sometimes from as many as four or five. The question was: "How would you rate this person in terms of influence in party affairs in the state (when a member of the national committee)? Among the top half-dozen leaders? Among the top dozen leaders? Among the top twenty-five leaders? Quite unimportant? Completely unimportant?"

The question is somewhat ambiguous, and the rating categories are less precise than we might wish to be the case. But the methodology, admittedly imperfect, is nevertheless as scientific as it needs to be to bear the fallible human judgments which are fed into it. The reporting system here is, in short, precise enough for the information reported. These are best guesses of knowledgeable people, of people who in every case know and have a feeling for the politics of the states and the committee members about whom they were asked. They were asked to make informed judgments, and one test of the value of our procedure is the fact that in many cases two or more such correspondents independently came up with the same judgment about the same members. In all, nearly one hundred persons supplied us with information—mainly unpublished and some unpublishable—about the 682 members of our sample. Despite this help, we have no judgments for a number of members about whom our informants knew very little.

The context for judging importance of individual political leaders is that of state-wide party activities. In the deliberately impressionistic way this was handled, we took the ratings of our informants without much effort to agree on terms and criteria for making judgments. Some of our correspondents asked us for guidance, however, and to them we suggested that the ratings be made on the basis of the individual's influence in party activity at the time when he first became a member of the national committee. Had we been able to standardize these criteria, the comparability of our nearly six hundred judgments would be greater. This was not possible, however, and the data which follow are, as we admit them to be, a collection of more-or-less sophisticated hunches and informed guesses. These ratings are political perceptions, not scientific fact.

Data in Table 5 do not include ratings on Republican National Committee members from Alabama, Arkansas, Georgia, Louisiana, Mississippi, North Carolina, South Carolina, or Virginia. Republican members from Florida, Tennessee, and Texas *are* included, however, because there has always been some Republican organization in Tennessee, and since 1952 real and vigorous Republican organizations are to be found in Florida and Texas. As a matter of logic we might have evaluated the Republican members in all the Southern states, for the question had to do with the importance of the members in party activity in the states, and a person may be important even in an unimportant party. But our sense of fitness triumphed over our sense of logic. It would not do, we thought, to put Sinclair Weeks or Arthur Summerfield into the same influence-rating system with, for example, the Negro Republican Committee members (living in Washington, D.C.) of the Mississippi "black-and-tan" party. Indeed, the white Republican National Committee members from Alabama and Georgia have been hardly more influential than the "black-and-tans"—or their state parties more worthy of being called parties. All this may be changing—in the interest of two-partyism, we hope it is—but, for most of the fourteen years under consideration here, it would have been an exercise of fantasy to talk about the state party influence of the Republican National Committee members from the Deep South states.

By our ratings it turns out that national committee*men* are important figures in the state parties. Of the national committeemen for whom we have judgments, more than 90 per cent in both parties are among the top twenty-five party leaders in the states; indeed, 42.1 per cent of the Democrats and 35 per cent of the Republicans are judged to be among the top half-dozen party leaders in their states. The Democratic percentage is higher because of the practice of some of the urban bosses and the Southern and Border State governors to take the office of national committeeman themselves.

We are not surprised that the national committeemen are, in general, powerful figures in state and local politics, although there is some literature portraying them as quite unimportant people (only ten Republicans of 117, and eight Democrats of 159, were described by our correspondents as quite unimportant). What does surprise us, at first, is the judgment that the Republican state chairmen are, on the whole, no more influential than the national committeemen of their own party. Our thinking is doubtless distorted by the pervasive use of an hierarchical model of state party organization in which we expect to find a neat pyramid, as in the textbooks, with the state chairman on top. Such a model may be very misleading, and our data suggest that

TABLE 5
INFLUENCE OF NATIONAL COMMITTEE MEMBERS IN THEIR STATE PARTIES

| | Republicans | | | | | | | | Democrats | | | | | | All members of both parties | |
| | NCM | | SC | | NCW | | All | | NCM | | NCW | | All | | | |
	N	%	N	%	N	%	N	%	N	%	N	%	N	%	N	%
Top six	41	35.0	32	28.1	8	8.1	81	24.6	67	42.1	1	.7	68	22.2	149	23.4
Top twelve	28	23.9	38	33.3	18	18.2	84	25.5	40	25.2	11	7.5	51	16.7	135	21.2
Top twenty-five	21	18.0	21	18.4	24	24.2	66	20.0	35	22.0	32	21.8	67	21.9	133	20.9
Quite unimportant	10	8.5	6	5.3	31	31.4	47	14.2	8	5.0	72	49.0	80	26.1	127	20.0
Completely unimportant	1	.9	0	—	6	6.0	7	2.1	2	1.3	9	6.1	11	3.6	18	2.8
No judgment	16	13.7	17	14.9	12	12.1	45	13.6	7	4.4	22	14.9	29	9.5	74	11.7
Totals	117	100	114	100	99	100	330	100	159	100	147	100	306	100	636	100

the national committeeman may be as influential as the state chairman.[19] The national committeemen of both parties tend to be older, to enjoy longer tenure, and, compared to the chairmen, to be more protected from the factional fights which rack so many state parties every two or four years. The very element that gives state chairmen power—the winning of majorities in state conventions or committees —may also limit their power (or at least their life expectancies). To the extent that the national committeeman can stand somewhat aloof from such crises and to the extent that his function and importance are seen to be related to national politics rather than to state politics— to that extent the national committeeman may prosper in an environment fatal to the state chairman.

The national committee*woman,* however, enjoys very little power in her state party. Nearly one-third of the Republican women and nearly one-half of the Democratic are described by our informants as quite unimportant. Six Republicans and nine Democrats were said to be completely unimportant. Some of the judgments were brutally candid about the lack of influence of national committeewomen: one, an Eastern Democrat, was described as "not well-liked—never had any power, and, though living, has completely disappeared"; another, a Rocky Mountain Republican, "was chosen because the party was sorry for her; she had no following and no influence"; a third, from a Pacific Coast state, was said to be "a cipher, who likes to sit at the head table."

Table 5 seems to carry two messages with regard to national committeewomen. One is that Republican women are judged to be somewhat more influential in the GOP than are Democratic women in their party. The other thought, inferred from the data, is that, if *these* women have little influence, then *no women have much influence in state political parties.* The national committeewomen are as important as any women in the parties, but of very little importance at all by comparison with the male party leaders. In most states, at most levels of party organization, women have *equal representation* with men; there is no evidence that they have ever had *equal influence.*

Our summary of the importance of national committee members in their own state parties might be as follows: they are apt to be as powerful as any other state party leaders of their sex. It is not fair to

[19] The Democratic national committeemen ($N{=}38$) and state chairmen ($N{=}33$) who responded to Henderson's questionnaire in 1957 generally felt that the offices were of equal importance. Henderson, *op. cit.,* p. 140.

compare the influence of national committeewomen with that of male state leaders who are not national committee members, but, when the men are compared with other males and the women with other females, then the national committee members may be said to be as influential as other state party leaders.

4

The National Party Chairmen: Responsibility without Power

Sen. Hugh Scott (R., Pa.) says that the chairman of a national party committee is a "thousand-fingered Dutch boy" who rushes about the political scene plugging up the holes in his party's dikes.[1] It is an apt figure and comes from a man who was himself Republican national chairman. It errs only in implying that the chairman is charged merely with defending ground already occupied by the party. Such is not the case; his job is to roll back the sea as well as to prevent its breach of the walls. It might be said, in fact, that the only clear objective of the national committee chairman is the sweeping command to advance the fortunes of his party. His primary goal is to hold the presidency if his party has it and, if not, to gain it. "About the only thing the two party chairmen have in common is their responsibility to win the next election."[2]

[1] Quoted in David S. Broder, "Changing Face of the Party Chairman," *New York Times Magazine,* October 18, 1959.

[2] *Idem,* "Strategists for '62 and '64," *New York Times Magazine,* October 15, 1961, p. 26. "The National Committee Chairman of a political party has only one function: to

In an ideal sense, all the energies and activities of the chairman should be related to the keeping or getting of the office of president of the United States. The presidency is the big prize on which much else depends, and the national chairmen are normally among the chief strategists and field generals in the struggle to keep or occupy the real estate at 1600 Pennsylvania Avenue, Washington, D.C. All the secondary objectives of the ideal national party chairmen should be related to the major objective of keeping or getting the presidency. The chairmen should test their every action against its probable consequences for the quadrennial national election.

The successes or failures of the party in congressional and gubernatorial elections are also important indexes of national strength. Thus the chairmen and their staffs get drawn into congressional and state campaigns. The national image of the party during the all-important presidential campaign will be a consequence of state elections and organizational *esprit de corps* as well as national politics.

The national chairman must attempt to reconcile the various and often competing interests of presidential, state, and congressional leaders. The ideal chairman must also provide satisfactions of a material and a psychological sort to campaign contributors, leaders of auxiliary party organizations, and leaders of groups whose members may be wooed by the party candidates at national and state levels. He must help in the distribution of patronage when success comes to the party. He must distribute the disappointments in time of electoral decline and failure. He must be attentive to the needs for recognition[3] to party leaders and the often sensitive personal feelings which are so important to the maintenance of party harmony and success at the polls. It may be very damaging to the party interests, which it is the chairman's responsibility to nurture and develop, for him to seat dignitaries wrongly at a national $100-a-plate dinner, for him to fail to give recognition to the appropriate leaders in the appropriate order when he journeys into a state for a political appearance, for him to fail to answer with all graciousness and speed the letters which come

---

win votes for the ticket—by organization, by personal standing, by persuasion, and by strategy." Editorial, *The Nation,* CLXV (August 23, 1947), 175.

[3] "Recognition" is a high-frequency word among politicians, little remarked by academic students of politics. It is an omnibus word which means, generally, the satisfaction of ego needs through flattering notice; recognition may range from a one-sentence thank-you note to the chairmanship of a major honorary group. (Job and contract spoils are not ordinarily thought of as recognition.)

to him from now obscure people who may tomorrow have influence in their states.

Such are the responsibilities and the dangers of the job of national party chairman. Ideally stated, the position seems one fit only for supermen. Because no supermen have been party chairmen, however, the ideal has not been reached. Some chairmen have been very inept indeed—badly prepared for the job, indifferent, and insensitive. Some of the chairmen have considered the job quite unimportant. It is said that Rep. Joseph Martin (R., Mass.) visited the national committee office only twice in the twenty-eight months he served as chairman. Some chairmen, at the other extreme, have been imaginative, energetic, and much in the public eye. Only a few have appreciated even the small opportunities a chairman has for bringing order, articulation, and responsiveness to a national party system which is un-national by design and experience. Chairmen who have made an effort to understand their job and to apply their talents often find their lot to be frustration, opposition, and derision.

The national chairman must be, indeed, "a thousand-fingered Dutch boy." His is a job "with great responsibility and little or no real power."[4] He may well be what former Chairman Alcorn calls him: "The least appreciated, most abused, and most harassed party official in the country."[5]

WHO GETS THE JOB AND HOW

The national party chairmanship is not a post for which a man may point his whole career, as an able young state legislator, for instance, may aspire to be governor or U. S. senator. There is no single road, or even any likely choice of roads, which leads to the national chairmanship. In the unpredictable storms of national politics, lightning may strike a man unawares and startle him into the candor of Frank McKinney when he was made Democratic chairman on October 31, 1951: "Unfortunately, I am not possessed with much information as to the operation of the headquarters, or of the National Committee, other than what I have learned in the past few days from a few of the members."[6]

The chairmanship of the two national party committees has been,

[4] Chatham, *op. cit.,* p. 300.
[5] Meade Alcorn, Lecture at University of Massachusetts, November 13, 1962.
[6] *Democratic Proceedings 1952*, p. 645.

historically, a specialized and part-time job of party financing and managing. It has been an office for which few were qualified and to which even fewer aspired.

Most of the chairmen in both parties have had one or more of the ingredients of what might be called "chairman availability": wealth, strength related to intraparty factionalism, or a personal nod from the president or nominee. Historically the strongest chairmen have had all three, although exceptions may be noted, especially among out-party chairmen. Without wealth or presidential favor Will Hays, John Hamilton, and Paul Butler were stronger and more successful than their contemporaries predicted, probably because they were toughminded, relentless, and *full time*.

A man must have a base from which to attain and keep the chairmanship. In the early years a wealthy man might buy the chairmanship of either party. At any time in the history of the committees, the president or the presidential nominee might bestow the chairmanship, like a royal favor, on a friend. But now as then, in times past as in times present, the most likely route to a national chairmanship has been related to intraparty factionalism.

Many chairmen have been leaders in the dominant party faction of the day: as chairman (and U.S. senator) Zach Chandler represented the Radical Republicans in their time of strength, as Mark Hanna represented the sound-money Republicans in their triumph, as Chairman Everett Sanders and Chairman John Hamilton represented the Midwestern Republicans in their control of the wreckage after 1932 and 1936, as Herbert Brownell and Senator Scott represented the Eastern internationalist Republicans in their not-quite recoveries of 1944 and 1948, as Stephen Mitchell in 1952 and Paul Butler in 1956 represented the frustrated national hopes of the Democratic liberals.

Factionalism will also produce neutralist chairmen. When there is no dominant faction or when the dominant faction for reasons of strategy chooses a chairman from another wing or from the unaligned, then the chairman may be the holder of the ring, the party harmonizer who is acceptable to all because he is agent for none. Eisenhower's most successful chairmen, Leonard Hall and Senator Morton, were middle-of-the-road acceptables, representing neither the Taftite congressional leadership nor the GOP liberals who put Ike over in 1952. Likewise, Rep. William Miller of New York was acceptable to Nixon, Rockefeller, Goldwater, and Eisenhower in 1961.

Among the positions of power from which chairmen may come and which help make them chairmen are member of Congress, state party organization leader, state official, and federal appointee.

Since 1848, seventy-three men have served as chairmen of the Democratic and Republican national committees. Though the Democratic committee is the older by eight years, there have been only thirty Democratic chairmen. Representative Miller is the forty-third Republican chairman.

The Republicans have more often had members of Congress as chairmen. Thirteen Republican chairmen were sitting members of Congress when chairman; three more chairmen had been in Congress, and one of these went back after serving as head of the national committee. Thus, sixteen of the forty-three Republicans (thirty-seven per cent) were or had been members of Congress when they served as chairmen of their national committee. Three other Republican chairmen were elected to Congress after their terms as head of the national committee.

The Democrats, by contrast, have had only six congressional incumbents as national chairmen; three more were members of Congress before they served as chairman, and one of these three, Cordell Hull, returned to Congress after his term as national chairman. No Democrat has been elected to Congress for the first time after serving as national chairman. Hence, nine of thirty (or 30 per cent) of the Democratic national chairmen were or had been in Congress when they served as committee head.

The greater influence of the congressional leadership in the Republican national party organization is more clearly seen in the years since World War I. Seven of the twenty-one Republican chairmen have been incumbent members of Congress and two chairmen, Sanders and Hall, former members. During twenty of the forty-four years since 1918, the Republican national chairmanship has been held by a member of Congress or a former member of Congress. The Democrats have had sixteen chairmen since 1918, of whom two were members and two were former members of Congress; their total tenure as chairmen was seven of the forty-four years.

Many of the chairmen serve part of their political apprenticeship in local and state party offices. Quite a few are veterans of several party offices or levels of offices—and Indianans Will Hays, Thomas Taggart (D., 1904–1908), and Paul Butler claimed to have started as precinct workers at the very bottom level.[7] Of the post-World War I Republicans, Will Hays, Hubert Work, John Hamilton, Harrison Spangler, Carroll Reece, and Wesley Roberts were state chairmen before becoming national chairmen; Claudius Huston and Arthur Summerfield were state finance chairmen, and Martin was executive secretary of the Massachusetts state committee in the early 1920's. Democrats James Farley, Howard McGrath, and John Bailey were state chairmen before and/or during their tenures as national chairmen. Ed Flynn, Robert Hannegan, and Frank McKinney were state king-makers and county or city bosses of great power.

It is not surprising that national party chairmen tend to come from men with considerable party experience in their states. Nor is it surprising that many chairmen have held *public* office in state or community before they reach the top of the party organization pile. Interestingly, very few governors or ex-governors have become national party chairmen. Two early Republican chairmen were concurrently governors of their states: Edwin D. Morgan, chairman, 1856–1864, and governor of New York, 1858–1862; and Marcus L. Ward, chairman, 1866–1868, and governor of New Jersey, 1865–1868. Republican Marshall Jewell had been governor of Connecticut before he held the national chairmanship from 1909 to 1912. Only one Democratic national chairman ever held a governorship; he was George White, chairman for a brief period in 1920–1921 and governor of Ohio from 1930 to 1933.

In the preparation of national chairmen, membership and leadership in state legislatures are as common as governorships are uncommon. Even Frank Walker and Clem Shaver, the least professional politicians (with Raskob) of twentieth-century Democratic chairmen, served in the state legislatures of Montana and West Virginia. Of the post-1932 Republican chairmen, Hamilton, Martin, Guy Gabrielson, Leonard Hall, and Alcorn had been members of their state legislatures, Hamilton, Gabrielson, and Alcorn serving as speakers of the lower houses of Kansas, New Jersey, and Connecticut.

The biographies of national party chairmen are filled with other political jobs, elective and appointed. From secretary of state, to

[7] A great deal of Horatio Alger tripe about the necessity of starting at the bottom in politics is talked and believed by professors and politicians alike. The political pros talk this way to encourage workers because workers are needed and would-be leaders are plentiful, and some seem to believe it. But any study of political biographies will indicate that most persons who get to the top start somewhere in the middle.

mayor, to county and state attorneys—even to Matthew S. Quay's election as prothonotary of Beaver County (the prothonotary nomination, then as now, going to a deserving party regular) from which he became, in time, U.S. senator and Republican czar of Pennsylvania.

If more testimony were needed to establish the pedigrees of national chairmen as political animals, one could find it in the federal appointments held by the chairmen on their way up the party ladders and on their way down. From cabinet offices—especially secretary of the interior or commerce and, of course, postmaster general—to local postmasterships and customs collectorships, national chairmen have had their share. Two presidents made their personal secretaries national chairmen; Taft gave Charles D. Hilles (1912–1916) the job quietly, with no fanfare, thinking, perhaps, there had been fanfare enough at the 1912 convention, after which Hilles was chosen. But the selection of George B. Cortelyou, Pres. Theodore Roosevelt's secretary, as national chairman in 1904 was accompanied by some characteristic bombast. "People may as well understand," wrote the hero of San Juan Hill to a friend,

> that if I am to run for President, Cortelyou is to be the Chairman of the National Committee. I will not have it any other way. . . . I regard opposition or disloyalty to Mr. Cortelyou as being simply disloyalty to the Republican Party.[8]

FUNCTIONS AND ROLES

It is difficult to say what a national party chairman should do. It is even hard to say what he does do. "There is simply no handbook of the powers and duties of the national party chairman."[9] Although no job description exists for the national party chairman's position, there are, however, some functions he may perform and some roles he may play if he wants to and if others will let him.

The major roles which a party chairman may assume are—ordered in their importance, we think—image-maker, hell-raiser, fund-raiser, campaign manager, and administrator.

National Chairmen as Image-Makers

The best national chairmen have been what Jim Farley called

---

[8] Chatham, *op. cit.*, p. 26, quoting Dorothy C. Fowler, *The Cabinet Politician: The Postmaster General 1829–1909* (New York: Columbia University Press, 1943), p. 279.

[9] Broder, "Strategists . . .," *op. cit.*, p. 26.

them—"drummers." Some may be chief money-raisers, some may be campaign managers of skill and renown, some may have special talents as administrators. But if they are to do the job well, they must be, first and foremost, good public-relations men.

This does not mean that they will necessarily be noisy or visible themselves. The in-party chairman, especially, may be well advised to be neither seen nor heard; the maximum party advantage may accrue, for him, entirely through the president and other party leaders in government. But the national chairmen, whether in-party or out-party, whether personally colorful or not, have a job which is fundamentally and increasingly that of directing and coordinating the public-relations efforts of the many different people and groups who bear the labels "Democrat" and "Republican."

The party chairmen have to maintain good relations with the opinion leaders of the big public, especially those who operate through and by the mass communications media, and with party leaders and activists at all levels who have to be supplied with how-to-do-it aids and satisfied in nonmaterial ways for the work which they do (or claim to do) on behalf of the national party interests.

The ideal national chairmen have to have a "feel" for mass communications. It is not just an historic accident that the first persons hired during presidential campaigns in the early part of the twentieth century were newspapermen and men engaged in the development of public opinion. It is not accident, in fact, that more than a dozen of the national committee chairmen themselves have been owners, publishers, or editors of newspapers and that many of the staff people who have worked for national chairmen, before 1930 on an intermittent campaign-year basis and subsequently on a year-round basis in Washington, have been newspapermen and others experienced in mass media.

Cordell Hull was the first full-time national committee chairman. He kept a "permanent" Democratic headquarters in Washington from November, 1921, to March, 1923. With the help of a secretary and a $25-a-week newsman named Richard Buchanan, Hull managed both the national committee and the Congressional Campaign Committee during 1922.[10]

Since World War I there have been few newspaper men as national party chairmen, but before then many chairmen were as-

[10] Cordell Hull, *Memoirs* (New York: Macmillan Co., 1948), I, 114.

sociated with newspapers: Republicans Henry J. Raymond (1864–1866), James C. Clarkson (1891–1892), Mark Hanna (1896–1904), Harry S. New (1907–1908), Victor Rosewater (1912), and John F. Hill (1911–1912); Democrats Benjamin F. Hallet (1848–1852), Thomas Taggart (1904–1908), Norman E. Mack (1908–1912), William McCombs (1912–1916), and Vance McCormick (1916–1919). Since 1918 only two chairmen, both Republicans, have been publishers of newspapers (not their principal jobs), B. Carroll Reece (1946–1948) and C. Wesley Roberts (1953).

The national chairman should be knowledgeable about public relations. He also relies heavily on publicity staff men and consultants. He needs good access to opinion leaders, especially to the Washington and national press corps, to radio and television commentators, to network officials, to the publishers and editors of specialized journals —trade journals, foreign language newspapers, and opinion journals— and to the public-relations men and advertisers who tie in with mass media organizations.

One of the peculiar and especially trying limitations of the national chairman's job is that he is expected to be an image-maker without being a policy-maker. An out-party chairman may occasionally make a sortie into policy-making terrain, but he does so at the risk of being shot at by his own army as well as by the enemy. The in-party chairman is ordinarily expected to make no forays into policy at all.

Eschewing policy, the party chairman is expected to deal primarily with what might be called public attitudes, loosely defined feelings or mental habits of goodness or badness, rather than public opinions. His job as party image-maker has its parallel in the "institutional advertising" of industrial public relations, where generalized good will, rather than specific sales, is sought. His hope is to make the audience identify or empathize with his cause by appealing to symbols with emotional content.

The prescription to avoid issues, yet to engage the emotions of the audience, results in an endless search for clever variations on a few themes. Republican chairmen and publicists find wasteful bureaucrats and big-government theorists behind all the evils of Democratic candidates and administrations. The Democrats see grasping big business and inattention to human needs in the background of all things Republican. Novelty of expression and the clever phrase are much in demand as the party chairmen and their assistants strive to get favorable attention for their own party and unfavorable notice for the opposition.

National Chairmen as Hell-Raisers

Second only to the importance of the national chairmen as an image-maker is his responsibility to be a hell-raiser. Hell-raising has to do with his style of politics among the party enthusiasts. To the wide, indifferent public he should be the leader of a party which dedicates itself to "responsible government" or "balancing the budget" or "states rights" or the "new" or "fair" or "square" deal; that is his job as image-maker. His job as hell-raiser is quite different.

Part of the accepted style of the national chairman is to be continuously, openly, and unremittingly partisan. When he speaks to the party faithful, he can be the very embodiment of the slogan, "My party, right or wrong." One of his leadership functions among the party devotees is to sharpen issues—even when the function of others, including the president and congressional leaders, may be to blur the partisan edges. The chairman can find countless angels on the side of his party, right inevitably and perpetually aligned with him and his people, and need have no word of praise for the benighted leaders and members of the opposition.

Is there a conflict, in logic and in practice, between the chairman's role as image-maker and his role as hell-raiser? If he is aggressively partisan enough to be the latter, may he not destroy his effectiveness as the former? The answer is yes and no.

There are, of course, limits even to the chairman's partisanship. The national party chairman cannot go so far as to attack the social and political consensus which is necessary for the operation of the body politic. His political sense will prevent such extremism. But to be a good fighting chairman, he must say and do many things which in other roles he would not say and do. His job is often to be a partisan's partisan: to oversimplify, to moralize, to attract the sympathies and the emotions (if not the intellectual assent) of the voters for his party and the candidates of his party.

The chairman must use his good judgment about when and how to meet his hell-raising responsibilities. But he also has going for him an elementary fact of social psychology: most people are not intensely partisan and do not know or care when the chairman is being so. Party stalwarts are few, but their contributions of talent and money are as essential for party success as are the votes of that greater number of people who support the party through an indifferent habit. Hell-raising is necessary to keep and increase the enthusiasm of the true believers. It is a matter primarily of knowing one's audience. At a rally of precinct captains or in his column in the party house organ, the chairman may be mercilessly partisan; at the national convention of the Association of Independent Druggists or in an article for *McCall's* magazine, he may be gently partisan—in the spirit of fun and toleration—but his statesmanship should prevail over-all. He has to be both image-maker and hell-raiser, but he does not have to be both at the same time. It depends on who is listening.

A second aspect of the chairman's hell-raising responsibility, closely related to the first, is his opportunity to provide a personal focus for the myths of party nationalism. If he has the individual and personal characteristics of an attractive leader, he may become, in a sense, the embodiment of the national party. The Jim Farley legend, carefully cultivated by Jim Farley, makes of him almost, but not quite, a national party boss, benevolent, genial, nurturant, and wise. Among recent out-party chairmen, Paul Butler was able to attain part of this same tinge of charisma, in large measure because of the kind of person Butler was and because he had no conflicting responsibilities to other wings of the party or to other conceptions of what a national party ought to be and do. Only someone with an intense passion for party ideology and/or loyalty can exploit the chairman's opportunities for the development of charismatic and symbolic leadership.

A national chairman who is only national chairman and who has thrown all his energies into that job has a considerable advantage over the national chairman who must divide his time, his loyalties, and his perspectives between that job and other leadership roles. A chairman who is a senator from Rhode Island or Kentucky or a congressman from New York, must be, some large part of his time, a senator or congressman. An out-party national chairman whose only job is to be national chairman may be able to provide some charismatic focal point for party loyalties and party enthusiasm. Such a personal focus will be especially important in maintaining *esprit de corps* between presidential campaigns when party activists cannot look to the candidate or titular leader for the maintenance of such *élan.*

National Chairmen as Fund-Raisers

There is only one clear tendency in the evolution of the job of national party chairman. That is the long-run change in the primary responsibility of the chairman from that of fund-raiser to that of publicist and chief partisan image-maker.

The nineteenth-century party chairmen were almost without exception chosen in part because of their demonstrated or presumed ability to raise money through personal contact. David, Goldman, and Bain say that "for many decades" the national committee chairman "was likely to be chosen primarily for his connection as a fund-raiser."[11]

Since 1900 rich chairmen have been the exception, in both parties. Chairmen now tend to be selected because they are friends of the president or candidate or because they have organizational skills, because they have influence with state and local leaders who control votes, or because they are acceptable compromises in times of factional stalemate. Other persons are relied on for contributions to maintain party organization and to finance campaigns. The treasurers and finance chairmen have taken over more of the solicitation of contributions, professional fund-raisers are used (especially by the Republican Committee), and the personal money-raising machinery of the presidential hopefuls is relied on after the nominee is chosen as well as before.

John J. Raskob, Democratic chairman, 1928–1932, was the last of the big-giver chairmen. A multimillionaire executive of DuPont and General Motors, Raskob had no political experience until he was maneuvered by William F. Kenney and Ed Flynn into a personal and political friendship with Al Smith.[12] Raskob's fortune, before the crash of 1928, "was reputed to be in the neighborhood of half a billion dollars."[13] For nearly three years, from 1929 to 1932, Raskob personally contributed $30,000 a month to maintain a full-time national committee headquarters. As a result of this unparalleled generosity, the Democrats were able to bring about the establishment of a permanent national headquarters several years before the Republicans managed to do so.

Of the chairmen since 1932 Democrats Frank Walker and McKinney were both wealthy men, and their friends felt the personal bite from each. Their ability to raise money was not overlooked by Roosevelt and Truman in appointing them, but neither was chosen for this reason alone. Likewise, Republican Summerfield, personally

[11] *Op. cit.*, p. 73.
[12] Edward J. Flynn, *You're The Boss* (New York: Viking, 1947), p. 65.
[13] Michelson, *op. cit.*, p. 14.

wealthy, deserved his reputation as a whip-cracking money-raiser. But these chairmen were selected for many reasons, of which fund-raising skill was only one.

Many recent chairmen have been men of modest income. Democrats Mitchell and Butler were working lawyers, and Republicans Alcorn, John Hamilton (1936–1940), and Guy Gabrielson (1949–1952) were lawyer-legislator-politicians in their states. Many of the chairmen have had comfortable private incomes from business or law connections, which have allowed them to serve the national committees without pay, as incumbent representatives and senators always serve. But several on both sides have opted for salary from the committees: Republican Henry P. Fletcher (1934–1936), Hamilton, William Boyle, Roberts, Mitchell, and Butler were all paid a full-time salary ranging from $25,000 to $35,000 a year.

The chairman has over-all responsibility for the money-raising enterprises, but the operations become, to a large degree, bureaucratized. Dinners are run by special honorary and working managers— often now, in both parties, under joint sponsorship with the Hill committees. The state quota systems are administered by the national treasurers, finance directors, or by deputies to the chairman. The sustaining-membership plans and small-gifts drives are punch-card, direct-mail activities or are decentralized down to the counties and precincts and shared by the lower levels of party organization. Such fund-raising is frequently a concern of the out-party chairman. The in-party chairman has other channels of fund-raising in the White House and national bureaucracy; these change the mode and effectiveness of his job as money-raiser, but they do not make the processes any less administrative and impersonal.

The national committees of the parties are still inadequately supported by too few contributors. But that is another story for another place in this book. Here we may only note that money-raising responsibilities do not constitute, as they once did, the chief duty of the national party chairman. The chairman's part of financing the party is increasingly diversified, systematized, and bureaucratized. His money-raising success is a result of his office and his institutional position rather than his personal friendships. This change is both a consequence and a reflection of the gradual development of regular continuous public-relations and service functions in the national committee headquarters.

National Chairmen as Campaign Managers

Whether the national chairman assumes major responsibility for campaign strategy will depend heavily on the prior relationship between him and the candidate. A new chairman, chosen by the candidate at the end of the convention, will typically have considerable influence in the direction of the campaign. Farley (1932), Hamilton, Martin, Herbert Brownell, and Summerfield illustrate the case for the out-party. Stevenson's choice of Mitchell illustrates the case for the in-party when the nomination is contested. When the in-party nomination is not contested, the president may plan the timing and direction of his re-election campaign as he chooses.

Sometimes, however, even when the nomination is contested, a new chairman chosen after the convention will have little influence in the campaign. Candidate John F. Kennedy chose Sen. Henry Jackson for purely strategic reasons having to do with party harmony and balance, reasons that did not require him to take a major part in the campaign. Hoover is said to have chosen Hubert Work, his doctor friend from Colorado, in 1928 on the condition that, as chairman, Work would not insist upon being campaign manager. The generalization seems to be that, when a new chairman is chosen after the convention, without having been part of the nominee's preconvention team, he is not likely to be given any campaign leadership role.

Given the likelihood of discontinuity of pre- and postconvention leadership, what can the chairman and the committee staff do before the convention to make stronger the prospects of the nominee whoever he may be? Some basic preparation for the campaign can be made by the chairman and his staff. Research on policy questions can be stepped up and backlogged for the use of the presidential candidate, the members of Congress, and the state and local candidates and speakers who will be on the hustings from August to November. Coordinated plans can be made with the Congressional and the Senatorial Campaign Committee for the use and deployment of field men, for the purchase of television and radio time, and for the employment of advertising and public-relations specialists. Rosters of potential campaign assistants, consultants, and workers can be made ready. Such planning, needless to say, must be highly tentative, changeable on the spur of the moment and often scrapped. But tentative planning is better than none at all, and an imaginative chairman may find ways to make his preconvention work valuable to the nominee and the new chairman.

In 1956 Paul Butler hoped to go beyond the stockpiling of research and documentary supplies. Before the convention he met with ranking strategists of all the potential candidates: James Finnegan of Pennsylvania represented Adlai Stevenson, Jiggs Donohue of Washington, D.C., was the Estes Kefauver agent, and Carmine De Sapio came for the Averell Harriman camp. The intention was to secure agreement on plans for the fall campaign, but nothing beyond platitudes eventuated. The campaign direction came largely from Philadelphia, with Butler's national committee staff playing a somewhat out-of-tune second fiddle in Washington.

In the preconvention days of 1960, Butler again offered to make national committee services equally available to all candidates. Once more his hopes for coordination and the systematic use of preconvention planning by the national committee were vain, as it turned out. The Kennedy organization imposed its will where it needed to— muzzled the Advisory Council; raided the committee where it pleased; took Richard Murphy and a few other top staffers; placated a few of the interests; gave the direction of a letterhead auxiliary group, Businessmen for Kennedy, to the old Butler-oriented faction of the committee, personified by Neil Staebler of Michigan and Drexel Sprecher, Butler's deputy chairman for organization; and for the most part ignored the rest of the committee, including the chairman. According to one staff man, "Robert Kennedy ran the national committee while Chairman Jackson went on tour to campaign for the ticket."[14]

The Nixon campaign was, for slightly different reasons, no better. Although Senator Morton had been Republican national chairman since early 1959, Nixon apparently never considered making him *de facto* campaign chairman. In late 1959 it was thought that Leonard Hall, a former chairman, would be in actual charge of the campaign. Retrospectively it is hard to tell who *was* in actual charge of the campaign. Those who were closest to Nixon were Robert Finch, Hall, and George Grassmuck. But no one was very close to Nixon. Hall, for example, thought he had persuaded Nixon not to fly to Alaska in the

[14] Daniel M. Ogden, Jr., "The Democratic National Committee in the Campaign of 1960," *Western Political Quarterly*, XIV (September 1961), Supplement, 27.

critical days of the campaign, but without Hall's knowledge Nixon got on the plane and the plane went to Alaska.

One of the Republican National Committee staff members, a professional of long standing, said about the relations between the Nixon preconvention staff and the RNC:

> After much backing and filling, they are coming in, we are going to restructure, we're going to do this, we're going to do that, in the end they ran it separately from 19th Street—no question about it. They ran it so separately that it began to gall on the part of many people in this physical headquarters. And remember that Bobby Kennedy was the young genius plugging the Democrat's loopholes. We did not have a similar person on our side. Bob Finch did very well as a campaign manager to the extent of his ability. But this is an example: he didn't come over from 19th Street even just to walk around and say, "Hello, I'm Bob Finch; we're on the team together." I presume he directed the entire campaign, but I can't tell you anything about it from a personal knowledge. I was here, and I might as well have been in Timbuktu. We were in different worlds. Many of their people were just names over the telephone to me, like John Hamlin and Peter Flanagan.

At a press conference on October 23, 1963, Republican Chairman William Miller announced, ". . . Each candidate, as soon as he announces himself, can appoint a liaison man to occupy a desk at Republican National Headquarters to make suggestions and keep the candidate informed on what we are doing."[15] On November 5, two days prior to the formal announcement of his candidacy, Gov. Nelson Rockefeller of New York appointed a Washington lawyer to represent him locally and form a liaison with the national committee.[16] The determination of Sen. Barry Goldwater of Arizona not to announce prematurely prevented him from taking timely formal advantage of Miller's offer, although, as in every campaign, it is to be expected that some national committee staffers are "neutral for Goldwater" just as some are "neutral for Rockfeller" in the preconvention period and that avenues of communication to the committee are not closed

[15] Transcribed from tape of press conference by courtesy of RNC staff. See also *Congressional Quarterly*, November 1, 1963, p. 1884.
[16] *New York Times*, November 6, 1963, and November 8, 1963.

to him. The results of this early liaison should be at least the dispelling of some of the suspicion and hostility toward the committee staff which characterized the Nixon campaign organization in 1960.

The long-run tendency is seemingly for the national chairman to play a smaller and smaller role in the conduct of the presidential campaign. The campaigning for the nomination tends to start early, frequently a full year or more before the election, and the hopefuls must build their own organization to the limits of their resources. Kennedy built up a field force in 1959; Rockefeller, in anticipation of 1964, had an organization in being early in 1963. The national chairman and his staff are prevented by the requirements of party harmony and neutrality to be an effective part of the preconvention campaign except for the first-term president who is widely thought to deserve a renomination.

Interestingly, in the face of the secular trend away from national chairmen as presidential campaign managers, there is recent evidence that the national chairman may be important in the coordination and nationalization of mid-term congressional campaigns. Hall in 1954, Alcorn in 1958, and both Miller and Bailey in 1962 played key roles in the congressional campaign. Sen. Vance Hartke of Indiana, chairman of the Democratic Senatorial Campaign Committee in 1962, said that "for the first time in history all three committees worked very closely together." The long-time chairman of the Democratic Congressional Campaign Committee, Rep. Michael Kirwan of Ohio, reported that Bailey and McCloskey, the national treasurer, in 1961 promised that they would give the Congressional Campaign Committee $250,000 plus $10,000 a month in 1962 if the Congressional Committee would not sponsor a separate $100-a-plate dinner. These promises were kept.[17]

Likewise, Republican Chairman Miller, a former chairman of his party's Congressional Campaign Committee who moved to the national office amid some charges that the Hill agencies were swallowing up the national group, played a key part in 1962 election strategy. He—and not Cong. Bob Wilson—was the chief spokesman for pre-election predictions and postelection analysis. Both national committees sponsored or participated in three-day "candidate schools" in 1962 and supplied much material aid as well as money to congressional candidates.

[17] Speech of Congressman Kirwan to the Democratic National Committee, Washington, D.C., January 19, 1963.

National Chairmen as Administrators and
Directors of Service Agencies

The national party chairmen are responsible, in theory if not in practice, for the work of seventy-five to one hundred people who have full-time jobs at the national headquarters. At campaign times they may also supervise some part or all of expanded forces numbering upward of three to four hundred.

The chairmen are at least nominally responsible for enterprises which have annual operating budgets of about $1,000,000 and which often have indebtedness of that much or more. Each chairman is, or would be if he took his job seriously, the center of a vast communications and service network which is directly in touch with a half-million or so Americans; sends out three to four million pieces of mail each year (more in campaign years); receives four hundred thousand to five hundred thousand pieces of mail each year, some thirty thousand to fifty thousand of which need typewritten and personalized answers.

Elsewhere the national committee personnel and staff activities are described in some detail. Here we consider only the chairman's responsibility to give direction and general supervision to the staff and the service activities of the national committee headquarters. If he has both the will and the influence, he can find work and challenge enough for much of his energies in the administration of committee activities.

He often does not have the will. More often, probably, he is a part-time chairman, prevented by the demands of other duties from applying himself wholeheartedly to his job as head of the national party bureaucracy. Sometimes he is chosen in the midst of an intraparty factional fight, with the expressed or implied understanding that he will do as little as possible in the committee headquarters.

To some extent the bureaucracy of the national committee will run itself. By chance or by policy a knowledgeable official can almost always be found to head the office force. Since 1940 the Republicans have generally designated a person to serve as executive director or chief of staff. The Democrats, too, have used the device from time to time, as when Gael Sullivan was executive director under Chairman (and Postmaster General) Hannegan, but the Democrats are typically less tidy in their tables of organization.

In 1962, the Republican top officers divided their duties roughly as follows: Chairman Miller made the appearances, the announcements, and the policy decisions; Executive Director William Warner devoted his time to a fund-raising effort which netted $750,000 in 1962 and over $1,000,000 in 1963—probably the chief factor in keeping the RNC doors open. Campaign Director A. B. Hermann shared with Warner the general management of the committee staff and directed the service functions. At the Democratic Committee, Chairman Bailey specialized in dealing with state organization leaders, and Assistant to the Chairman Charles Roche (with some difficulty, amid power scrambling on all sides) handled most of the staff management.

With competent assistants a chairman can divest himself of most or all of the supervisory functions. To the extent that the services performed by the committee for other elements of the party system are standardized and routine—the maintenance of up-to-date lists of party officials, voting records, election statistics, and the like— the bureaucracy may function adequately. But the chairman's direction is needed for the innovation of new services and the adjustment to new power balances among party leaders and groups.

In addition to his responsibilities for staff supervision, the chairman must attend to the desires and needs of important state and local party figures. For the in-party chairman this is primarily a matter of carrying out or interpreting the wishes of the president in his relations with party leaders. A state chairman or governor of an important state can always get preferential treatment at the hands of the national party chairman or, at the very least, can be heard and have his wishes seriously considered. Only on rare occasions would a national party chairman ignore or bypass or fail to clear with the state party chairman when he engages in any conversations or political activity in his state.

The national chairman's responsibility to service party leaders is illustrated by his relations with the congressional leadership of his party. Communications between congressional leaders and the national chairman tend to be more systematic and adequate than those with state leaders, though even here the reciprocal flow of information is much less than perfect. By and large the congressional party leader's wishes, demands, and perquisites are both more visible and more insistent; to that extent, Hill relations are more manageable than are those with state party leaders. The congressional voice is at least clear. The congressional leadership is almost never challenged by other congressmen, whereas state party leaders are in constant debate and conflict over who has which mandate to do what. Also, each congressman is a leader in his own right by virtue of election in his constituency and as such may command the services of the national chairman and committee staff.

Accordingly, the staffs of the national committees will respond unstintingly and with alacrity to almost any request from offices on Capitol Hill. The relations between the chairmen and the congressional party leaders are both facilitated and impeded by the existence of party campaign committees in the House and Senate. Much of the history of national party organization could be written around the attempts—as often unsuccessful as successful—to coordinate and integrate the objectives and activities of the Hill committees with those of the national committees. The national chairman figures prominently in those relationships and is in many cases the key to the success or failure of their coordination.

The ultimate importance of the chairman as administrator and agency head is related to his other responsibilities. The major functions of the national party apparatus are, as we have seen, those of general public relations (image-making), communications, and—to the extent possible—integration of party activity. To carry out these functions at all adequately, the chairman should be in reasonably effective command of his organization. A chairman who cannot give part of his time to supervision is in danger of losing some of his all-too-little opportunity to rationalize a party system which, even under the best of circumstances, doggedly resists rationalization.

5

The National Party Chairmen: In-Party and Out-Party

We have described the job of the national party chairmen in terms of the five main roles which they may play. To understand further the behavior of the chairmen requires us to distinguish between the in-party situation and the out-party situation. The chairman of the in-party, that is, of the party which has the presidency, will have a mixture of responsibilities and opportunities very different from the chairman of the out-party. How the national chairmen play their roles will be determined, in large part, by the presence or absence of a political superior in the White House.

IN-PARTY CHAIRMAN CAUGHT BETWEEN THE WHITE HOUSE AND THE FIELD

The in-party chairman has one big advantage over the chairman of the out-party: he knows who the boss is. There is no ambiguity of leadership in the party which has the presidency. The president is the leader. He may delegate his leadership responsibilities as he likes, but the ultimate responsibility is his, and he may claim and take full credit or blame for the party decisions which are made during his administration.

Like the chairman of the out-party, the in-party chairman will be expected to offer many kinds of services, personal and material, to congressional and state party leaders. His main job, however, is to satisfy one man, the president. No matter how he treats the other leaders of the party, he can retain his post and his influence as long as he manages to hold the good will and confidence of the president.

Adviser to the President

The chairman of the president's national committee may or may not be a close adviser to the president. Generalizations here, as elsewhere, are difficult to make. One might suppose that the national chairmen who were associated with a victorious presidential candidate in the early days of his career and candidacy would have more influence after inauguration than those who were made chairmen purely to improve the political or financial outlook of a candidacy in its later stages. This does, in fact, appear to be the case. One of Jim Farley's great sources of strength was his intimate association with the Roosevelt campaign in 1932 and, indeed, with the F.D.R. drive for the presidency which started with Al Smith's defeat in 1928. In the same way, Chairman Howard McGrath seems to have had increased influence on Truman's political life after Truman's surprise victory in 1948. Eisenhower's campaign manager, Arthur Summerfield, refused to continue in that post after he was offered the postmaster generalship in 1953, and it is difficult to speculate on the influence he might have possessed as national chairman had he continued in that office. Given Eisenhower's apolitical bent, it seems reasonable to believe that Summerfield might have been a powerful national chairman had he elected to hold both the chairmanship and the postmaster generalship at the same time.

A key variable in the assessment of the influence held by the in-party chairman is his personal closeness to the president. Farley, as we suggested, was a close *political* adviser of Pres. Franklin D. Roosevelt, but he seems not to have been a close *personal* friend of Roosevelt. Ed Flynn, Bronx County and New York boss, became national chairman when Farley resigned after the 1940 convention. Flynn was a near friend of Roosevelt. According to Moley, Roosevelt

. . . probably tried to restrict his contacts with Farley to set political strategy meetings in his office. Flynn, Roosevelt's other major political adviser, always seemed bored with politics, had read widely and could amuse Roosevelt with items far from statecraft and politics. He was always a close social companion, from Albany to Yalta.[1]

There was also a mutuality of political interest for both Farley and Flynn with Roosevelt. They needed the F.D.R. magic, but he also needed to keep them in line and working for the national ticket. During Flynn's incumbency as national chairman (1940–1943), White House policy seems to have been directed much more toward the allied war effort than toward the attempt to maximize party advantage.[2] Flynn's job was to keep the party machinery tuned and idling for the inevitable speed-up after the war. As a Northern big-city regular, he was just the man for that job.

Flynn's successor, Frank C. Walker, was a good friend of Roosevelt and a great admirer of the President. Sherwood says that Walker was one of Roosevelt's "principal political advisors" in late 1931 and 1932, along with Louis Howe and Jim Farley.[3] Walker was a good administrator and mediator among New Deal bureaucrats, but Sherwood appears to have exaggerated Walker's importance as a political adviser. His partisan experience and knowledge were small, and Michelson declared, with greater authority, that Walker succeeded Flynn in 1943 "with no enthusiasm." He was, said Michelson, "a quiet, shrewd, very successful businessman . . . who was catapulted into the big Democratic game by his admiration for FDR. . . . He did not want to be Postmaster General or national chairman, but could not refuse the President's request."[4]

Robert E. Hannegan, Roosevelt's last chairman and Truman's first, took office on Walker's retirement in January, 1944. He had the backing of Ed Flynn and Chicago Mayor Edward Kelley, as well as that of Sen. Harry S. Truman. He had switched to Truman in the latter's critical primary race for senator in 1940, and the support of Hannegan, St. Louis city chairman and boss, may have been the margin

---

[1] Raymond Moley, *27 Masters of Politics* (New York: Funk & Wagnalls, 1949), p. 113.

[2] There is no implication in this statement that Roosevelt became less partisan during the war, only that he recognized, as did all political leaders, that the vigorous and successful prosecution of the war was the best way to maintain popular and electoral strength for the party.

[3] Robert E. Sherwood, *Roosevelt and Hopkins* (New York: Bantam Books, Inc., 1950), I, 40.

[4] Michelson, *op. cit.*, p. 148. Walker was national chairman for only twelve months, January, 1943, to January, 1944, during which time the Democratic National Committee never met.

of Truman's victory. Thus in 1942 a grateful Senator Truman insisted
that Hannegan be made collector of internal revenue for eastern
Missouri. Sixteen months later he became commissioner of internal
revenue in Washington, recommended, Flynn says in a bit of pious cant
so characteristic of his book, "entirely because of the fine record he
had made in Missouri."[5]

According to Jonathan Daniels, Hannegan was "at least as close
to President Truman as Jim Farley ever was to FDR,"[6] but other
observers dispute the point;[7] in any case, Hannegan was not the most
powerful adviser in the Truman circle.

Howard McGrath became chairman at Truman's direction in
October, 1947. McGrath was the boy wonder of the Rhode Island
Democracy, having been vice-chairman of the State Central Committee before he was out of law school. He became state chairman
at twenty-seven and governor at thirty-seven. Although only a first-
term senator when he became national chairman, he had been U.S.
solicitor general and had, through his party and gubernatorial experiences, a firm knowledge of politics in most of the states and in
Washington. After playing an important part in the campaign of 1948,
he supervised the distribution of patronage, being especially tough on
Dixiecrat bolters who wanted to get back into the party. As with many
chairmen who have attempted simultaneously to hold other full-time
jobs, McGrath felt unable to perform well under such pressure, and
he resigned in August, 1949.

McGrath's successor as in-party chairman, William Boyle, like
Hannegan, had had a political career in Missouri, and Truman brought
him to Washington. He had assisted McGrath in the 1948 campaign,
planning Truman's whistle-stop tours and directing them on board
the trains and by telephone from Washington. In February, 1949, he
joined the Democratic National Committee staff as executive vice-
chairman, presumably to be groomed as McGrath's successor, at a
reported salary of $30,000 a year. Six months later he became chair-
man. In midsummer of 1951 Boyle became involved in a conflict-of-
interest scandal and shortly resigned because of "ill health."

[5] Flynn, op. cit., p. 178; and Harry S. Truman, Memoirs (Garden City,
N.Y.: Doubleday & Co., 1958), I, 324.
[6] Jonathan Daniels, Frontier on the Potomac (New York: Macmillan Co.,
1946), p. 125.
[7] E.g., Fred Rodell, "Robert E. Hannegan," American Mercury, LXIII
(August 1946), 134, 140.

Boyle was succeeded by Frank McKinney, a top political pro from Indiana. McKinney came in with some new-broom enthusiasm, under orders to revitalize party organization in preparation for the 1952 election. McKinney seems to have been part of the Truman plans to control the convention of 1952 and choose the candidate. However, Adlai Stevenson and Frank McKinney were very different breeds of politician, and the candidate's decision to dissociate himself and his campaign as much as possible from the Truman administration resulted in the scuttling of Frank McKinney along with most of the rest of the Truman crowd. Stevenson was scuttled, in turn, by the voters in November, 1952, and the in-party chairmen for the next eight years were Republicans.

Arthur Summerfield, Eisenhower's successful campaign manager, was perhaps the most well-known Republican state organization leader in 1952. He had attained a kind of legendary success as fund-raiser for the Republicans in Michigan and as regional director of the Republican Finance Committee. His selection as national chairman by Eisenhower in Chicago was a recognition of this organizational prowess; it was also a reward for a timely shift of the Michigan delegates to Eisenhower at the 1952 convention. After the Republican victory Summerfield was offered the postmaster generalship. He accepted and without much hesitation determined to give up the chairmanship on the grounds that, if he held both offices, he could not do a good job in either. As postmaster general, Summerfield continued to exercise considerable political authority and influence in the White House.

Summerfield's successor, C. Wesley Roberts, had one of the shortest of modern tenures as national committee chairman. Almost before he had found his desk at 1625 I Street, reports from his native Kansas implicated him in a conflict-of-interest charge in the state legislature, and the political heat rose to quite startling degrees. Eisenhower and his White House advisers sacrificed Roberts without observable reluctance.

Leonard Hall became Republican chairman on April 10, 1953. He brought with him a reputation as an exceptionally talented organization man, having held many party and elected posts including those of town chairman, county sheriff, and New York state assemblyman. He was also highly regarded by his fellow partisans in the House of Representatives, where he had served for fourteen years as congressman from his Long Isand district, the New York Second. Among his rewards in Congress had been the chairmanship of the Republican Congressional Campaign Committee.

Hall's abilities were recognized by Democratic leaders as well, and he has been called the most successful in-party chairman in the twenty-three years since Jim Farley.[8] Hall was not personally close to Eisenhower,[9] but Ike's reluctance to accept the responsibilities of chief of party and his penchant to compartmentalize leadership roles resulted in a good deal of influence for Hall when party matters were seen to be related to executive policy.

Meade Alcorn's qualifications for national committee chairman were those of a very successful state party chairman in the critical state of Connecticut. After the Republicans won the presidency but lost the Congress in 1956, Alcorn's record in Connecticut, as one of the few states where the congressional delegation improved, recommended him as Hall's successor. Alcorn's relationship with President Eisenhower and White House officials seems to have been largely *pro forma*. He was the political consultant within the context of the staff procedures favored by Eisenhower. Alcorn says that he attended cabinet meetings when political items were on the agenda, and he was called in for partisan jobs which were thought to be inappropriate for regular cabinet members.

As he had been made national chairman by his success in the election of 1956, so National Chairman Alcorn was unmade by lack of success in the elections of 1958. After some attempts to revive the party organization, he resigned in April, 1959.[10]

Alcorn's successor, Sen. Thruston B. Morton, came from the congressional wing of the party. An affable and well-liked moderate, Morton was acceptable to the Eastern liberal presidential-wing Republicans. Morton leaned very heavily on his professionals at the national committee, as any chairman who is an incumbent senator or congressman is forced to do. Morton managed to play the delicate role of balancer of party interests rather successfully from mid-1959 through the elections of 1960. A Nixon moderate by character and by political training in Kentucky, Morton was acceptable as chairman

[8] Cabell Phillips, "Party Chairmen: Study in Feuds and Funds," *New York Times Magazine,* July 1, 1956.

[9] He was not Eisenhower's first choice for the chairmanship but had been strongly backed by Joe Martin and other Republican congressional leaders. *New York Times,* January 12, 1957.

[10] See Philip S. Wilder, Jr., *Meade Alcorn and the 1958 Election* ("Eagleton Case Studies in Practical Politics" [New York: Henry Holt, 1959]).

during the campaign. He seems not to have been especially influential in campaign decisions, not so influential as Nixon's friend Robert Finch, who was campaign director, and Leonard Hall, who had the title of campaign chairman in 1960.[11]

After the Republican defeat of 1960, Morton was asked to stay on for a while, until the factional alignments became more clear. He was asked to stay, in part, because he was "a moderate whom all the party's factions can support," and his immediate resignation amid the bitterness of defeat might have touched off a bloody struggle for the succession to his job.[12] He resigned June 1, 1961, when New York Rep. William B. Miller was elected.

Democratic presidential nominee John Kennedy had two major reasons for making Sen. Henry "Scoop" Jackson of Washington his national chairman on July 16, 1960. First, Jackson was a personal friend from bachelor days in the House and a freshman senator with Kennedy in 1952. Second, Jackson's name had been suggested with some enthusiasm by Westerners as a potential ticket balancer before Senator Johnson agreed to run in the vice-presidential spot. Jackson was therefore entitled to some kind of recognition in Los Angeles in 1960. The national chairmanship was third-place prize for failure to capture the second place at the convention.

The understanding between Kennedy and Jackson was that Jackson would hold the chairmanship for the campaign. Shortly after Kennedy's inauguration Jackson is supposed to have told the President that he would be willing to give up the post. Jackson offered his resignation on a *pro forma* basis, hoping that the President would insist he remain. The story has it, however, that, when Jackson said he would quit, President Kennedy put his arm around his friend's shoulder and said: "That makes it easy for me, Scoop. Now I know what to do with John Bailey."

It had not been easy for Kennedy to find the proper place for John Bailey. Bailey's interests are not those of a state or federal administrator. His very considerable talents have been effectively utilized in party organization, in the development and maintenance of electoral machinery, and in the back-room negotiations which characterize all politics and which are especially prevalent in New England. Bailey has very little interest in programs and policy. He

---

[11] Theodore H. White, *The Making of the President 1960* (New York: Atheneum, 1961), pp. 62–63.

[12] *New York Times,* January 7, 1961, and March 21, 1961.

enjoys the prestige and power which come with winning elections. His sensitivity is the sensitivity of the experienced ringmaster who knows his performers and their skills and limitations and is able to combine them in such a way that the total production is pleasing to the eye, harmonious in execution, and successful at the box office.

Despite his early championship of the senator from Massachusetts, Connecticut State Chairman John Bailey had never been a close friend of John F. Kennedy. It is probably true, as alleged, that an important influence on Kennedy's decision in 1956 to try for the presidency in 1960 was the memorandum in which Bailey argued that a Catholic could win. Bailey's analysis of the demographic changes since 1928 and the ways in which a Kennedy campaign could be much stronger than the Smith campaign seems to have been substantially accurate. It was the first such analysis by a knowledgeable professional whose judgment was respected by Kennedy and his political advisers.

Despite this early and consistent support, Bailey's advice was not especially sought or followed during the campaign. Nor did he figure prominently in White House strategy during the Kennedy administration. The Kennedy family members and the President's friends from Massachusetts had much more to say about political decisions than did National Chairman Bailey. The President's brother-in-law, Stephen Smith, and Richard Maguire, national party treasurer, were among the most influential.

It is at least possible that President Johnson will find more use than President Kennedy did for Bailey's skills and experience. Bailey's usefulness to President Johnson is related to his influence among the professional political leaders, especially those in the big Eastern states, and his unquestioning sense of personal and party loyalty. Bailey's strengths lie in his ability as political negotiator and broker among the urban Democrats of the Northeast, and it is here that Johnson is relatively weak and Kennedy was relatively strong. Bailey was somewhat redundant in the Kennedy scheme of political power. In Johnson's he is complementary.

The chairmen of the in-party disagree about the organizational arrangements and devices best suited to coordinate national party affairs. For example, some believe that the chairman ought to attend cabinet meetings; others think that would generally be a waste of time. Whatever their views of the best formal arrangements, they would all agree with Leonard Hall: "The important thing is to have the ear of the President. That's all you need."

In-Party Chairman as Presidential Fall Guy and Trial Balloonist

Whether the in-party chairman is a close adviser of the president or, as is more common, a political organization man, part of his job will be to take political pressures and to hold aloft some of his dike-wet fingers from time to time to test the winds of public reaction to presidential policy.

On June 7, 1962, at a press conference, President Kennedy repudiated his national party chairman, John M. Bailey. Bailey had implied that Gov. Nelson Rockefeller, a leading contender for the Republican presidential nomination in 1964, had shown some anti-Negro bias. Bailey had intimated in a speech that Rockefeller had been in favor of the creation of a federal department of urban affairs until he found that a Negro was to head it. At the White House press conference six days later, a newsman said that Bailey had "accused Governor Rockefeller of racial prejudice toward Negroes" and asked the President whether he "felt even in an election year that this was a justified statement."

The President's answer throws some light on the relationships which may exist between the party leader and the party chairman. The President said he had "never seen any evidence that Mr. Rockefeller is prejudiced in any way toward any racial group." He could have ended his answer at that point or expanded his own view of Mr. Rockefeller's character. He seems to have felt, however, that the matter was set in a partisan context and that he, in his own way, might make some partisan response. Thus he added:

> I am glad to make that statement and I am sure that some of the statements the Congressman—chairman of the Republican committee—has made about me will be, I am sure, similarly repudiated by leading Republicans. I have been waiting for it for about a year and a half. [Laughter][13]

This is a revealing statement. It indicates that the most highly politicized presidents think of the chairmen of the national committees as having some special roles as partisans with a capital "D" or capital "R." The national committee chairman of the in-party does not share

[13] *New York Times,* June 8, 1962.

the inherently contradictory position which the president has as leader
of the party and simultaneously as leader of all the people. There
need be no ambiguity of representation for the chairman; his con-
stituents are Democrats or Republicans. The president, in a very different set of roles, cannot allow his friends and enemies to be drawn
so partisanly. Eisenhower, the least political of modern presidents,
seems heartily to have disliked being a capital "R" Republican. Tem-
peramentally and by experience nonpolitical, surrounded by former
army associates and wealthy businessmen, committed to a sense of
staff which delegated responsibilities widely and thoroughly, Eisenhower seems never to have been able to think of himself as having
the major responsibility of nurturing and strengthening the Republican Party.[14]

Pres. Franklin Roosevelt, by contrast, loved a good partisan fight,
but he also very keenly appreciated the need to maintain some per-
sonal distance from the most highly partisan behavior of his chairmen.
When he proposed Farley as chairman in 1932, he declared: "If the
National Committee does something that I don't like, I shall disavow
Jim Farley and it."[15]

President Kennedy, like F.D.R. and Truman, knew that an important part of his job was to be the head Democrat. Like F.D.R.,
but unlike Truman, he had enormous party and public prestige
(despite his hair-thin popular majority in 1960) with which to exploit
his institutional position as president. But if he used his party strength
too often or too blatantly, his public strength was likely to be weak-
ened. It is a common notion among the people that sharp party
attack and counterattack is mud-slinging, and the president cannot
be thought of as a partisan mud-slinger. One important component
of Truman's public image was the view of the many middle-class
"independent voters" that he was too much the politician and too
little the statesman.[16]

Knowing that he is head of his party, the president also wants

[14] P. S. Wilder, Jr., "The Republican National Chairmanship Under
Eisenhower" (unpublished manuscript). Wilder points out that the Republican
congressional leaders, mainly Taft supporters in 1952, were pleased with
Eisenhower's lack of interest in being the "authoritative spokesman for
Republicanism."

[15] *Democratic Proceedings 1932*, p. 598.

[16] Characteristically, this seems not to have bothered Truman. "A statesman," he said, "is a dead politician."

to be a statesman. He must maintain some detachment, in the public view, from the grosser aspects of party battle at the same time that he maintains control over party pronouncements and policy. Thus he needs a system of institutional buffers and personal front men. The national chairman must expect to be the fall guy at times, leaving the more prestigeful role to the president he serves.

We may cite one other recent example of the use of the in-party national chairman as trial balloonist (and perhaps fall guy). In early 1963 Chairman Bailey toured upstate New York with State Chairman William H. McKeon to demonstrate, as Bailey is reported to have said, "that Mr. McKeon was the party leader in the state."[17] Earlier the Kennedy administration seemed to have acquiesced in the implied claim of New York City Mayor Robert Wagner to be head Democrat in that state, but the White House enthusiasm for Mayor Wagner lagged with the poor showing of his candidate in the 1962 New York gubernatorial race, and Bailey's strategic job in 1963 was to keep the situation fluid until a better judgment could be made for the 1964 races.

How much of a fall guy the chairman needs to be will depend on the personal relations that exist between him and the president, whether he has party power in his own right (as a congressional leader, as a possible rival or successor to the president, as chairman of an important state committee), and the stage the presidential four- or eight-year cycle happens to be in at the moment. Presidents can afford to be more openly partisan during congressional campaigns, when Congress is not in session, and on certain occasions like Lincoln or Jackson Day dinners, which are traditional party feasts.

Kennedy's willingness to repudiate his national chairman, and his puckish request to "leading Republicans" to repudiate their own national chairman, demonstrates again the highly partisan and vulnerable nature of the chairman's role, as well as the fact that there is no single person who stands, vis-à-vis the out-party national chairman, as a president stands to the in-party chairman.

[17] *New York Times,* April 26, 1963. During the same week that Bailey was testing the political winds in New York, the assistant to the chairman, Charles Roche, was participating in some AFL-CIO conferences in the South, where there was talk of a purge of Southern Democratic congressmen who had poor presidential-support records. In this case even the chairman disavowed the role of trial balloonist, *Congressional Quarterly* reporting (April 26, 1963) that Bailey "publicly disclaimed responsibility for or knowledge of any purge."

In-Party Chairman as Postmaster General

A tradition is supposed to have grown up, by the late 1940's, that the national chairman of the in-party be given the cabinet office of postmaster general. The first national chairman to serve in the cabinet was Zachariah Chandler, Republican chairman from 1876 to 1879, who was not postmaster general but secretary of interior from 1875 to 1879. Chandler resigned the chairmanship when he was re-elected to the Senate in 1879 (where he had served from 1857 to 1875).

Two chairmen were ex-postmasters general when they assumed the party post. Marshall Jewell, Republican chairman from 1880 to 1883, had been Pres. Ulysses S. Grant's postmaster general from December, 1874, to July, 1876, but had fallen out with Grant, who forced his resignation. Jewell was part of the victorious anti-Grant coalition in the convention of 1880. Hubert Work, Republican chairman from 1928 to 1929, had also been postmaster general before his term as chairman.

First to serve in both offices concurrently was Henry C. Payne, who, according to the way one prefers it, was Republican national chairman for four months or one day in 1904. Payne was Theodore Roosevelt's postmaster general from January, 1902, until his death during the campaign of 1904. He was vice-chairman of the national committee when Mark Hanna died on February 15, 1904, and was acting chairman until the convention began on June 21.[18]

To George B. Cortelyou is usually given the honor of being the first chairman–postmaster general. Cortelyou had been Pres. Theodore Roosevelt's personal secretary and was named by the President for the campaign of 1904, becoming chairman on June 23. He continued to serve as chairman after his appointment as postmaster general in March, 1905, but resigned the chairmanship when he became secretary of the treasury in March, 1907. His successor as chairman, Harry New, publisher of the *Indianapolis Journal* and national committeeman from Indiana, held the chairmanship for only slightly more than one year (March, 1907, to July 4, 1908). Long afterward, in Coolidge's administration, having in the meantime served a six-year term as senator, New became postmaster general (1923–1929).

---

[18] He seems to have been chairman in the formal sense only one day, being elected by the committee on June 20, 1904. See William Ward Wight, *Henry C. Payne: A Life* (Milwaukee: Burdick & Allen, 1907), p. 161.

New's successor as Republican chairman, Frank H. Hitchcock (July, 1908–March, 1909), a career bureaucrat, friend and protégé of Cortelyou and his assistant postmaster general, actually resigned his national chairmanship when he became postmaster general.

The only other Republican chairman to hold that job and the postmaster generalship simultaneously was Will Hays (chairman February, 1918, to June, 1921), and he held both jobs for only three months at the end of his tenure as head of the Republican National Committee.

The summary record, then, of Republican chairmen–postmasters general is that of two persons, Cortelyou and Hays, and their total of dual incumbency was only two years and three months. Two Republican chairmen, Hitchcock and Summerfield, resigned the party job when appointed postmaster general. If there has ever been a tradition of chairmen–postmasters general, it must have been a Democratic tradition.

The Democratic chairmen who were postmasters general were Farley, Walker, and Hannegan. Their total time in the dual capacities was ten and one-half years, but Farley alone accounts for seven and one-half years of this "tradition." We would suggest that a tradition which rests so heavily on the experiences of a single chairman is hardly a tradition at all. To be sure, Farley made good use of his position as postmaster general to distribute the jobs and keep the organization in tune. As head of the Post Office Department, he had a pass with which he rode free on any railroad, ostensibly visiting post offices, but also talking from place to place with state and local leaders. He claims the Pullman charges and other incidental costs on these non-political-political junkets were paid by the Democratic National Committee.[19]

For patronage purposes it is important that the in-party have knowledgeable and reliable agents in the top administration of the Post Office Department. Postmasterships, temporary clerks, and rural mail carrier appointments provide much of the raw stuff of federal beneficence for the party faithful. But this does not mean that the postmaster general himself need be the principal distributor. In fact, it might be said that the major tradition is that of assigning an assistant postmaster general to the patronage operations of the Post

[19] James A. Farley, *Behind the Ballots* (New York: Harcourt Brace & Co., 1938), p. 281.

Office. Both Teddy Roosevelt and William Howard Taft seem to have done so, tying the national committee in through an interlocking bureaucratic leadership. Democratic Chairman Walker had his political leg-man, Ambrose O'Connell, in the Post Office Department and the national committee simultaneously. Clarence G. Adamy, patronage officer at the Republican Committee during the Eisenhower administration, dealt regularly with Summerfield's assistants in the Post Office Department. Richard Murphy, director of the DNC's Young Democratic Division from 1956 to 1960, is now assistant postmaster general for personnel; Harold Jinks of Arkansas, former regional representative of the Democratic National Committee, is now director of the Rural Mail Carriers Division of the Post Office; and Deputy Postmaster General William Brawley was actually shifted to the Democratic National Committee staff during the 1962 campaign.

It is unrealistic to suppose that there is some special political magic or tradition, good or bad, about the national chairman himself being postmaster general. The patronage and party-building ties between committees and the Post Office Department may be more effectively kept if the two offices—each of which may have a big enough work load in its own right—are not held by the same man. A good case can be made for the in-party chairman's not being postmaster general. In any event, there seems now to be no presumption that he shall be.

OUT-PARTY: CHAIRMAN AS LEADER AMONG LEADERS

The nature and importance of the work of the national chairman of the party in power will be determined in large measure by his relationships with the president. The strengths and weaknesses of the president will be reflected in the pattern of in-party leadership which the chairman shares with the president and other party dignitaries. The chairman of the out-party finds a very different political environment, however. He is at the mercy of long-standing, deliberate, and institutionalized fragmentation of national political power. The built-in conflicts and tensions in the separation of powers and the federal system have produced, since the very beginning, leadership antagonisms which underlie and determine the context for all particular problems and party issues of the day.[20]

[20] The literature on out-party leadership is large. David and associates have made a special contribution. David, Goldman, and Bain, *op. cit.,* chap. 4, pp. 75–110.

Who's Head of the Out-Party?

There are four offices and institutional positions which can provide those who occupy them with some chance of engaging successfully in the struggle for out-party leadership. Those who can contend for the national direction of the out-party are: (1) the titular leader, the defeated presidential candidate; (2) the national party chairman; (3) party leaders in the two houses of Congress; (4) successful party leaders (mainly governors) of major states.

The titular leader's strength will depend almost wholly on the degree to which he is thought to be available as a candidate in the next presidential race. If he lost badly, the presumption is against his availability and against his being able to exercise very much influence as titular leader.[21] Even if he lost only narrowly, his importance in party councils and decisions will be influenced by such factors as his age, the timing of his nomination, the unhealed intraparty conflicts growing out of the nomination and campaign, and the growth or appearance of other candidates.

Occasional factors will be present, too, and will have relevance to the influence of the titular leader. The personal and institutional strengths of the congressional leaders, of the party chairman, and of the major governors will have a bearing on the question, as will the general social adjustment and occupational role which the titular leader finds himself required or able to assume after his defeat. A defeated presidential candidate who is at the same time a leading senator will be able to maintain his strength as titular leader by combining it with his influence as a Senate leader. Likewise, a losing candidate who continues as incumbent governor of a major state, as Dewey did after his defeat in 1944, will enjoy unusual strength.[22] The titular leader who has no other position is apt to lose influence rapidly unless he can maintain visibility by being appointed to office or by private activity of significance. Thus did Richard Nixon attempt in 1962 to find another platform, namely the governor's office in California, to maintain visibility and availability for 1964.

[21] Sen. Richard Russell of Georgia, after Stevenson's defeat in 1952, said that Stevenson was the titular leader of the party and titular meant "title without authority."

[22] Perhaps the major reason that Thomas E. Dewey was the first of all defeated Republican presidential candidates to be renominated (in 1948) was the strengthened position he enjoyed as both governor of the Empire State and titular leader.

Former presidents who were not defeated in re-election bids (and were therefore not titular leaders by definition) have sometimes maintained great influence in their parties. Ulysses Grant stayed around to badger Rutherford B. Hayes from 1877 to 1881 and nearly lost the election for James Garfield in 1880; Theodore Roosevelt tired quickly of retirement and *did* lose the election for William Howard Taft in 1912. Eisenhower, ever the hero of the Republican faithful, was still the national head of the GOP in October, 1961, according to chairman Miller;[23] Richard Nixon affirmed, even before his unsuccessful race for the California governorship in 1962, that "General Eisenhower is the leader of our great party."[24]

The influence of the national chairman of the out-party, like that of the titular leader, depends on both the man and the other relationships he is able to maintain or establish on his own after the campaign and defeat. His influence will be increased to some extent, like that of the titular leader, if he simultaneously holds another position—for instance, senator or congressman—which has in its own right a claim to national party prominence. On the other hand, the out-party chairman has responsibilities which cannot so easily be met if he is a leader in another institutional role. In his image-making and hell-raising requirements, the national chairman must be more partisanly oriented than a congressional leader can usually afford to be. Hence the influence of combined authority which comes to a chairman who is also a congressional leader may be negated by other imperatives of his congressional role.

If the chairman is a near political or personal friend of the defeated candidate and the defeated candidate himself remains important in party circles, the likelihood for independent exercise of leadership on the part of the chairman is considerably reduced. In such cases the chairman must accede in his diminished importance; or, feeling his own opportunities in the eclipse of his friend and former principal, he may attempt to challenge the titular leader. Under these circumstances John Hamilton challenged Alf Landon's leadership of the Republican Party from 1937 to 1940.

If the chairman has not come to the position at the sufferance of the defeated candidate, but subsequently by election of the committee itself, his influence will depend very largely on that which he

[23] *Washington Star,* October 18, 1961.
[24] At the Gettysburg meeting, June 30, 1962, where the National Republican Citizens Committee was founded.

brings with him to the committee from his state or national activities and that which he can amass through adroit playing out of his position as chairman. Paul Butler's strength did not depend on any notoriety or any personal power which he brought with him from Indiana or from earlier political experience. Butler depended on a skillful concentration of the diverse and seemingly trivial powers which the chairman may exercise either because no one else cares to take advantage of them or because the scattered nature of power in the American parties makes such an effort of concentration so time consuming that no one other than a full-time party chairman can hope to undertake it. Sidney Hyman, in a penetrating article on Butler's leadership, illuminates the unique opportunities of this sort which are available to the chairman.[25]

The checks and balances of the federal system and separation of powers create a power vacuum which cannot be adequately filled by any of the leaders who occupy formal positions in the federal or state governments. Under the best of circumstances a president may bridge the gap and draw into his hands, from many sides, powers sufficient to carry out a limited program of reform—or sometimes quite considerable reforms, as Franklin Roosevelt did in the period from 1933 to 1937. But the president himself is so circumscribed by checks and balances that he cannot adopt the behavior which maximizes *party* advantage in every circumstance. And when the party does not have the presidency, there are no formal positions and no individuals who are compelled to resist the fractionalization of power and to lead the party in a clear and consistent manner. The chairman may be in the best position to fill the vacuum of out-party leadership. To do so, he must use the mass media to gain support from the large and ill-defined public which identifies in an electoral way with the party, and he must hell-raise, fund-raise, manage, and administer unceasingly.

The congressional leadership positions of the out-party have their own strengths and weaknesses. They are strong because no other national party leaders can command so much attention by virtue of their work and their offices. They have the visibility (if also the vulnerability) of the important policy matters with which they deal. They are strong, too, because they operate from a base which is constitutional and has significance in the consciousness of the attentive and

[25] Sidney Hyman, "The Collective Leadership of Paul M. Butler," *The Reporter*, December 24, 1959, pp. 8–12.

inattentive publics which make up the democratic society. The popular view of Congress is more favorable than the popular view of parties and partisanship. The party aspect of congressional leadership can be camouflaged from the disapproving publics by the constitutional and historic importance of Congress. No mere party leader is in a position to gain protection of this sort.

A congressional party leader has, in addition to this institutional protection, the decided advantage of being able to speak when he pleases from a national perspective without being responsible to a national public. When Lyndon Johnson was majority leader of the Senate, he was electorally accountable only to the voters of Texas, but he was able to play his national and his Texas identities off against one another as no national leader can do and as no senators in nonleadership positions can do. If the congressional leader comes from a safe congressional district or occupies a safe Senate seat— which tends to be the case because of the operation of seniority in the selection of party leaders—he may be very free to direct his image and his career along lines which maximize his influence both nationally and in his state or section.

Against these advantages must be set certain disadvantages of congressional leaders who compete for national out-party leadership. The most important of these disadvantages are closely linked to and are part of the structural-functional patterns which also provide the strengths of congressional leaders. The opportunity, even necessity, for being constantly in the mass media (which give the congressional leaders visibility and general prominence) may make it very difficult for them to engage in the kind of partisan hell-raising which, from the more narrow context of leadership in the out-party, is necessary to invigorate and arouse the faithful.

Historically, too, though this may be changing, the congressional leaders were thought to be less available as presidential candidates than other prominent members of their party, such as governors. Congressional leaders were thought to be less available because, in the course of an average to lengthy career in the Senate or House, they would have to become identified with sectional or policy interests which would weaken their claim to be attractive to voters all across the nation.[26]

[26] There is some evidence and some speculation, since World War II, that the importance of international affairs in the selection of presidential candidates makes senators, especially, more available as presidential candidates. Senators,

The claim of congressional leaders to party leadership goes beyond the arguments derived from the institutional arrangements of Congress. The congressional leaders assert, with some force and justification, that the party record, on which the presidential candidate must run in the next election, is largely made by the members of the out-party who are in the Congress of the United States. This is especially true when the out-party happens to have a majority of one or both houses of Congress or when, by the effecting of a coalition with less loyal members of the other party, the out-party is able to control the legislative program of Congress during all or half of the four years between presidential elections. The argument of the congressional leaders is simply that the gross image of the party during this period will be gradually built up by the policy debates and the projection of issues and arguments which take place in the Congress.

The key difference which separated the points of view of Sam Rayburn and Lyndon Johnson, as Democratic congressional leaders from 1956 to 1960, from the point of view of Paul Butler, as national chairman during that period, was precisely over this matter of how the party record should be created and who should be primarily responsible for its creation. Rayburn and Johnson were of the opinion that the party should be a constructive opposition, quietly reacting to the policy proposals of the president's party. Butler's notion of opposition was that the party should be anything but quiet and should be willing to take the initiative in suggesting policy and in bringing new policy ideas to the electorate and to the congressional forum as well. Johnson and Rayburn said, in short, that the Democratic record should be built up by moderate, considerate, and thoughtful handling of those issues which the Republicans were prepared to raise in their presidential program. Butler would not leave the initiative to the Republicans, but conceived it to be the function of the opposition—especially the opposition which, as was the case, had a nominal control of the two houses of Congress—to be an active source of policy ideas and proposals. Butler thought, at the very least, that it was the duty of the Democratic Party to raise policy matters which could be debated in Congress and openly in the mass media. Butler's point of view reflected, of course, that of the presidential party. The view of the congressional leadership reflected the practices

---

it is said, give more continual attention to foreign policy matters and tend to be familiar with the details of international relations.

of the House and Senate, where various kinds of complex, but not necessarily national, coalitions are sufficient to carry the day.

The final group of claimants to national out-party leadership is made up of party figures outside Washington, D.C., who have national prominence because they are possible presidential candidates. Because of the importance given to the large states by the electoral college system, the governors of these states have been historically more available for presidential nomination than perhaps any other party leaders.

The governors of New York, California, Massachusetts, Pennsylvania, Ohio, Michigan, and Illinois must be considered by party leaders when a presidential candidate has to be chosen. How long or seriously these governors will be considered depends on a number of things: the governors themselves as men, and more importantly as vote getters; the ideological and policy positions which they have taken and which may have national significance; such personal factors as age, religion, and ethnic background; and many intangible factors relating to the support which they claim or have from party leaders and important voting blocs in the states thought necessary for presidential victory.

Like congressional leaders, the governors of major states find that their institutional positions both help and hinder their aspirations for out-party leadership. They are tied to their states more precariously than are the senators or congressmen who gain leadership positions in the Congress, but who are protected and screened from the state issues which fall with all their force on the governors. Saddled by the manifold problems of their states, the governors are not afforded an opportunity to become conversant with the national and international problems which are dealt with daily by the congressional leadership and which now figure so prominently in presidential campaigns.

On the other hand, the governor, precisely because he is actively engaged with a variety of problems understood by state party leaders, by other governors who tend to be important in their state delegations to the national conventions, and by the delegates themselves, is able to gain both sympathy and support from other state-oriented people on whom the presidential candidate depends for election. The congressional leaders necessarily lose some of the feeling for state campaigning and for state party organization which the governor must constantly deal with. In short, congressmen lose some of their state perspective, and state party organizations with state perspectives nominate and elect the president of the United States.

If a governor has the opportunity to look ahead, has the resources, and has some measure of good luck in his political career, he may be able to indulge in presidential aspirations. Such a governor may organize for out-party leadership in a way that congressional leaders and other leadership claimants cannot organize and plan. In this regard any governor of New York is in a good position to seek the national leadership and presidential nomination of his party.

The likelihood of governors claiming and exercising a large measure of national party leadership seems to have diminished in recent years, and one is obliged to believe that of the four positions which may be springboards of out-party leadership—titular leader, national chairman, congressional leader, major state governors—the governors have become less important with the changing significance of international affairs, with the nationalization of mass media and governmental policy issues, and with the over-all tendency toward centralization of institutions and issue discussion in the nation's capital.[27]

Special Need for Image-Making, Hell-Raising, and Administration

In the out-party the chairman has special needs and opportunities to provide a national focus for party affairs. The in-party's image and prospects will rise or fall mainly on the strength of the president's programs and popularity; there is little the chairman can do, independently of the White House, to affect the party's fortunes.

Not so for the out-party. The out-party leadership vacuum invites increased activity by the chairman. The various elements of the presidential party, though frequently embittered, confused, amateurish, and poorly led, require a spokesman. The major pressure groups aligned with the party especially need an office and official for the articulation of their national interests. Business groups need the Republican National Committee more when there is no Republican in the White House; labor and liberal groups take renewed interest in the Democratic Committee and chairman when that party is out of power. For these reasons there is a tendency, or at least an opportunity, for the national chairman of the out-party to indulge more vigorously the chairman's roles as image-maker, hell-raiser, and administrator.

[27] See Louis Harris, "Why the Odds Are Against a Governor's Becoming President," *Public Opinion Quarterly*, XXIII (Fall 1959), 361–370.

(He may or may not have increased fund-raising or mid-term campaign managing responsibilities.)

In out-party years national committees increase their publicity activities. The Michelson propaganda job on the Republicans was the principal effort of the invigorated DNC from 1929 to 1932. Throughout the thin years of 1952 to 1960, the Democrats published their brilliantly satirical *Democratic Digest* at a loss of more than $300,000 in the years 1956–1959 alone. After the Republican defeat in 1960, the newsletter *Battle Line* was revived by the RNC to carry the partisan message to the country, especially to sympathetic local leaders and party workers.

New programs and staff increases have come mainly in out-party years. Hull's establishment of the first "permanent" national headquarters occurred directly after the Democrats had lost what Teddy Roosevelt called the "bully pulpit" of the White House. Raskob's second "first permanent" headquarters was an out-party development. Hamilton's reorganization and elaboration of the Republican committee were likewise signal events of out-party years. The quite understandable tendency is for the out-party chairman to reinforce his claims to national leadership by expanding the tested programs and introducing new ones.

The out-party chairman's efforts to fill the national leadership vacuum are not limited to increased internal vigor and exhortation. Improved relations are sought with the big public. Image-building may fall to the chairman in the absence of presidential leadership. Attention and support may be attracted by issuing policy statements, whether *ad hoc* pronouncements of the committee or its chairman or products of some advisory group. Two of the three attempts by the Republican National Committee to formulate goals and principles of Republicanism have occurred during out-party years. To date the most successful of national policy devices, the Democratic Advisory Council, flourished—amid intraparty conflict, to be sure—during out-party years, but disappeared without a trace after the Democratic victory of 1960.

Beyond the obvious and conscious increase in image-making and hell-raising by the out-party chairman, he has more mundane and less dramatic devices for increasing his influence. His daily management of staff and service output may more directly reflect his own views and may be subtly used to improve his stature in the party.

Any chairman has great discretion in the management of the service functions of the national committee, but the chairman of the out-party may almost completely control the aid and services which are available to party organizations and activists from the national headquarters. The chairman of the out-party can use these services to enhance his own position as party leader and to reduce the influence of other claimants. In both the kinds of material which issues from the committee and the kinds of relations that are established with party leaders at the national and state levels, the national chairman can encourage his friends and discourage those who are not; the out-party chairman is thus in an improved position to determine the meaning of the party in the minds of his fellow partisans and in the mass electorate as well.

OVERVIEW II: POWER AND RESPONSIBILITY

Our first overview of the national party chairman's job indicated that it was one of uncertain dimensions, dimly and distortedly perceived by party enthusiasts and the public, but nevertheless one from which great accomplishments were expected although it had almost no traditional power or regular support. In our more detailed look at the chairman's job, we found it to consist of five major roles: image-maker, hell-raiser, fund-raiser, campaign manager, and administrator. The opportunities and limitations of these role responsibilities of the in-party chairman were seen to differ greatly from those of the chairman of the out-party. We can now summarize the findings of our survey of the national party chairmanship.

Who Speaks for the Party?

Whether or not we have national parties in the United States, the parties which we have do, or ought to, represent something more than valueless, issueless groups of technicians concerned only with winning elections. The ancient saw that we have two parties in the United States because there are two sides to every office, the inside and the outside, does not provide an adequate basis for examining American politics. Political parties, however blurred in their images, must purport to stand for something more than the naked acquisition of power.

Who should define what the parties stand for? It is easy to say that the national chairman should be a political mechanic, concerned only with winning elections and uninterested in policy or program. It is not easy to conform to such an axiom, nor, in our view, would it be wise. The five roles which make up the chairman's job are in part those of a mechanic, but in part they also require the chairman to be a policy-maker. Campaign direction and fund-raising, the main duties of the early chairmen, have increasingly given way to responsibilities which involve adroitness in the leadership demanded and made possible by the advanced technology of a big democracy.

The in-party chairman both gains his influence and wields it primarily through his links to the president. These are mainly informal and vary widely from president to president and chairman to chairman. Some presidents have found it desirable to make these links more formal by giving a cabinet post, usually that of postmaster general, to their party chairmen. In a staff conference at the RNC, Chairman Morton once declared (we paraphrase):

> In the days when I was assistant secretary of state under John Foster Dulles, I found frequent necessity to attend cabinet meetings. I sometimes feel that Mr. Dulles traveled so frequently and so far to avoid the tedium of cabinet meetings. I am not at all anxious to incur the obligation regularly to attend such meetings. However, I think it important that the national chairman of the party in power be apprised of the agenda for cabinet meetings and be able, at his discretion or the request of the president, to attend and voice his opinion concerning the political implications of the policy alternatives discussed. Having informed the cabinet and the president on the political significance of their decision, he must then accept and support whatever choice they determine to be in the national interest.

The tradition of giving cabinet status to national chairmen by making them postmasters general has been easier put aside than can be the practice of considering their views on policy issues of moment. The national chairman of the in-party should be a chief political adviser to the president in fact as well as in theory. In turn, if he is equal to his job, he will be best informed on the strengths and needs of the president's party which, along with the out-party, provides the essential life force of American democracy.

The party out of power is peculiarly at the prey of public demand that it have a spokesman. The position of titular leader is largely mythological; the idea of the titular leader in the United States has only a little more viability than the idea of a shadow cabinet. Only when a defeated presidential candidate can keep his visibility, a party nucleus, and public support does the theory of titular leader fit the brutal facts of political life. Otherwise, through whom shall the out-party speak?

Complicating the problem is the frequency with which elected members of Congress are selected as party chairmen. It is difficult for a congressman who is also a national chairman to vote his constituency interest or his conscience in matters coming before the House without seeming thereby to give a clue to what his party stands for. It may be an oversimplification for the working press and American public to impute to him a policy-making role for the party when he is acting as congressman, but this they do, and this imputation he cannot avoid.

A policy-making role will be ascribed to any out-party chairman, whether or not he occupies an elective office such as congressman, since we live in an age in which party chairmen necessarily perform on a national stage. They must appear on "Meet the Press," "Face the Nation," and a dozen other mass media productions. They must speak at rallies and debates and forums across the country and, in doing so, must respond not to the question which we present here—"Who speaks for the party?"—but to "Where does the party stand?"

The party which does not have the presidency—whether or not it has a majority on the Hill—is under heavy pressure to produce a spokesman. It is unlikely that the so-called titular leader can serve as the single dominant spokesman for the party. The party's representatives on the Hill are persons with electoral mandates and hence authorized to speak for the party on some policy matters, but their constituencies are too restricted to permit them to speak with national authority.

For the party out of power, the chairman is the one person who has day-to-day responsibility for drumming up the party's fortunes on a national basis. To him people will unavoidably look for policy guidance as well as for the magic formula of electoral victory. He may share his policy-making responsibility with advisory groups and committees, and neither he nor his advisory groups will ever exercise the responsibility with ease. They will constantly be subjected to criticism from those with electoral mandates. They will always be in the unhappy position of attempting to fill an unfillable void.

6

National Conventions and Campaign Organizations

Although the staging of the national nominating conventions is one of the national committees' chief functions, until recently the lore of convention-staging was never written down. Most of it was known only to such long-time committee executives as William J. Donald of the Republican National Committee.

Reviewing Donald's career at the RNC is like reading the history of the Republican Committee over a twenty-five year period. A native of Scotland, he was brought to the RNC by Chairman Hubert Work when Work moved from the Department of Interior to the party post in 1928. Donald soon became the indispensable member of the committee staff. At times, in the lean years after 1932, he is reputed to have met the payroll of the RNC staff out of his own pocket, and certainly he went without salary for months at a time. Donald served a succession of chairmen and was responsible for national conventions until, in the mid-1950's, a severe heart attack signaled to him the need to prepare a successor. Josephine L. Good was brought to the

107

committee in March, 1956, from her position as confidential and administrative aide to Postmaster General Arthur E. Summerfield, and Donald began imparting to her from his memory the myriad detail and the chronology of activity leading up to the most spectacular event in American politics.

In 1960 Miss Good became executive director of the convention. Between 1956 and 1960 she transferred to paper a kind of blueprint for staging a national convention. Such a document has not yet been prepared by the DNC. Our account of the work leading to and following the national conventions is based largely on Miss Good's records.

From the point of view of the national committee, the problem of staging a national convention is largely one of moving and quartering troops—some twenty thousand to forty thousand of them, including delegates, minions, mass media people, the head of state, prospective candidates, and thousands of hangers-on, assembled to see the nearest that the American democracy has been able to contrive to the Roman circus. The term is all the more descriptive because of the popular conception of the national convention as a forum for speech-making and for logical discourse, understood in the context of the mass psychosis which perceptive observers, such as Lord Bryce, have always seen in a national convention. It is a ritual of words, banners, and other more subtle forms of communication, all glossing a power struggle such as must periodically take place in every political society.

SHEETS, BEDS, AND TELEPHONES

Captain Bluntschli of George Bernard Shaw's *Arms and the Man,* combining as he did qualities of practicality and courage, was willing to eat chocolates to survive and to count his inheritance in terms of

> . . . Nine thousand six hundred pairs of sheets and blankets, with two thousand four hundred eider-down quilts. I have ten thousand knives and forks, and the same quantity of dessert spoons. I have three hundred servants. I have six palatial establishments, besides two livery stables, a tea garden, and a private house.

Simultaneously he counted his achievement in terms of

> . . . four medals for distinguished services; I have the rank of an officer and the standing of a gentleman; and I have

three native languages. Show me any man in Bulgaria that can offer as much!

His position is not dissimilar from that of a national committee seeking the presidency.

It is a function of the national committee to make possible one of the most important decisions in Western democracy, namely, the nomination of a candidate for president of the United States. But it is also the committee's task to be sure that the nomination takes place in a context in which there are enough sheets and enough telephones for all. The national committee is at once general officer and innkeeper in the struggle to determine who will compete for the first position in the first democracy of the free world.

The organizational and housekeeping problems of staging a national party convention do not vary much between the parties. What is true of a Republican convention, with a change of time, place, labels, and actors, is true of the Democratic convention. To avoid a pedantic comparison of the two 1960 conventions and to give a little drama to our account, we take, in case-study form, the story of the Republican National Convention, Chicago, 1960.

HArrison 7-1960

If you wished to contact one of the thousands of people assembled in Chicago to perform a function in connection with the Republican National Convention of 1960, your problem was a relatively simple one. You asked your local operator to get you the convention operator in Chicago. One of a flock of Illinois Bell Telephone operators received your call and channeled it to the national committee staff at HArrison 7-1960, to the convention at the convention hall, or, after scanning a card register kept current on an hour-to-hour basis, to one of the delegation headquarters hotels or mass media offices. There your party was quickly reached in person or by messenger.

Simple and sensible as this service might seem, it did not "just happen." It was the product of a planning cycle which, for the Republican National Committee, extended back four years in time and reflected 104 years of experience in staging presidential nominating conventions. For the host city, for the newspapers and broadcasting media, for such private firms as Illinois Bell, which provide services essential to the conduct of the convention, it reflected at least a year of planning and liaison with the national committee and its subsidiary groups.

The introductory description in terms of military logistics and the preoccupation of Captain Bluntschli, the "Chocolate Soldier," with sheets and blankets are all the more appropriate at the national convention of the party in power. It must call in the Army Signal Corps to set up a communications center capable of keeping the president in touch with the White House and his global responsibilities during his visit to the convention. Arrangements must be made with the Secret Service, and the Air Force must provide transportation, all of this to be coordinated with a harassed national committee staff and all attendant costs to be reimbursed to the government out of the national committee treasury.

To trace the course of planning and preparation for the 1960 Republican National Convention, it is necessary to shift from HArrison 7-1960 in Chicago, to NAtional 8-6800 in Washington, D.C. At either number one will encounter the same busily cheerful voices, since the national committee switchboard operators move to the convention city, taking with them their familiarity with certain voices and personalities and a highly developed capacity to initiate the process of screening which determines who will handle the incoming calls for the chairman at the national committee.

The Convention Cities

Three constants confront the planners of a national convention. One, the convention will be held in a presidential election year. Two, the formula for apportioning delegates is prescribed in the rules adopted by the previous convention or subsequently by the national committee. And three, there are only eight or nine cities in the United States which can seriously be considered as convention sites. Some of the requirements for a convention city follow.

There must be at least ten thousand first-class hotel rooms near the convention hall or within reach of fast transportation to the convention hall. Among the hotels there must be a capacity to provide at least one suite for each state headquarters, the size and elaborateness of the suite depending on the size of the state delegation. Collectively the hotels must be capable of catering to the politicians' penchant for holding special breakfast, luncheon and dinner meetings, ranging in size from five to three hundred or more. Each candidate for the office of president and vice-president must have campaign headquarters facilities at one of the central hotels. The guideline the national committee provides is to plan on at least four to six such candidates. Unstated, but a political fact of life, is that hotel facilities, like the convention hall facilities, must be available without discrimination based on race.

It is essential that there be one hotel which is suitable as the convention headquarters hotel. It must be centrally located. It must be able to provide the Arrangements Committee staff with office space eight to ten months ahead of the convention and space for the Housing Subcommittee six months prior to the influx of delegates. The convention officials will require twenty-five to thirty suites in the headquarters hotel, and national committee members and staff will require rooms for approximately two hundred and fifty persons. The hotel must have public (theater-type) meeting space for two meetings of the national committee and one meeting of the Credentials Committee. It must also have meeting space for the Arrangements Committee and other groups, ranging from fifty to one hundred persons, any four of which might be meeting simultaneously.

Of equal importance to the housing of the convention officials and the national committee and staff is the provision of some fifty thousand square feet of working space for the press, radio, and television. Parking space and lobby space to accommodate information desks are another headache for the headquarters hotel.

And, of course, there are other requirements. The city should have a convention hall capable of seating at least fourteen thousand, with about eighteen hundred of these in box seats. It must be air-conditioned. The press will require approximately one hundred thousand square feet of space in the convention hall or immediately adjacent to it. The national committee chairman, the chairman of the convention, and other officials require office space in the convention hall, and one must count on three or four simultaneous caucuses numbering fifty-nine to one hundred people each. Radio and television will require rooms in which to conduct interviews; those filling the fourteen thousand seats will wish to take at least one meal a day in the immediate vicinity of the convention hall. The post office, Western Union, the telephone company, will all require space.

The forgoing are minimal requirements. The Republican National Committee lists under "Information Required" concerning the convention hall questions which are hardly subtle in their implication of further requirements. Does the hall have an organ? If so, describe.

Is there a permanently installed bandstand? Describe seating facilities. What are the rest-room facilities? Describe fire safeguards and give number of entrances and exits. Also, what arrangements are made for cleaning the hall? Wiring facilities must be adequate to permit installation of microphones at the seat of each delegation chairman. Will special cables for television be necessary?

There are requirements of transportation to the convention city and from the hotels to convention hall. Airport facilities, railroad stations, their locations, and the cost of taxi and bus transportation to the hotel center are factors which influence a city's qualifications.

Inevitably the presentation made to the Site Committee by the mayor, chamber of commerce head, and others will come to the matter of money. The Republican National Committee asks a minimum guarantee of about $350,000 from the convention city. The actual offers received for the 1960 and 1964 conventions have exceeded this amount. Indeed, the Atlantic City offer of $690,000 for the Democratic National Convention is the highest in history. The contribution may take the form of a combination of cash and service, including such considerations as free rental of the convention hall, free cleaning of it, complimentary space at the headquarters hotel, and so on. There is no legal requirement for accounting for the funds contributed and received by the Arrangements Committee as the result of such a guarantee. Presumably the donors are not contributing to a political party, but are attempting to benefit local business by bringing the convention to the city. Prior to 1956, when Meade Alcorn was vice-chairman of the Arrangements Committee (the chairman of the Republican National Committee is the chairman of the Arrangements Committee), no accurate records of disbursements from Arrangements Committee funds were kept. In 1952, for example, the doorkeepers at the Republican National Convention were paid in cash. In 1956 they were paid by check at the end of the convention. Disbursements are made by the treasurer of the Arrangements Committee on certification of the vice-chairman. Any funds remaining with the Arrangements Committee at the end of the convention are kept in a bank in the convention city and may be drawn on only by the chairman, vice-chairman, and treasurer of the national committee.

The requirements outlined above suggest why in 1960 the Republican National Committee received convention invitations only from New York City, Philadelphia, Chicago, Miami Beach, Los Angeles, and San Francisco. And, of course, there are more subtle considerations influencing invitations and selection. Atlantic City has one of the best convention halls in the country and plenty of hotel rooms, but these are matched by a determination to keep the summer business. Thus the local businessmen and officials are reluctant to tie up the city with a convention between the last week of June and Labor Day. The Republicans did not wish a June convention date in 1960, and Atlantic City withdrew its bid. For 1964 Atlantic City and the Democrats compromised with a late summer convention to begin at the beach resort on August 24. After considering bids from Atlantic City, Chicago, Detroit, Miami Beach, Dallas, Philadelphia, and San Francisco, the Republicans in 1964 succumbed to San Francisco's cash offer of $650,000 and scheduled a convention to open at the Cow Palace on July 13, thus allowing time for fund-raising and organizing the campaign once the candidates are selected.[1]

Political considerations are weighted in some fashion along the way to selection. It is good if the governor is of your party, although not essential that the mayor be. Thus in 1960 the Republicans were greeted in Chicago by a Republican governor, but by a Democratic mayor who was later accused of stealing a substantial number of Republican votes. In Los Angeles in 1960 the Democratic delegates were greeted by a Republican mayor and a Democratic governor who had not shown agility in joining the Kennedy campaign boom. It appears more difficult in recent years to engineer the choice of convention city to further the candidacy of any prospective nominee. The Site Committee is chosen with the purpose of excluding from it representatives of states from which nominees are likely to come. Indeed, the Nixon candidacy in 1960 sufficed to rule out Los Angeles and San Francisco as Republican convention cities. New York was similarly disadvantaged by the dark horse candidacy of Nelson Rockefeller.

There are supposed advantages in holding a convention in a city other than that which hosted the opposition party and in holding it later than the other party. In 1956 the Republicans, determined to keep the campaign short, investigated the filing dates for getting candidates' names on the ballots in all states and discovered the first deadline for filing nominations in the general election, just as in the primaries, was New Hampshire's. Fortunately the secretary of state for New Hampshire was a delegate to the convention, and it was possible to hand him, on the convention floor, the certificate of nomina-

---

[1] *Washington Post,* June 26, 1963; *Washington Star,* June 23, 1963.

tion of Eisenhower and Nixon, thus pushing the convention up to the last possible moment and at the same time complying with the New Hampshire law on filing.

There are publicity considerations, too, for the Site Committee. The advent of radio and television coverage of national conventions introduced another kind of time problem—that of daily scheduling to maximize the audience over the four U.S. time zones. On this criterion Chicago is the ideal convention city. The GOP found it necessary to run the 1956 San Francisco convention by rigid script in order to assure that the sessions were keyed to prime viewing hours across the country. Chicago allows more flexibility in convention proceedings consistently with ensuring that convention highlights will occur during prime nationwide viewing time. However, even for Chicago-based conventions, the heavy hand of television, rendered still heavier by America's complicated time-zone and summer "fast-time, slow-time" local options, may force the preconvention settlement of intraparty fights and suppress the last vestige of true extemporaneity from the conventions as the price of pacing the show to maximize Trendex ratings.

The Chronology of Convention Management

The Site Committee, on April 11, 1959, recommended to the Republican National Committee that the 1960 convention be held in Chicago. The recommendation was accepted. The convention took place July 25–28, 1960. The formal process of planning it commenced when Meade Alcorn appointed the Site Committee on August 27, 1958, fewer than two years after the most recent presidential victory for the Republicans and a few months short of the congressional and state elections which turned out so badly for the Republican Party.

The Site Committee, composed of three men and three women, met in January 1959, in conjunction with the Republican National Committee meeting in Des Moines, Iowa, and heard presentations from Los Angeles, San Francisco, Chicago, Philadelphia, Atlantic City, New York, and Miami Beach. As we have indicated, the committee was as much concerned with the cash payment which could be offered by the cities as in the physical arrangements available. Ideally—in a sense not to be approximated by reality—the committee will entice a city into paying all of the costs of a convention, with a surplus assured to enable the next Arrangements Committee to take up its tasks.

Some of these expenses have been alluded to earlier. The cost of transporting the president may amount to $15,000. The cost of moving the national committee staff to the convention city by chartered plane—an economy—must be met. In 1956 and 1960 the head stand for television, which obstructs the view of delegates but enables television viewers to have a clear view of the platform, proved more expensive than anticipated. Prior to the nationwide televising of national conventions, which began in 1952, teleprompters were unnecessary. Today it costs about $10,000 to install one. Telephone service for the 1960 Republican convention was budgeted at $20,000. Little wonder that the national committee, which, after the 1956 convention, picked up an Arrangements Committee deficit and put $2,000 in the bank to start the next Arrangements Cimmittee, in 1960 found itself again picking up a deficit and depositing a modest $1,800 to start the 1964 operations.

The possession of a piece of paper known as "the Call" legitimizes a delegation to the national convention. One of the principal functions of the national committee under the rules adopted at each national convention is to issue the Call. This is done through the Committee on Call, appointed by the chairman in the same manner in which he appoints the Site Committee. Thruston Morton appointed the Call Committee for the 1960 convention in May 1959, and for the first time a woman, Mrs. Consuelo Northrop Bailey, national committeewoman for Vermont, was named as chairman.

The Call is as obscure as it is integral to the constituting of the quadrennial governing body of the party which, like the cicada, spends months in chrysalis and, upon emergence, lives but a few days. So obscure is it that people appointed to chair the Committee on Call have been known to ask, "What is the Call?" Rule 24, adopted by the Republican National Convention of 1960 provides that "The National Committee shall issue the Call for the next National Convention . . . at least four (4) months before the time fixed for said Convention." Both parties treat the document with veneration in all stages of its preparation. The Call specifies the apportionment of delegates among the states and territories in conformity to the mode adopted by the convention or the committee. The mode of distribution of the Call lies in the discretion of the Committee on Call and the national committee and might vitally influence the character of the delegation from any state. Possession of the Call is one of the primary factors to be considered in deciding a delegation contest. So sensitive is the handling of this document that national committee staff members have been known to claim that, were the chairman of the party to request extra copies of the Call, he would first be asked why he wanted them, then refused them, and finally granted them only under protest.

Traditionally the Call states the time and place of convening of the convention, the rationale for composing the convention, the formula for choosing delegates, rules for filing credentials and contests, and a statistical table presenting the apportionment of delegates among the states and territories. It is, in effect, a call to the recipients of it to take the steps outlined in it toward selecting delegates to the next convention. Thus, presumably, it goes only to those persons in positions of legitimate party authority to discharge this duty. Its possession is prima facie evidence that the recipient and his state's delegation appear at the convention as a result of legitimate processes of notification and selection.

The Call is delivered by registered mail, return receipt requested, and the envelopes are stamped with the day and hour of mailing. In 1952 one copy went to each Republican National Committee member, with extra copies to the senior member for him or her to transmit to the chairman and the secretary of the state central committee. In 1952 two delegations appeared from Texas, South Carolina, and Mississippi, each with a copy of the Call. This resulted in crucial delegate contests which may have determined the outcome of the convention.

By 1960, as a result of the rules change in 1952, most state chairmen were members of the Republican National Committee. In consequence, a change was made in the system of distributing the Call. One copy of the Call was sent to each national committeeman and committeewoman and one copy to each state chairman. In departing from the practice of relying on the senior national committee member from the state to deliver the Call to the state party authorities, the national committee gave added stature and power to the state chairmen. For example, the changed method of distribution solved the "Mississippi problem." The long-time national committeeman from Mississippi, Percy Howard, a resident of the District of Columbia, a Negro, and head of the Republican National Committee–supported "phantom" party in Mississippi, did not recognize the white chairman of the party in Jackson. In sending a copy of the Call directly to Chairman Wirt Yerger, the quadrennial contest between the Howard delegation and the Mississippi delegation was ended. It is entirely possible that this method of distribution, which solved certain problems in 1960, especially for the party in the South, may create future problems. For example, in distributing the Call for 1964, the national committee could find itself in the unenviable position of deciding which of two rival claimants to the state chairmanship should have his claim legitimized by the receipt of the Call.

As if these delicate considerations were not enough, each twenty years the committees confront a problem of apportionment which can be decided only on an *ad hoc* basis. Delegates are chosen in part by congressional district. The decennial census and the problem of re-apportionment of congressional districts in the states did not affect the selection of delegates in 1960. Before *Baker* v. *Carr* it might have been assumed that the congressional apportionment problem would not affect the composition of the convention in 1964, by which time reapportionment in the states would have been completed. Indeed, there are only one or two states which may be in litigation on apportionment problems in 1964. No problem exists for 1968. But each twenty years, when the convention is held in the second year of a new decade, the parties encounter a situation in which states are mapping a redistricting at the time the Call is issued, and in some states it is therefore necessary to adjust delegate distribution after reapportionment.

After distribution of the Call certain rules are followed which aim at protecting the integrity of the convention. Where delegates are elected in state convention, forms are provided authenticating the election of delegates, and these forms must be certified by the secretary and chairman of the convention. In those states in which delegates are elected in a primary, a list is certified by the secretary of state. There are many unusual or unique problems of certification. For example, California can be counted on to bedevil those who must make up the roster of alternate delegates at the Republican National Convention, for it selects alternates at the last moment in the site city, when it has been discovered who is at hand.

An unofficial sheet of delegates is prepared in the site city for the press. Where there are contested delegations, both are listed. The temporary roll of delegates is completed in the site city the night before the convention opens. It contains a section on disputed delegations, as decided by the national committee. The national committee must put off the printing of the permanent roll until the Committee on Credentials has decided whether to accept the temporary roll. If the fight over contested delegations goes to the convention floor, the permanent roll cannot be printed until this is settled. In effect, the preparation of the permanent roll of delegates begins with the distribution of the Call but does not end until it accurately reflects the report of the Credentials Committee and the results of any convention floor fight.

Such are the vagaries of politics that, all of these shoals having been avoided in 1960, the permanent printed roll was not distributed on schedule because the truck carrying it was caught in the traffic generated by President Eisenhower's visit to the convention, and the police would not let it through.

On May 25, 1959, the Republican National Committee Chairman Thruston B. Morton announced the appointment of four committees for the 1960 convention, "including a 50-member committee on arrangements which will handle the advance setting-up of the Convention." The other committees were those on rules (forty-four members), contest (seven members) and Call (forty-four members). Traditionally the chairman of the national committee serves as chairman of the Arrangements Committee, and the person who does the work is the vice-chairman of the Arrangements Committee who, for the Republicans in 1960, was Jaren L. Jones, national committeeman for Utah.

The range of logistical problems confronting an Arrangements Committee is well illustrated by the subcommittee organization of the Republican Arrangements Committee in 1960:

> Subcommittee on Badges
> Subcommittee on Concessions
> Subcommittee on Convention Program Planning
> Subcommittee on Decorations
> Subcommittee on Housing
> Subcommittee on Press, Periodicals, and Photos
> Subcommittee on Radio, TV, and Motion Pictures
> Subcommittee on Tickets
> Subcommittee on Transportation

An effort is made to secure representation of each state on the Arrangements Committee. Although, as suggested above, the vice-chairman must bear the brunt of the responsibility, the executive secretary of the committee is a salaried member of the national committee staff, charged with convention-planning responsibility. In 1960 this position was filled by Josephine Good, who went on to become executive director of the national convention, the first woman ever to hold such a position. The secretary lives and works in the convention city for some six months prior to the convention, and the vice-chairman must be able to make frequent trips to the city and to spend full time on convention affairs immediately prior to the convention.

Clearly it is impracticable for a committee of forty to fifty people to transact day-to-day business or even to meet at short intervals. The officers and chairman of the subcommittees of the Arrangements Committee form an executive committee and are empowered to act for the full committee. The vice-chairman and the executive secretary make the day-to-day decisions. In the Republican Party, this committee traditionally has a heavy sprinkling of women members on the national committee.

Tickets are one of the big headaches of a national convention. Their mere manufacture can be a problem, for, unless expensive processes (including engraving) are used, the tickets may be quite easily counterfeited. In 1960 the Democrats contracted to have their tickets manufactured by a Philadelphia bank-note company. But the Republicans determined to have their tickets show the union bug of the Allied Printing Trades Council for fear of labor demonstrations in Chicago.

"No matter how many tickets you have, there will be a fight over them." There are two basic forms of tickets: those for spectators and those (usually called badges) for delegates, alternates, and convention officials. Indeed, the number of floor seats and spectator seats available in the convention hall is a major factor in determining the choice of convention city. The Repubicans had three thousand fewer tickets to distribute in 1960 than in 1956, simply because the Cow Palace in San Francisco is larger than the International Amphitheatre in Chicago. Exacerbating the problem was the fact that, like 1956, there was an incumbent president who must be in the position to distribute some tickets, and, unlike 1956, there were also candidates for the nomination, each of whom had an undefined entitlement to tickets. The number of incumbent governors will vary for each party from convention to convention and will influence the ticket distribution. Like a theater manager or producer of a show, incumbent politicians must be in the position to give tickets away—a form of largesse which can be much more influential than money.

A formula must be developed, and cheating resorted to only after the formula has been applied. For the 1960 Republican National

Convention, space was assigned in the following order before giving the states their quota of guest tickets: (1) the press; (2) delegates and alternates; (3) officers of the convention; (4) the administration— president, vice-president, cabinet members, undersecretaries and wives (one ticket each); independent regulatory commission members pay for their independence, for they must get convention tickets through their state chairman or the chairman of the national committee; (5) Arrangements Committee members (who, like theater producers, get the choice seats); (6) national committee members and spouses; (7) members of Congress and governors; (8) Republican Finance Committee members; (9) in theory, ten tickets each for the announced candidates for the nomination (this is a rule to be gotten around); (10) the citizens committee which raises the money promised to the party by the site city and which therefore can expect or extort tickets to the convention;[2] (11) the "honored guests"—the Hoovers and Mrs. Coolidges; (12) the diplomatic corps (Republican National Committee policy is never to refuse an embassy request for tickets, which means occasionally raiding the allotment of the national chairman); (13) special groups—tickets to the Women's Division for prominent women, to the party's youth group, to farm groups, to party policy-making groups, and so on.

Although the national committee staff may be inclined to complain that they are last on the list of allocations, they have surreptitious ways of getting people into conventions through the use of badges and the like. One of the ironies of the national convention, especially since the advent of television, is that, difficult as it may be to determine the proper allocation of badges and tickets, convention authorities frequently encounter problems in filling the convention hall in order to avoid the appearance of lack of interest at various times during the proceedings. Young Republicans and regional whips whose job it is to keep delegates' and guests' seats filled attempt to cope with this problem.

The problem of allocation does not end with the delegates and spectators. Competition is keen for positions as pages, sergeants-at-arms, and doorkeepers. Each state is allocated one position for each ten delegates or major fraction thereof. The national committee member from the state who serves on the Committee on Arrangements fills the state's allocation. Pages tend to be high school and college students.

[2] In 1960 the Chicago citizens committee was promised five hundred tickets and was given another two hundred-fifty when fund-raising difficulties were encountered.

They receive no wages or expense allowance. The assistant sergeants-at-arms and assistant doorkeepers receive $150 if the chief sergeant-at-arms and the chief doorkeeper certify that they have actually performed their duties. In addition, honorary assistant sergeants-at-arms are appointed from each state on the same formula as ticket distribution. No official functions attach to this position, and no seats are assigned. It is a way of gaining admission to the convention hall only. Members of the House and the Senate are bombarded with requests that they use influence to secure these appointments for constituents.

The representatives of the mass media must be accredited and allocated working space and seats. This chore is handled by the Standing Committees of Correspondents, of Radio-Television, and of Photographers in charge of the press galleries of Congress. Superintendents and assistants are appointed to police the galleries at the convention. Some eighteen hundred convention hall seats were requested for working members of the press in 1960, with an additional sixty-two guest seats for media officials.

This is, as we indicated, a back-stage narration of the problems of planning the national convention. The story of the 1960 convention proceedings has been so well told that no justification exists for retelling it here.[3] After the convention, while the nominees recuperate, their preconvention campaign staffs prepare for the arduous months ahead, and the national committee staff enplanes for Washington, wondering what the next months have in store for them. The vice-chairman and executive secretary of the Arrangements Committee briefly remain to make final settlement and reminisce about the near disasters and singular achievements in the management of the convention.

Forty or fifty truckloads of equipment must be removed from the convention hall. Details to be squared away include $4,500 termination fee for the RNC switchboard; $12,000 in hotel bills for the RNC staff; $25,000 for the unbudgeted use of two closed circuit television screens in the convention hall to enable delegates and guests better to appreciate the also unbudgeted and extremely expensive animated narration of the republican platform, insisted on by Platform Committee Chairman Charles H. Percy.[4]

[3] See White, *op. cit.*, and Tillett, *op. cit.*
[4] See, e.g., Austin C. Wehrwein, "G.O.P. Convention Still Lingers On," *New York Times,* August 7, 1960.

NATIONAL COMMITTEE STAFFS AND
PRESIDENTIAL CAMPAIGNS

On Monday, December 19, 1960, the Electoral College met in state capitals from Maine to Hawaii and elected John F. Kennedy president by 303 to 219 votes.[5] The President-elect, whose selection had now been nearly formalized (the president of the Senate had yet to perform the duty of tallying the votes in the presence of both houses of Congress), had been elected by the narrowest percentage margin of the popular vote in history. Nixon-Lodge had polled 49.55 per cent of the total popular vote and Kennedy-Johnson 49.71 per cent.[6]

So close was the election that any explanation of the deciding cause of Nixon's defeat seemed plausible. Indeed, some refused to concede defeat. A switch of 11,874 votes in five states would, without giving Nixon-Lodge a majority of the popular vote, still reverse the decision in the election.[7] Admitting that Kennedy would be inaugurated on January 20 and would "stay inaugurated," Republican Chairman Morton nevertheless charged "shocking irregularities and frauds" in voting in various states.[8] Some days later he lamented that it would take two years to discover whether the twenty-seven electoral votes of Illinois and the twenty-four of Texas should not have gone to Nixon-Lodge.[9]

In the same month in which *The Washington Post* reported the results of the Michigan Survey Research Center report which found that Kennedy's Catholicism cost him a million votes, *The Washington Star* published a story based on RNC Research Division analysis under the caption "G.O.P. Sees Nixon Loss Due to Religious Issue."[10] Earlier that year the defeated candidate was quoted as believing the cause of his loss to be "a pro-Kennedy attitude by reporters covering

[5] Hawaii's three electoral votes, then in doubt, subsequently were cast for Kennedy by a margin of 115 out of the 184,705 votes cast in the Islands.

[6] Republican National Committee, "The 1960 Elections" (April 1961), p. 1.

[7] *Ibid.;* the states were Hawaii, Illinois, Missouri, New Mexico, and Nevada.

[8] *Washington Post,* December 9, 1960.

[9] *Ibid.,* December 12, 1960. Morton's fatalism is significant. It may be that the distortive element built into the Electoral College system is beneficial in that, in close elections like that of 1960 and probably many to come, the gap between winner and loser in the electoral vote is sufficiently great that little incentive exists to a Hayes-Tilden type Donnybrook in an effort to reverse the result, as might be the case were the popular vote directly determinative and as indecisive as it was in 1960.

[10] *Sunday Star,* April 9, 1961; *Washington Post,* April 24, 1961.

the campaign."[11] Long after the expiration of Chairman Morton's two-year period for ascertaining the "real" result of the vote in Illinois, Texas, and other states, interest in such inquiry had abated. But former Republican staff people continued to believe that the decisive cause of the loss of the 1960 election lay in the Vice-President's failure to mobilize such resources as the Republican National Committee staff and his refusal to delegate decision-making responsibility even within his personal campaign staff.

Presumably it is a function of the national committees to stockpile experts and expertise on campaign management. A political expert obviously cannot make contributions to a political campaign unless he is able to communicate his opinion and advice to the person or people who make campaign decisions. This means that the decision-makers must be willing to receive ideas, advice, and even criticism from the expert. It means also that the expert must be *persona grata* to the person he is to advise, for no claims to expert knowledge suffice if the personality of the expert offends and alienates the individuals who are to draw on that fund of knowledge, experience, and skill.

Staff campaign experts are of three kinds: strategic, tactical, and operational.

Strategic experts are the top-level generalists, the Jim Farleys, the Leonard Halls, the Robert Kennedys. What these people share is a certain claim, grounded on training, talent, and experience, to knowing the temper of the times and the mood of the people. Presumably these are the people whom the candidate will consult on how to win the independent vote, on whether to ignore the South or to attempt to capture it, on whether to emphasize the labor or Negro vote.

The second group might be called tactical experts. The tactical experts are those whose scope is limited and whose experience is deep. They will tell you what television time to buy, how much television to buy, and how far in advance of campaign needs you should purchase it. They will conduct polls and advise the candidate of their implications concerning the course of the campaign and the type of appeal which should prove effective in courting the voter or various categories of voters. They may be experts at framing efficient campaign itineraries, balancing the dictates of time and distance against speaking opportunities and political imperatives. Indeed, at a lower, but by no means unimportant, level, it will be a tactical expert who will

[11] *Ibid.*, January 2, 1961.

see that the campaign plane is properly equipped to accommodate electric typewriters and mimeograph machines. Probably most of the work of the candidate's press assistant falls into the tactical category, although, of course, he also has opportunity to offer strategic advice.

One of the most important people in the second category will be the public-relations expert who plans and executes the mass media campaign for the party. In 1955, in anticipation of the 1956 campaign, the Republican National Committee negotiated contracts with the major television networks, securing at a reasonable cost all of the time which would be required in the course of the 1956 effort. In 1960 the cast of characters and the stage were much the same; Eisenhower was in the White House, Nixon was running for president, and the same faces were to be found either at the national committee or on the Nixon staff. Yet it was not until September, 1960, that commitments could be made for television time. The reason was not a lack of expertise, but the fact that both Eisenhower and Nixon felt unable (or unwilling) to authorize these commitments far in advance.

The third group of political campaign experts are the operational experts. These are the persons on the electoral firing line. They generally operate at the local level, although they may be located at the national committee headquarters or in separate campaign headquarters. These are the individuals who know approximately the number of votes by which the Democratic majority in Chicago will be depressed if an expenditure of X thousand dollars is made by the Republicans for poll-watching on election day. They are the individuals who know how to get out the vote and how to hamper the efforts of the opposition to do so. They may be skilled in the technique of stealing votes (fortunately less common now) and will certainly be skilled in the techniques of preventing others from doing so. Some regard these experts as party hacks, but others believe them to be the key figures in winning elections in the United States.

A special comment may be made of the functions of the fund-raising expert in a campaign. The fund-raisers do not necessarily exercise a restraining influence on campaign expenditure. One reason for this is that the peaks and valleys of monthly receipts in a campaign year fluctuate so radically that a kind of political survival instinct dictates that funds be obligated whether or not they are on hand. Second, the two party committees, like the American organization man, have discovered credit-card living. Thus it is not at all abnormal for them to use a multiplicity of telephone and airline credit cards to achieve movement and communication which might be drastically curbed were cash on the line demanded. Indeed, it is sometimes easier to fly the party chairman to Alaska than to send out a mass mailing, for the government has not yet developed a mail credit card and is old-fashioned enough to demand cash on the line.

In most cases the fund-raisers of the candidate organization and the national committees go into an election hoping to win, anticipating victory, but cognizant of the possibility of failure and aware of the fact that in the months following Election Day they may find themselves members of the out-party, desperately continuing their effort to raise funds but then attempting to raise funds to eliminate a deficit incurred in an unsuccessful campaign. Thus, as of the end of October, 1960, with Election Day imminent, the Republican National Committee found itself with a debt of $1,183,000 and little by way of immediate resources with which to meet it. The DNC's debt of nearly $3,000,000 was paid off more quickly and more easily than the Republican debt of less than half that amount.

In our earlier discussion of the role of the national chairman as campaign director, we noted that the former practice of the candidate's placing major responsibility on the national chairman has given way in modern times to the frequent relegation of the chairman and national committee staff to a poor place in the shadows. More often than not the candidate's own preconvention manager becomes the *de facto* campaign manager without also becoming national chairman, and/or the national committee staff is paralleled (replaced, to a considerable extent) by an augmented personal campaign organization. Thus the national committees were used only minimally in the Democratic campaigns of 1952, 1956, and 1960; and, during the past three presidential elections, only in 1956 have the RNC staffers been in the front lines of the Republican campaigns.

One is tempted to conclude, from the well-documented evidence of the past fifteen years and from the scattered reminiscences and accounts of earlier campaigns (Democratic 1912, 1916, 1936, 1940, 1944, 1948, and Republican 1928, 1932, 1940), that *the national committee staffs serve as the core presidential campaign organization only when a president in a re-election bid has complete control of the committee staff and apparatus.* And, since the passage of the Twenty-second Amendment, such a situation can prevail, at the most, in only 25 per cent of the cases over a twelve-year cycle. Thus the common case is for the preconvention campaign organization of the candidate to absorb, be equal to, or be superior to, the regular national committee organization, but only in most unlikely circumstances to be absorbed by the regional committee organization. In the common case the most we can rationally hope is for the candidate's campaign organization to absorb the national committee effort.

In the uncommon case, that is when the re-electable president builds the regular committee organization specifically for campaign purposes as Truman did in 1948 and as Eisenhower allowed to be done in 1956, something like a model of campaign organization may be seen.

We can illustrate this distinction between the model campaign and the more common uncoordinated effort by contrasting the 1956 and 1960 Republican campaign organizations. Probably one of the most efficient campaign organizations was that which managed the re-election of President Eisenhower in 1956. This is not to suggest that he would not have been re-elected had the campaign organization supporting him been inefficient. Indeed, he might have been re-elected had he had no campaign organization at all. It remains true, however, that the Republican National Committee in the 1956 campaign was probably as well organized and as effective as it ever has been. In that campaign Leonard W. Hall of New York was chairman. Below Hall several divisions were arranged. The Campaign Division, under the direction of Robert Humphreys, had responsibility for plans, programs, and the implementation of policy incidental to the campaign. The Executive Division, under the direction of Chauncy Robbins, a veteran national committee staff man, had charge of such matters as patronage and budget. The Public-Relations Division, under L. Richard Guylay, had charge of the mass media aspects of the campaign, including radio and television, billboards, newspapers, the production of display materials, art, and literature.

The organization of the Republican National Committee—which in 1956 was the campaign organization—was that simple. All the other activities of the committee, including specialized appeals to minority and ethnic groups, Young Republican activities, and activities directed especially at women, or at professional groups, were arranged under one or more of these divisions. The national campaign telephone directory for 1956 is probably one of the best campaign organization charts ever produced, and it is significant that its major heads relate to campaign functions.

Of course, the 1956 campaign organization was misleadingly simple. What really mattered was not the symmetrical arrangement of the telephone directory or the patterns of organization charts, but that people knew to whom to go for prompt decisions in various areas of activity, and, in many instances, it was possible to make decisions with confidence months prior to the time when they were to take effect. The fact is that the campaign was planned. In 1956 the charts and directories were indicative of the sense of direction which pervaded the campaign.

The telephone directory of the 1960 campaign was also indicative—but indicative of confusion. It was an alphabetical listing of everyone of significance in any of the various cooperating, competing, and at times conflicting campaign organizations scattered about Washington. It can be argued that a lack of campaign organization—or perhaps too many campaign organizations—was the hallmark of the 1960 Republican campaign.

It could also be said that a lack of clear-cut campaign organization was the hallmark of the 1960 Democratic campaign. However, if there was lack of organization and if there was an impression of chaos in the Democratic campaign, at least in the Democratic campaign of 1960, unlike the Republican campaign, people were delegated authority to speak for the candidate, and individuals had authority to frame decisions.

7

Public Relations, Research, and Patronage

PUBLIC RELATIONS

The Public-Relations Division is the evangelistic arm of the national committee. Depending on whether his party has the White House, the function of the public-relations director is to view with alarm or review with pride and confidence the endeavors of the incumbent administration and the state of national affairs. It is also his job to maintain a steady flow of hard-hitting propaganda aimed at keeping the party in public favor.

The public-relations director will ordinarily report directly to the chairman of the national committee, although for general policy he may not be a close adviser to the chairman. He will maintain liaison of sorts with the president's staff if his party has been fortunate in the outcome of the most recent presidential election. He will either manage public relations for his presidential candidate in campaign time or attempt to integrate his program as closely as possible with responsible persons on the candidate's personal campaign staff. He must have adequate relations with the party's campaign and policy committees on the Hill if his effectiveness is to be maximal. The national chairman should, as far as possible, be in gait with the White House, titular leader, or candidate, as the case may be, and with the party leadership in Congress as he issues pronouncements on public policy and the conduct of public affairs.

The forgoing suggests many and frequent opportunities for misunderstandings and lack of communication in the parties' activities. However circumspect may be the conduct of the public-relations function when the party has a strong titular leader or the presidency, in the absence of either a national chairman labors under heavy inducement to act as the voice of his party. Thus, implicit in the existence of an extensive public-relations staff at the two national committees is the premise that the chairman is, perhaps intermittently at the convenience of the president or titular head or in a sustained manner and free of external control, the spokesman for his party. The existence of this function also suggests that both parties cherish certain assumptions concerning the efficacy of words, emanating from the mouths of various political personalities in various combinations and permutations, to sway the American voter and influence the image of the party.

At the Democratic National Committee, the Press and Publicity Division, sometimes called the Public Affairs Division or sometimes simply the Publicity Division, is a thing of several parts loosely coordinated by its nondirective director, Sam Brightman. Brightman is the current ghost of the Democratic National Committee, able successor to Michelson and Redding. He has had various titles—assistant publicity director, publicity director, deputy chairman, assistant to the chairman—since joining the committee staff in 1947. Modest and retiring in speech and demeanor, he is a brilliant phrase-maker, verbal stiletto artist, the chief conceiver and promoter of the *Democratic Digest* in its most vitriolic days, and a man with a sure sense of the Washington press corps. Brightman is, in short, the kind of man the transient chairmen find it hard to get along without. The other assistants and deputy chairmen are political in the purest sense, momentary brokers for the shifting coalitions which happen to share influence with the president, the chairman, the titular head, the congressional leaders, and the other national spokesmen. Brightman differs from these. He is a specialist in Washington publicity, not in West Virginia or California or Massachusetts politics, although he knows a great deal about politics in those places. His clients are the press and television and magazine newsmen in Washington. He was one of them before he went to work for the Democratic National Committee. He is a master at exploiting the bad press breaks of the opposition; at describing such "pseudo events" as statements, press conferences, announcements; and at ghosting the alternately deft and heavy-handed "fighting speech" that chairmen like to give in Minneapolis and Seattle for the delight of the party faithful. Brightman cannot easily be turned out by the new chairman as the assistants of the old chairmen so commonly are.[1] He has something to offer which they do not. Political brokers are many in Washington; experienced and talented political craftsmen are few.

Brightman's division consists of three major parts: the writing and press section proper, the research division, and the library. Brightman's time and effort tend to be concentrated on the creation of speeches, releases, and the periodical organs which wax and wane with the political moons and the financial fortunes of the committee. The current regular piece is *The Democrat,* pale successor to the *Democratic Digest* of opposition days. Normally six to ten people might be employed in the writing and press section of the Public Affairs Division.

Michelson and Brightman are typical of the success which the Democrats have had in attracting vigorous, competent, zealous public-relations officials and keeping them at the national committee through the bad years as well as the good. L. Richard Guylay is probably the outstanding publicist of the Republican National Committee. He was available for a period from 1955 to 1957 and then during the key months of the 1960 campaign.

In the 1952 campaign, Guylay was preceded by Robert Humphreys, one-time national affairs editor of *Newsweek* and organizer of the Publicity Department of the Republican Congressional Committee. Humphreys, who was to exert great influence at the Republican National Committee for many years, moved on to become campaign director of the committee in 1954. He subsequently took his enthusiasm for Bach to the National Cultural Center, of which he was director for a short time, before introducing further variety into his career by taking on the job of script-writing, directing, and stage-managing the "Ev and Charlie" show, the periodic appearances of the minority leaders of the Senate and House before the press. In the interim between imaginative wielders of the publicity hatchet, the Republican

---

[1] It is a frequent practice of the top professional people at the Democratic National Committee to submit their resignations, in a spirit akin to that of British cabinet solidarity, when the chairman submits his own. This practice is not true to the same degree at the Republican National Committee.

Committee has been served by competent and loyal men, it is true, but
men whose real interests sometimes lay in newspaper work rather than
partisan public relations or who have lacked the incisiveness, imagi-
nation, drive, and forcefulness of personality needed to do a job on the
opposite party.

The ultraconservative organ *Human Events* was not being unduly
captious when, in its January 20, 1961, issue it admonished the Republican National Committee that it needed a Charles Michelson.
What the magazine did not address itself to is the problem of recruiting a Lou Guylay or Jim Haggerty to take over public relations at the
national committee for four or eight years at a salary not in excess of
$30,000 annually and sacrificing, for the chancy prospect of con-
tributing to a Republican presidential victory, perhaps $100,000 a year
or more of income. Charles Michelson worked in the primitive days
of the development of party machinery; it is doubtful that he experienced the frustrations, setbacks, and harassment which must be experienced by a dynamic public-relations director as he seeks to exploit
issues and events without affronting enough factions of his party to
lose his scalp to some combination of them. Perhaps the best hope of
the Republican National Committee is to take a flyer on one or a succession of the bright young men for whom the public-relations directorship would be a steppingstone toward a career rather than a lateral
move or a way station between newspaper jobs.

However forceful, imaginative, and dynamic its chief, public relations in the national committees is eight parts routine to two parts
flare. In addition to liaison with the public-relations operations in other
party organizations, the division is responsible for maintaining a current file of miscellaneous information ranging from biographies of national committee members to the itinerary of the chairman's latest
speaking trip. The news ticker must be reviewed periodically during
the day and preliminary assessments made of those stories which offer
an opening the party can take to snap at the opposition and keep in
the news. There is a constant spate of publications to get out, some
periodical, some occasional. Montages of favorable news stories will be
pieced together for duplication and mailing to one or more segments
of the half-million names in the mailroom files. For a number of years
in the 1940's and 1950's, the Republican National Committee maintained a radio and television service which catered to the needs of
the congressional delegation. This was taken over by the Congressional
Campaign Committee as that body expanded. The speaker's bureaus

in both committees comes under the jurisdiction of public relations, and with it come all the problems of attempting to get constituency-oriented representatives and senators to take radio and television spots and to speak before obscure party groups around the country. This comes to a climax in the weeks preceding Lincoln Day and Jefferson Day; indeed, the national Congress traditionally transacts no important business during the week of February 12, thereby helping Republicans to accept speaking assignments around the country.

As the campaign year approaches, a well-run (and perhaps this cannot fairly be separated from well-heeled) public-relations division will concentrate on lining up Class-A television time for the contest, seeking to get the maximum coverage for the convention, and preparing to inundate the country with literature ranging from bumper stickers to fact books which serve as a handy source of canned speeches. Foresight in reserving television time can be an embarrassment if supporting funds do not pour in. In 1960 the Republican National Committee became involved in a fracas with C.B.S. when, in the last week of the campaign, it sought to cut to a half-hour an hour block of time which, during the summer, it had reserved for 10 to 11 P.M., election eve. The network took the position that the national committee must pick up the tab for the full hour unless the sponsors of the originally slotted program cared to use the time. The Democrats were luckier in securing a cut. Their program was scheduled to begin at 11 P.M., at which time networks cease programing, and thus the original order for time had not dislocated a scheduled program.[2] Such are the vagaries of the medium, and they must be mastered or they will master the parties in campaign time. Time- and space-buying usually has been handled through advertising agencies at both committees. Until 1960 Batten, Barton, Durstine and Osborn did much of this work for the Republicans, but a separate agency, Campaign Associates, Inc., was set up to handle the 1960 campaign. In January, 1963, Chairman Miller announced that the Leo Burnett Company of Chicago, the nation's sixth largest agency, would handle the committee's advertising account until January, 1965.

RESEARCH

Research at the national committees has come to be regarded as an adjunct of public relations. In theory and largely in practice, the research director is responsible to the head of public relations, who, in

[2] *New York Times,* November 3, 1960.

turn, has direct access to the chairman. At the Republican National Committee, the public-relations bull pen is adjacent to the suite of offices which house the chairman and his chief assistants. The research component of public relations is located at the back of the building, only less remote from the vortex of committee activities than the switchboard and the mailroom. At the Democratic National Committee the research offices are also physically as far from the chairman's office as it is possible to be. Research is a much underrated and much abused function at each national committee. There is an irony in this. The national party leaders cannot lead effectively unless they appreciate the objective facts of life concerning the situation of their party in a congressional district, in a state, and nationwide. They must know how members of the other party are voting in Congress. They must have competent analyses of the content of bills in the legislature and of partisan speeches and reports. They must be able to frame an intelligent judgment of the state of the economy and have available the demographic data which would influence decisions of sound public policy. Research is vital to the national committees, but it is public relations that is appreciated.

At any given time eight to twelve persons may be found in the Research Division of the Democratic National Committee. The output of this section consists of voting records of Republican (but not Democratic!) congressmen and senators and the collection and analysis of material on all major issues and many minor issues which might figure in partisan debate. The preparation of memorandums and background papers for the chairman and his chief lieutenants, for the White House, for congressional leaders, for state party leaders, and for distribution to the party laborers across the country may be demanded of the Research Division staff. The activity of the division and the use to which its products are put will depend greatly on the perspicacity and aggressiveness of the director and those who set tasks for his staff. The militant out-party chairman who has an astute research director, as was the case with Paul Butler and William Welsh in 1958, can grind out from the national committee's Research Division a great deal of helpful campaign material. Here again the in-party chairman and research director have different and less visible roles to play; the White House staff may use committee research people for "back-up" work but most likely will want to place its own stamp on the finished product. The congressional leaders always have other research assistance—the Library of Congress, their own and committee staffs, and the party campaign committees on the Hill. Moreover, with their own man in the White House, all in-party political leaders have easy access to the research talents of the administrative agencies (the Budget Bureau, the Census Bureau, and the Council of Economic Advisors are especially helpful).

The Democratic Congressional and the Senatorial Campaign Committee have very small staffs, however, and a vigorous research director at the Democratic National Committee may be of considerable help to the rank-and-file congressmen and their leaders when a highly partisan stance is indicated. Beyond that the national committee's Research Division thinks of itself as being especially available to nonincumbent congressional candidates; in 1958 and 1962 each Democratic candidate received an elaborate book explaining the votes of record of the previous Congress and indicating how his opponent voted on every issue.

Although both parties undoubtedly underappreciate the research function, it is treated with greater respect at the Republican National Committee, and the Republicans, who for so long have been tarnished with the reputation of anti-intellectualism, have for many years enjoyed the services of one of the superior research units in Washington. From the early 1940's until 1960 the Research Division was directed by Floyd McCaffree, a Michigan Ph.D. in political science who subsequently went to college teaching. McCaffree's chief associate and the new director of the division is William B. Prendergast, a product of Notre Dame, the University of Louvain, and The University of Chicago, where he took his Ph.D. Prendergast, who has run for the Maryland Senate and for Congress, has been responsible for a series of election studies which have such a reputation of accuracy and objectivity that college professors around the country seek to have their names on the mailing list for the biennial editions and *The New York Times* treats their appearance as an occasion for presenting its readers with a scholarly review of the most recent election returns.

Theodore H. White, in *The Making of the President 1960*, an eminently fair study though written by an admirer of the Kennedy effort, says:

> This writer should commend to the reader also the researches of the Republican National Committee and their summary of the 1960 election called *The 1960 Elections*. Over the years I have found the research staff of the Re-

publican National Committee the finest source of quick
accurate tabulation and analysis of returns in Washington.
It is remarkable that the high command of the Republican
Party, which supports the finest research staff in Washington, should pay so little attention to their researches, while
the Democratic National Committee, full of men who love
politics, should have so primitive a research staff and resources.[3]

Such is the lack of feeling—perhaps the phrase should be active contempt—for the research function that a recent research director at the
Democratic National Committee learned that he had been replaced
only by reading the circular file of carbons of memorandums.

Advance, a Republican political journal independent of the party
committees, pointed to the difficulties of the Republican research effort
and to the intraparty rivalries which contribute to keeping the national
committee research activity within narrow bounds:

> The problem of Republican research is not merely one
> of degree. The charge that GOP research is inadequate
> cannot be answered by pointing to Senate Policy Commit-
> tee "Blue Books" or to the lamentably rare but sometimes
> excellent, House Policy Committee studies. The problem
> results from a fundamental disorientation in the party's
> approach to its task. It is reflected by the predicament of
> Dr. William Prendergast, the able research director of the
> Republican National Committee.
>
> The top research official in the party, with a long repu-
> tation for excellent but neglected accomplishment, his pres-
> tige is a measure of the Party's evaluation of the importance
> of research. The last two research directors of the Conserv-
> ative Party in England are now prominent in the British
> cabinet and one, R. A. Butler, is considered heir-apparent
> to Prime Minister Macmillan. The staff of the Conservative
> Research group, excluding clerical help, numbers over
> twenty full-time scholars. Yet Prendergast's budget is so
> small that he cannot even compete with individual Con-
> gressmen to keep good men on his four-man staff, or pub-
> lish or publicize his research results. His services are so

undervalued that they are regularly sought by fewer than ten Senators and Congressmen, the most frequent being Senators Morton (Ky.) and Scott (Pa.) two previous national chairmen.

When the National Committee does call on its staff for original research effort, the Congressional Leadership charges usurpation of its prerogative to make policy (or evidently to decline to make it). Such an instance was the Republican State of the Union address prepared for delivery two years ago by Chairman Miller before Kennedy's speech. Containing several Republican legislative proposals, it was considered an encroachment on the policy-making authority of Congress and vetoed by the Leadership. The National Committee has been more reticent since then.[4]

There is also a tendency, witnessed by the authors at first hand, to fail to include the research director in many staff conferences at which his division could be expected to have much to contribute by way of fact and judgment. There is not a like tendency to fail to include the director of public relations. The research activity, outstanding at one national committee and at least adequate at the other, is conducted under the shadow and within the various limits of the public-relations function. Frequently research is just not taken into account by the public-relations people. This leads to a natural resentment. The line of demarcation between research and public relations has been humorously defined as the production of facts as distinguished from the distortion of them. What slights the researchers and on occasion can threaten to embarrass the national committee is failure to permit them to perform the production job prior to the chairman's breaking into print with a press release on a given matter or incident.

Most research is conducted on demand. As indicated earlier, in each party there is little range of discretion allotted to a research director and relatively little attention paid to whatever efforts he may independently make to bring to the chairman's attention the desirability of an imaginative research program which, coupled with effective public relations, could identify the party with the principal fears, anxieties, aspirations, and demands of various groups of the electorate and forge an ideological weapon for victory. This neglect, although

[4] *Advance, A Journal of Political Thought*, Spring 1963, pp. 7–8.

much criticized by those familiar with the role of research and the forging of ideas and new issues in certain party systems abroad, is probably understandable and inevitable in a political system in which the parties have not yet been able to differentiate their positions on a significant range of issues.

PATRONAGE

The distribution of party patronage is one of the jobs to which the national chairman of the in-party must give some time. In this responsibility, as in all his others, the power is not his directly or by right; he and his committee staff constitute one channel through which the job-givers (the top levels of the federal executive, headed by the president himself) and the job-seekers make contact, conduct their negotiations, and come to some agreement. The national committee becomes, to the extent the president and his most influential advisers desire or allow, the unofficial employment agency for filling certain jobs in the executive branch of the United States government.

Some presidents expect their national chairmen to handle practically all of the patronage business. Historically, strong chairmen gained their reputations as strong chairmen in large part because they were given much responsibility and freedom in rewarding the party faithful for what George Washington Plunkitt always referred to as "patriotism," that is, undeviating loyalty to one's political friends.

Mark Hanna's influence in patronage is legendary. A sympathetic biographer attributes Hanna's success to three ingredients: an unswerving attachment to party regularity, a known formula for the allocation of jobs, and human understanding and tact in dealing with applicants. Hanna worked exclusively with the regular party organizations.

> He cooperated with some of the worst elements in his party as well as the best. He conceived it as his business above all to keep the Republicans united . . . [and] they could be kept united only in case the existing local organizations were accepted and possible corruption overlooked.[5]

The patronage distribution formula was in effect in the North and working well enough when Hanna became national chairman in 1896. He organized a new and effective system for the South:

[5] Herbert Croly, *Marcus Alonzo Hanna: His Life and Work* (New York: Macmillan Co., 1912), p. 300.

The local offices were usually filled on the recommendations of the defeated congressional candidate, and Mr.
Hanna expected by the recognition of these leaders of for-
lorn hopes to induce a better quality of men to run for the
office. For the higher Federal offices, such as the United
States Judges and Attorneys, the recommendations were
usually accepted of a Board of Referees—consisting of the
defeated candidate for Governor, and chairmen of the State
Committee, and the member of the National Committee
from that state.[6]

Jim Farley's system for handling the tens of thousands of would-
be federal job-holders after Roosevelt's election is still cited in textbooks and by political dopesters as a testimony to Farley's political
adroitness and a procedure to be emulated. Farley's system, in theory,
was quite simple: major appointments would "be discussed directly
between the President and myself and other high government officials"
and all other job applicants would be cared for at the national committee headquarters. He found, however, that the great throngs of job-
seekers could not be handled at the committee. He and his assistants
met the "rush of deserving patriots" in private rooms off a large,
crowded, reception hall at the Post Office Building. The views and
recommendations of senators and representatives were first sought and
respected insofar as possible; then, as now, the state chairmen and national committee members were annoyed by the preferential treatment
accorded national legislators. When thus cleared by Farley and his
assistants, the applicants were sent directly to employment officers in
the administrative agencies. Farley admitted that the system was "substantially the same as that which the Republicans employed"; he
gained his reputation as an organizer of spoils because he perfected the
machinery at a time when there were many job-seekers and many jobs.[7]

The field of forces in patronage distribution includes, most importantly, (1) those who think themselves qualified, by virtue of help

---

[6] *Ibid.,* p. 298.

[7] Farley, *Behind the Ballots, op. cit.,* pp. 226–236. It has been estimated that
Farley had seventy-five thousand patronage jobs available to him after Roosevelt's inauguration. Henry says, "Farley conducted the largest, most systematic,
and the most overt patronage operation in history." Laurin Henry, *Presidential
Transitions* (Washington: Brookings Institution, 1960), p. 432. The number of
1933 patronage jobs and job-seekers has been variously estimated, but essentially
remains a matter of guesswork.

which they gave to the winners and (for rationalization comes to the aid of job-seekers, as it does to all men) their personal abilities to hold governmental office; (2) those who wish to uphold the principle of nonpolitical merit in governmental service; (3) those who wish to maintain their own personal or institutional patronage-securing powers in the face of presidential change of the *status quo*.

The environment in which these forces play is exceedingly complex, as are all things governmental in the 1960's. The number of federal jobs is great and increasing. The legal and administrative patterns by which the hiring and firing of employees of the United States are accomplished are complex, protean, and only dimly understood even by those who are engaged in their perpetuation and change. After nearly one hundred years of civil service reform and antipatronage rhetoric, the pursuit of job spoils (for there are other, perhaps more important, spoils) is not the kind of endeavor most men can engage in openly and unashamedly. The rivalry of claimants, the relationships of sponsors, and the self-protective attitudes of holdover or newly appointed bureaucratic employers—all these make it difficult to cast the struggle as one between the angelic incomers and the devilish outgoers. At the highest level the new president cannot tolerate the continuation in office of those associated with the administration of his predecessor, nor can he fail to choose a new team which represents, over-all, his own point of view and the general policy on which his campaign was based. Equally, however, he is compelled by the dynamics of the coalition of interests whose efforts resulted in his election to recognize leaders of these interests, representing, as they invariably do, a wide range of ideological and policy positions. Thus, Eisenhower was obliged to have his "plumber," Labor Secretary Martin Durkin, in his 1953 cabinet, and Kennedy was obliged to have his Southerner, Commerce Secretary Luther Hodges.

The national committee chairman and his associates in the party headquarters may be participants in the selection of top-level presidential appointments, but the more common situation is that the patronage machinery of the committees is brought to bear lower in the rankings of jobs to be filled. Unless the chairman was, and remains after inauguration, a close adviser of the president (a situation which seems less common now than in the past), the chances are that his services will not be needed in the choosing of the highest political appointees. Eisenhower took little interest in the patronage game. It is reported that on one occasion Chairman Hall was urging that reward for party work be among the criteria considered in appointments, and Ike rather snappily replied that he did not "like the spoils system."[8] Eisenhower's repugnance to the spoils system meant that he was not very willing to value partisan reward in filling executive and administrative posts. Recruitment was therefore not a party question and therefore not a matter, at the highest levels, for the Republican National Committee to handle.

The Kennedy practice with regard to patronage and the Democratic National Committee was quite similar, but for other reasons. Although Eisenhower's background resulted in an unfamiliarity with electoral politics of any kind and a continued indifference during office to partisan questions, Kennedy's background resulted in his indifference to regular party organization and his reliance on a personal organization. Despite early and long labors on Kennedy's behalf, Chairman Bailey was never included among the close advisers on whom the late President relied for key appointments.

By midsummer of 1963, with more than two years of experience, the patronage operations of the Kennedy Democrats in Washington had shaken down into a pattern of sorts. Top-level jobs were handled almost exclusively at the White House, with two kinds of procedure. Middle-range jobs were divided between congressional forces and party-organization forces which might or might not act through the machinery provided by the national committee. Lesser jobs were dispensed through congressmen or other party figures, such as presidentially appointed administrators, or directly through the national committee. Most of the middle- and lower-level appointments were at least cleared through the national committee even when it was not a principal channel for bringing applicant and job together.

Thus the White House handled all appointments requiring presidential nomination plus other jobs of a sensitive political nature. Kenneth O'Donnell, assistant to the president, acted as the chief patronage officer for these high-level appointments. He would routinely concern himself with other applicants as well—personal or political friends of President Kennedy or applicants in whom powerful congressional leaders had a special interest. When, for example, a minor conflict arose in early 1962 over the selection of a federal judge in Arizona, Sen. Carl Hayden and Secretary of the Interior Stewart Udall failed to agree on a nominee. Hayden's favorite was given the judgeship, and

---

[8] Wilder, "Republican National Chairmen . . . ," *op. cit.*

Udall's choice was made ambassador to a newly independent African nation.

Simultaneously, at the White House a top-level recruitment effort was made to attract experts and experienced administrators who were not self-starting job-seekers. Daniel Finn, a Kennedy egghead import from the Harvard Business School, was in charge of this operation, described as a nonpolitical effort to get the best brains in the country into the administration, but requiring coordination and clearance with other parts of the hiring effort.

Inevitably some conflict occurred among the three centers of patronage activity—the White House, Congress, and the national committee. Of the three operations that at the national committee was the least important because it was the least influential. The President's interests could have been maintained for a long time without the national committee, but he could not have hoped to develop a satisfactory record in Congress without the aid and good will of the congressional leaders and key individual members.

The national committee patronage dispensers had a different view of it. They needed the President and the sympathetic attention of his men if they were to satisfy the job demands from state organizations and from national committeemen and -women. The endorsement of the national committee, however, was not so influential with the hiring officers in the agencies as was the endorsement of the applicant's senator and congressman. Thomas Brislin, chief patronage officer at the Democratic Committee in 1963, put it directly: "A smart congressman doesn't send his people here; he has more influence in the administrative departments than we do." Another Democratic National Committee staffer said, "Tom is in charge of petty patronage—the kind the White House can't be bothered with."

Brislin and Paul Corbin were, in 1962 and 1963, the key patronage advisers and assistants for Chairman Bailey. Corbin had been hired by the Kennedy organization during the 1960 primary campaign in Wisconsin. He had had some experience in party work and in the labor movement in Wisconsin. Some of the Kennedy success in Wisconsin seems to have been attributed to his political adroitness, and Robert Kennedy especially appreciated Corbin's unsentimental and hard-headed approach to political problems. At first part of the White House staff, Corbin was moved to the national committee in late summer, 1961, at about the time the *Milwaukee Journal* printed some less-than-complimentary articles on his relations with both the late Sen.

Joseph McCarthy and Communist-led organizations in Milwaukee.[9] Someone close to the President, probably Robert Kennedy, determined that Corbin should ride out that storm and make himself useful if possible, but at any rate quiet, at the national committee headquarters. As one of a half-dozen assistants to the chairman, he was assigned to patronage among other duties.

Brislin, also assistant to the chairman, seems to have had major responsibility for patronage until he left the committee in late 1963. He had served as Cong. Donald Irwin's administrative assistant before Irwin's defeat in the Connecticut Fourth District in 1960. A quiet, no-nonsense type from the coal-mining area of Pennsylvania, Brislin understood patronage. He appealed to Bailey as a man who would never let sentiment stand in the way of maximizing electoral advantage. "You go where the votes are" was Brislin's formula for settling patronage disputes between states.

The amended formula at the Democratic National Committee's employment service was, "You go where the votes are—if the leaders there are agreed." But state leaders do not always agree among themselves about how the prizes should be divided. Patronage was a headache for Brislin and Bailey in the biggest state of all (before 1963), where the leaders of the New York Democracy were in more than ordinary conflict; caught among the Tammany-Wagner-Kennedy cross currents, the national committee found that it was nearly impossible to "go where the votes are" in that instance. Likewise, conflict in Ohio between Cuyahoga (Cleveland) County Chairman Ray Miller and State Chairman William Coleman and between Gov. Michael DiSalle and Sen. Frank Lausche produced a virtual impasse in federal patronage in that state. Oregon leadership, too, was torn, with Sen. Wayne Morse, Rep. Edith Green, and National Committeeman C. Girard Davidson agreeing only to disagree.

Some other important states, though, were problem-free. When the state system of patronage flow is worked out (but, note well, at the state level and not by any national authority), some jobs can be found —at least enough to keep the most persistent quiet if not happy. In Michigan the state committee cleared applicants through a consortium

---

[9] *Milwaukee Journal*, August 24, 1961, as reprinted in the *Congressional Record*, August 29, 1961. The *Journal* described Corbin as "an aggressive, successful, and widely experienced political technician. He has worked in politics of several shades, including that of the late Senator Joseph McCarthy, since becoming a naturalized American in San Diego in 1943 after immigrating to the United States from Canada."

of governor, former governor, state chairman, national committeeman,
and top labor leaders. In Pennsylvania Gov. David Lawrence and
the Philadelphia boss, Cong. William Green, proposed, and the national committee disposed. In California another pattern prevailed;
the congressional delegation caucused formally and informally on
names, and Gov. Edmund "Pat" Brown went along.

It should not be thought that the turnover of jobs in the federal
government is very great when there is a partisan change in the White
House. Despite much talk of sweeping spoils in 1953, the best estimates
would put the turnover in that year and in 1954 at about five thousand
jobs. In the comparable period 1961–1962, only about six thousand
jobs (including honorific and nonpaying appointments) had been filled
on a patronage or semipatronage basis by the Democrats.

Clarence G. Adamy, patronage chief at the Republican National
Committee during almost five of the Eisenhower years, estimated in
1959:

> There are only 2,860 government positions appointed by
> the President which are selected by him or by his ap-
> pointees as a matter of personal choice. This includes 1,629
> Presidential appointees and 1,231 schedule "C" positions.[10]

The difference between the Adamy estimate and the number of positions filled by the Democrats in 1961–1962 is not nearly so significant
as the difference between these and the volume of jobs at James Farley's disposal in 1933. Adamy complained that the president and his
appointees could together appoint only .1 per cent of the federal
employees on whom they must depend to carry out administrative
policy. In 1933 Farley complained of having only one hundred and
fifty thousand exempt positions—20 per cent of the seven hundred and
fifty thousand Federal jobs—to distribute among "'at least 1,500,000
men and women applicants."[11]

Farley spoke of these jobs as "one of the chief assets of a party
in office"—an asset to be skillfully expended through the national committee and with the principal purpose of rewarding loyal Democratic
supporters of Roosevelt, preferably F.R.B.C. (For Roosevelt before
Chicago) applicants. Distribution of the patronage then, as now, must

[10] Clarence G. Adamy, "Whose Clerks Are They?" (Republican National
Committee, 1959).
[11] J. A. Farley, "Passing Out the Patronage," *American Magazine*, CXVI
(August 1933), 20.

be weighted to accommodate varying regions of the country, states, party factions, and elected officeholders on the Hill. There is the further traditional and sometimes tongue-in-cheek caveat to the effect that the applicant must be qualified to hold down the job he seeks.

Adamy makes a more modern and sophisticated defense of patronage and an appeal for its enlargement. His argument is cast in terms of the "impenetrable inflexibility" of the bureaucracy and the need that the president, whatever his party, has for a sufficient number of his men in policy-influencing positions throughout the government to ensure a sympathetic effort on its part to understand, appreciate, and administer his programs. Adamy contends that the president has little power to control his administration.

> The President has lost the power to control his adminis-
> tration. He cannot insure that positions vital to the execu-
> tion of his program are occupied by persons sympathetic
> to him and his political philosophy. . . . His power to
> hire and fire is infinitesimally small when measured against
> the number of administrative officials who exert a vital in-
> fluence upon public policy.[12]

Farley was concerned with patronage almost solely as a party-building device; Adamy, interested in strengthening his party, expresses a major concern about the power of the party to rule effectively, having won the presidency, with the restricted number of offices available for patronage appointment. Stanley Kelley points to a growing tendency of Republican and Democratic presidents to revert to the nineteenth-century emphasis on patronage as a device for trading favors with party leaders and the rank and file of the Hill.

Distribution of patronage, or at least maintenance of the patronage accounts, is straying from the national committee to the White House, says Kelley. During the Truman, Eisenhower, and Kennedy administrations, there was a trend toward focusing on a White House staff member or members

> . . . responsibility for recruiting and receiving nominations
> of political appointees, making preliminary appraisals of
> their qualifications, and clearing their appointments with
> party officials, agency heads, members of Congress, and,
> in some cases, interest group leaders.[13]

[12] *Op. cit.*
[13] "Presidential Legislative Leadership: The Use of Patronage," a paper

When this activity is put next to the growing White House interest in full-time liaison with the Congress, what develops is

> . . . an institutionalization in the White House of responsibility for handling requests for favors—patronage—by members of Congress and the close integration of that activity with Administration lobbying—the trading of patronage appointments for legislative support of the President's program.[14]

There is, of course, no patronage operation formally conducted at the Republican National Committee today. Prior to the 1960 elections, patronage and the employment office for national committee staffing were combined. The major portion of the work of patronage in the last years of the Eisenhower administration was accepting 57's (federal employment application forms) from applicants for clerk-typist and stenographer positions with the government. The staff would make routine telephone calls to the Hill and to contacts in the various agencies of government. The committee did little more for the applicants than they could have done for themselves although, inevitably, some contacts would give preference to a 57 forwarded from the national committee. The truth is that competent secretarial help is so much in demand in Washington that one does not require political pull to secure such positions in government. After the 1960 election the committee closed out its patronage operation, which in the interim after Adamy's departure to join a trade association had been conducted by his former assistant, Mrs. Ethel Friedlander.

Probably no national committee staffer is likely to be happy with his administration's handling of patronage. Farley claimed to have one and one-half million patronage applications in 1933. It seems to the national committee staff that they have that many each time their party captures the administration afresh. And during the tenure of the administration, applications pour in, and pressures are applied from the Hill, outmatching the willingness or capacity of the various agencies to absorb new employees.

The Civil Service Commission, for its part, is very much in the picture, as Dorothy Davies, a White House aide, discovered in April, 1963, when the commission decided she had been a bit too blatant in

---

delivered at the 1962 Annual Meeting of the American Political Science Association, Washington, D.C.
[14] *Ibid.*

associating a political test with summer employment for students.[15] By and large the merit system functions effectively to protect career civil servants, if not from occasional political pressure for contributions, at least from too obvious reprisals for resisting such pressures. It serves also to moderate the inevitable pressures, for no political official wishes to so violate employee tolerance for political pressure that he tempts the employee to complain to the Civil Service Commission or the newspapers.

The fact is that qualified people are in much demand at all levels of government. There is no reason that on entry into federal employment a qualified person should not be of the president's party. It is also a fact that there are thousands of exempt positions in government from which people may be dismissed without cause or from which they are expected, upon request, to resign. For the most part these are and should be filled by members of the president's party. Additionally, the mobility of government employment in the United States (unlike, for example, Great Britain) is such that there is constant movement in and out at all levels, presenting opportunities which may appropriately go to qualified applicants of the president's party.

In sum, we do not think that patronage in the federal government is a matter of great moment. Compared with the importance and consequences of patronage in some states like Pennsylvania and Massachusetts, the spoils system of the federal government is very small indeed. Non–Civil Service jobs or noncompetitive jobs are of only trifling importance in the conduct of partisan politics at the presidential or Congressional level. Even when federal patronage is used for all it is worth, as in the 1962 primary race between Edward Kennedy and Edward McCormack in Massachusetts, its influence is relatively small. In many, perhaps most, cases it produces more conflict than satisfaction.

We would not argue that no nonpolicy jobs be given out through the national committees and other federal patronage machinery. There is a need for recognition of state and local partisans who are moved by Plunkitt's "patriotism" to serve their country. But the market place of federal patronage works tolerably well. Demand and supply seem, in the mid-1960's, to be in something of a working and probably salu-

[15] The commission, with front-page stories in the Washington papers, withdrew from all agencies permission to hire summer students, offering to restore such authority on an agency-by-agency basis when the agencies had shown that they were not applying a political test in connection with such employment.

tary equilibrium. If a few hundred of the party faithful become post-masters, customs collectors, appraisers, savings bond directors, or regional heads of Federal Housing Administration districts, we will not fear for the future of the country.

In former times, when the general level of education was lower and in periods of unemployment when applicants virtually required jobs whether fit or not, the spoils system was no doubt an impediment to good government, and in some states and communities it remains so today. But in the federal government we have seen no evidence of in-competence, inefficiency, or venality which can be traced in significant degree to patronage. It may be, in fact—and the argument for this could be made, though we do not make it here—that the major cause of inefficiency and incompetence in the federal service is precisely that officers have insufficient discretion to hire and fire and move with political impunity. Civil Service rigidity is probably a bigger problem now than is the spoils system.

Nor should it be thought that job patronage is an important source of support and strength in contributions or delivered votes to the presidential candidate or to the national party committees. For a few very top jobs of cabinet rank or near equivalence, some deals may be made before or during the convention or during the campaign. But this is rare. The outright buying of jobs with campaign contribu-tions is so scarce at the national level, however common it may be in some localities, that it deserves no consideration. Patronage is largely programmatic, designed to create a team which will be effective for obtaining the ends sought by the administration, or symbolic, designed to give rewards to representative party leaders and workers who are both the beneficiaries and living proof of party success.

National party chairmen of recent years would probably all agree with the commentary made by the last party chairman to have big spoils at his disposal:

> Those people who are inclined to imagine that patronage, and patronage alone, is the only thing that keeps a political party knit together are off on a tangent that is about as far wrong as anything humanly could be. I am convinced that with the help of a few simple ingredients like time, patience, and hard work, I could construct a major po-litical party in the United States without the aid of a single job to hand out to deserving partisans.[16]

16 Farley, *Behind the Ballots, op. cit.,* p. 237.

8

Groups
and the
National Committees

Whatever the background of the chairman and president, whichever the party, the national committee will be found to support programs designed to create and maintain a favorable party image with such groups as labor (not elaborated here), women, youth, sections of the country, and, more recently, intellectuals. It is the purpose of this chapter to describe certain of these programs. The efforts are disparate, and the programs wax and wane, sometimes with and sometimes without relation to one another. Changes of elected and appointed staff spell changes of organizational ability and ideological commitment. These in turn can cause the national chairman's interest in a group to expand or to become attenuated.

WOMEN AT THE
NATIONAL COMMITTEES

Youth groups and the women's organizations are headquartered at the two national committees and partially supported by them. They might be termed satellite party organizations as distinguished from independent, non-
149

sponsored party groups which may or may not be friendly to the elements running the party apparatus. The Republican Workshop, which
flourishes in the Midwest, is an example of an independent but friendly
party group. It began as the Republican *Women's* Workshop, with
emphasis on the discussion group approach to involving people in Republican politics. The existence of the workshops as competitive groups
was a constant source of concern to the Republican Women's Federation, but a friendly truce was maintained, and all that the Workshops
wanted and want from the national committee was and is reciprocal
friendliness. Some independent auxiliary groups, as indicated above,
reject the incumbent leadership of the party insofar as it is identifiable
and would seek to capture the party through the vehicle of an organization or a candidate. Thus the Young Americans for Freedom
(YAF) regard themselves as a conservative rival of the Young Republican Federation, quite willing to infiltrate the latter and take over.

The first enterprise of a national political party to woo women
voters was the campaign division established at the DNC in 1916.
Known then as the Women's Bureau, it was created to seek women's
votes in the eleven Western states where women were given the
franchise before the Nineteenth Amendment. A quasi-official statement of the Democratic Office of Women's Activities (OWA) goals
declared in 1959 that it "concentrates on bringing women into the
Party, helping them to function effectively on all levels of the Party
structure, encouraging them to seek both public and Party office." It
is telling evidence of the internal tensions and lack of self-understand-
ing at the Democratic National Committee that this quasi-official
statement was a draft (dated September 15, 1959) of a "proposed illustrated, accordion-fold, pocket size leaflet to explain to Party members the operation of the national headquarters." Short accounts of the
work of each division were to be included in the publication. Disagreement among staff members about what should go in the piece, lack of
money, and nobody to push for it very strongly, resulted in its death
in embryo. To this day, after more than one hundred and fifteen
years, the Democratic National Committee has never issued a document describing its staff divisions and functions for the party or general
public.

The Office of Women's Activities (which is called the Women's
Division by other staffers) has produced over fifty pieces of how-to-
do-it literature, conducts regional workshops and conferences, sponsors
a mammoth biennial campaign conference for Democratic women, and

handles special projects through a selected mailing list of over thirty thousand names of lady Democrats and Democratic sympathizers. Democratic women's clubs and state federations of women's clubs (like the Young Democratic clubs and unlike the Republican women's clubs) are chartered by the state committees rather than by the national committee and are serviced by the Office of Women's Activities. Since 1957 all Teen Dem clubs (party groups of prevoters, organized mainly by high-school-age enthusiasts and rarely having permanence) have likewise been serviced by the OWA.

A perennial but usually gentle controversy exists at both national party committees over the objectives and activities of women's divisions, indeed, over the question of their very existence. Some argue that politics ought to be sexless and that properly there are no women's activities, no special tasks for women, and no motivations, inspirations, or rewards in politics which do not apply equally to men and women. Others view this as naïve and unrealistic; they claim that women are, in fact, discriminated against by males in politics and by an all-too-common view, shared by females, that politics is a dirty and unladylike enterprise; they argue that women therefore need special encouragement and assistance and that they should, as it were, huddle together for warmth while they pioneer in the cold, forbidding, and male-dominated world.

The controversy over women's divisions is a little like the arguments about strategy for improving race relations. Politics should, perhaps, be sexless, as the laws should be color-blind. But politics and the attitude patterns underlying politics are not sexless, as the laws and attitude-patterns underlying the laws are not color-blind. It is probably fortunate that the women's divisions at both national committees have in recent years been run by tough-minded (though sweet-speaking) directors who recognize, though they deplore, the need for special attention to the problems and opportunities for women in political life.

On the Republican side the rivalries of satellite and independent auxiliary organizations are more obvious, if not more pronounced. For, although women abound at every staff level and in all divisions of the RNC, two areas of the national committee exist specifically and exclusively for women. They are the Women's Division and the headquarters office of the National Federation of Republican Women, a party satellite organization.

The Women's Division has been a part of the national committee since 1919, a year after the RNC established permanent headquarters in Washington, D.C., and a year prior to adoption of the Nineteenth Amendment. The NFRW has been in existence since 1938, when the Women's Division organized it as a device for knitting together a host of local Republican women's clubs. It is not entirely correct to include the NFRW in the structure of the national committee staff except for the reasons that their headquarters is in the RNC offices, their officers and staff are included in RNC programs, and everyone from the national chairman on down seems to consider them a part of the committee although the Women's Division is likely to consider the NFRW its own independent campaign and an educational arm.

The Women's Division is traditionally headed by the assistant to the chairman or the assistant chairman, whichever title the national chairman happens to bestow, and is appointed by him and serves at his pleasure. The Federation of Republican Women is directed by an elected national president who serves at the will of the NFRW's biennial convention. National committee funds finance the full operation of the Women's Division and about two-thirds of the costs of the NFRW office. And both offices employ public-relations directors and comparatively good-sized staffs. The Women's Division today averages eight full-time employees, and the NFRW staff slightly fewer. The two offices are adjacent, and their staffs are incongruously competitive.

The Women's Division works primarily with Republican women who are candidates for public office, members of the national committee, or leaders in state Republican or women's organizations. It maintains extensive files on women active in political or civic life and helps women requesting information, whether affiliated with the party or not, always attempting to attract them to the Republican Party. Interestingly enough, Mrs. Clare B. Williams, the Republican national committeewoman for Florida and the assistant chairman from 1958 to 1963, privately expressed the wish that the Women's Division be abolished since it tends to foster the idea that the political woman differs from the political man, but this conviction has not hampered her willingness, as director, to fulfill and enlarge its role. While heading the Women's Division, Mrs. Williams displayed a capacity for staging well-organized women's conferences for two thousand women on an annual basis, something which is done only occasionally by her counterpart organization at the Democratic Committee, and for raising and spending large sums of money in her activities. Often criticized for the thousands of dollars put into any one of the annual women's conferences, she never failed to bring in considerably more money than was spent on a convention which tied up the Sheraton Park or the Statler-Hilton for three days each spring. Her year around projects have ranged from pyramid organizations for building funds from single dollar bills to shadow voter programs for drawing attention to vote fraud and first lady campaigns to assist wives of candidates and indirectly their husbands. Although such programs turned out surprisingly successful, Mrs. Williams remained a controversial figure in some quarters and nowhere so much as in the National Federation of Republican Women.

The Federation of Republican Women is a proud, hard-working organization of volunteers, which dislikes being compared to the Young Republican National Federation, even though by some methods of calculation the Young Republicans can claim to be the more experienced organization by three years. The local Republican clubwoman sees the NFRW office as a staff of caseworkers for her problems in party organization. She receives how-to-do-it kits, position papers, and a monthly newsletter from the national office, and she attends its biennial conventions, which tend to conflict with her campaign schedule every autumn of an even-numbered year.

The NFRW office devotes itself to the work and program of organized Republican women, assisting, as it were, the Women's Division. Between 1938 and the early 1950's, the two women's offices worked together smoothly, with the NFRW accepting the lead of the Women's Division. But personality strife during the early 1950's led to a rivalry which prevails today. At the time the Women's Division was under the leadership of Bertha Adkins, the national committeewoman for Maryland who later was to serve as under secretary of health, education and welfare. The Federation of Republican Women was directed by Mrs. Carroll D. Kearns, wife of the then congressman from Pennsylvania. Mrs. Kearns simply contended that her position as an elected officer of Republican women throughout the country should not be subordinate to a woman chosen only by the Republican national chairman. This contention led devotees of Miss Adkins to suggest that Mrs. Kearns took this view more because of her estimation of her position as a congressman's wife than as president of the NFRW, and the battle was on.

Mrs. Kearns left the presidency of the NFRW in 1956 and was succeeded by Mrs. Peter Gibson of Michigan, a woman who worked willingly with Miss Adkins and the Women's Division and with Mrs.

Williams, who was appointed by Meade Alcorn when Miss Adkins moved to the Department of Health, Education, and Welfare in 1958.

In 1960 Mrs. Gibson left the presidency, and Mrs. J. B. Parks of Colorado was elected her successor. Mrs. Parks, who is a sister of Sen. Gordon Allott, had no known feelings about the Women's Division at the time of her election; indeed, she had the active behind-the-scenes support of Mrs. Clare Williams. After a few months in office Mrs. Parks developed a keen sense of autonomy for the NFRW. The Women's Division response was to outdo Mrs. Parks on program ideas, conferences, and whatever Mrs. Parks might be planning.

Some people close to the scene see the NFRW-WD dispute, if it may be so depicted, as that of a conservative versus a middle-of-the-road struggle. The NFRW is the more conservative, and the Women's Division works to keep it from sounding off on policy.

YOUNG REPUBLICANS AND YOUNG DEMOCRATS

As a stable political force at the national level, the Young Republicans date from 1946, when they received the trapping of permanence, with office space at the national committee, with biennial conventions (to determine who was to fill the space), and with the recognition of having their national chairman made an ex officio member of the Executive Committee of the national committee.

The establishment of a stable group of young Republicans was attempted by national senior Republicans two decades before the YRNF chairman moved into his headquarters in 1946. In 1931, Robert H. Lucas, executive director of the RNC, issued a call for a conference of young Republicans. Three hundred men and women designated by the members of the national committee met in Washington in June of that year. No permanent national organization survived early efforts, although distinguished alumni of various conferences in the 1930's included Robert A. Taft of Ohio, Styles Bridges of New Hampshire, Edward S. Shattuck of California, Harold E. Stassen of Minnesota, Gordon L. Allott of Colorado, and Walter J. Mahoney of New York.

The convention in Milwaukee in 1947 was the first of the regular biennial conventions and marked the practical beginning of the YR's on the national level. The Young Republican National Federation exists very largely in the persons of its paid staff in Washington, where they occupy two pens and an inner office tucked up against the volumes of the RNC library. Low salary and conflict among young officers and staff and the inexperienced elected leadership tend to encourage high turnover in personnel and a generally low level of performance. Expenses are provided by the national committee, even, in many cases, without expectations of concrete accomplishment.

The Young Republican organization follows closely the lines of the senior party. A hearty senior party organization in a state almost without exception encourages thriving Young Republican organization. The latter is organized along the strengths or weaknesses of the Republican Party in the area—by clubs in the cities, by county-wide groups in rural areas, in the colleges in both areas. The members of individual clubs meet in annual convention or, possibly, more frequently to secure the election of state officers. The collegiate organization maintains a separate hierarchy and cooperates with the regular Young Republican organization in a manner and to a degree determined by the vagaries of personality and local politics. The latter circumstance also largely determines the nature of liaison between the senior party and the Young Republican movement as a whole.

A distinctive liberal movement among YR's is found in the colleges of the Northeast, centered around Harvard and its undergraduate Young Republican Club. Opposed to this group is a conservative faction (probably a majority of YR activists in 1963) led by the Young Americans for Freedom organization. The YAF was established during the presidential campaign of 1960 on the invitation of William Buckley, the editor of *The National Review,* and, although its membership is bipartisan, its leaders are active in the Young Republican movement. In the early 1960's Young Americans for Freedom grew rapidly in all areas of the country, drawing heavily on the membership of already established Young Republican clubs, especially in colleges. At the 1961 YRNF convention Young Americans for Freedom elected the college chairman for the Young Republicans and in 1963 won the YRNF chairmanship by a close vote in a convention marked by name-calling, fist fights, and charges of fraud.[1] Sensing that the convention would be a Goldwater rally, Governors Nelson Rockefeller, George Romney, and William Scranton had politely refused invitations to participate. California State Republican Chairman Casper W. Weinberger, virtually host to the convention, was glaringly absent, as was National Chairman

---

[1] See the authoritative review by long-time student of YR politics, Biehl P. Clarke, *Political Intelligence* (III, No. 8 [Washington, D.C.: Civic Affairs Associates, Inc., 1963]).

William Miller who, a few days before the convention, reversed his earlier acceptance of an invitation to address the closing banquet.[2]

The Young Democratic Clubs of America have had permanent staff at the Democratic National Committee only since 1956. The YD's had been organized or reorganized (no one is quite sure) in the early 1930's during the Roosevelt energizing of the party. Before 1956 it had been the practice to bring in an executive secretary for Young Democratic activity during the campaigns. The secretary and one or two clerks would normally have a six- to eight-months tour of duty. They were hired by the national chairman after consultation with the national officers of the Young Democrats (chosen for two-year terms in the late fall of the odd-numbered years). The staff in 1952 had consisted of two people, Executive Secretary Howard Whitecotton, a McKinney appointee from Indiana, and a campaign director for college clubs.

Paul Butler's preparation for the 1956 campaign included plans for the more permanent staffing of YD activities. Butler thought that a regular division of the committee should be created for Young Democratic affairs. His suggestion, adopted by the YD national president, David Bunn of Colorado, was that the committee establish a Young Democrats division whose executive director would also be the executive secretary of the Young Democratic Clubs of America. The YD director would be given national responsibility for liaison with other college and youth groups and would handle such projects as the first voters drive, as well as serve the YDCA in his capacity as secretary of that auxiliary federation.

Richard Murphy was hired by Butler for this assignment in January, 1956, and there began the closest professional and personal relationship that Butler enjoyed on the staff during his five and one-half years as chairman. In his twenties Dick Murphy was already a seasoned organization leader, public speaker, and political veteran. Elected to Phi Beta Kappa at the University of North Carolina, he had been raised in the excitement of Frank Graham's political renaissance of the North Carolina Democratic Party; he had fought the fight against enemies of the right and left in the National Students Association and was rewarded with the office of national president in 1950–1951. Sharp-witted, urbane, dedicated at once to liberal issues and the per-

[2] See, for example, "Leaders' Snub of Young G.O.P. is Significant," *Chicago Tribune*, June 30, 1963; "Mob Rule Tactics Cited—Young GOP Convention Shocked Ex-Leader," *Minneapolis Tribune*, July 7, 1963.

sonal excitement of politics, Murphy complemented and strengthened the qualities by which the older Butler gained both his devotees and his enemies. Murphy wrote many of Butler's speeches and consulted with him as closely as anyone else on the permanent staff. The Kennedy campaigners found Murphy a model new frontiersman and took him quickly into their group after the Los Angeles convention in 1960. In January, 1961, he became assistant postmaster general for personnel, the chief hirer and firer in the Post Office Department.

Young Democratic clubs are chartered by state Democratic committees. Butler and Murphy wanted it otherwise and proposed the national chartering of YD clubs when the DNC rules were written in 1956. Southern states and the strong organization states such as Illinois and Pennsylvania combined to defeat the proposal. The national committee nevertheless grants direct charters to college YD clubs when application is made to Washington. Generally, however, to be accepted by the state committees means to be accepted by the national committee's YD Division. With official recognition comes eligibility to attend the biennial National Young Democratic Convention where, typically, the senior party leaders attempt to influence the resolutions in the direction of moderation and are frequently embarrassed by their failure to do so. Presumably the more liberal center of gravity among the Young Democratic clubs has some effect on the intraparty dialogue of which platforms and campaigns are parts. It would be hard to specify just what this effect may be.

Some Young Democrats, we know, become old Democrats in the course of years. And yet the percentage of YD leaders who become leaders in the senior party does not seem very great. Of the 140 state and national YD officials listed in the 1940 souvenir convention book, thirteen were recognized immediately by the Democratic author of this volume as having held important state or national party office subsequently. The YD national treasurer of 1940 was John M. Bailey of Connecticut.[3]

Whatever the influence and importance of the national Young Democratic efforts, the total cost is not great. In Butler days the Young Democratic Clubs of America were allowed to keep the approximately $20,000 per year received in dues to spend for travel of officers, meet-

[3] *The Democratic Book 1940* (Chicago: Bipartisan Committee for the Democratic Convention, 1940), pp. 106–107. Only one of the 140 persons, Price Daniels, then Texas state YD president, was recognized as having subsequently held a major elective office.

ings of the Executive Committee, and costs of conventions. Staff and administrative expenses in Washington were paid by the national committee and were estimated to have totaled from $35,000 to $50,000 a year.

NEGRO VOTE OR SOUTHERN VOTE?
BIPARTISAN DILEMMA

Reporting from the scene of a meeting of the Republican National Committee in Denver, June, 1963, Rowland Evans and Robert Novak found

> . . . a self-conscious lack of support, either private or public, for Negro rights at the meeting of the Republican National Committee here last week. And for good reason.
> Far from desiring to out-do Democrats as crusaders for racial equality, substantial numbers of Party leaders from both North and South see rich political dividends flowing from the Negrophobia of many white Americans. These Republicans want to unmistakably establish the Party of Lincoln as the white man's party.[4]

Evans and Novak link what they discern to be Republican strategy on the race issue to three assumptions: (1) the Democrats have captured the Negro vote, and there is no sense trying to compete for it; (2) Democratic administration support of Negro rights will cause the Democrats trouble in the South; (3) Northern whites are beginning to feel threatened by Negro demonstrations and Negro job competition. *Ergo,* the Republican Party should woo the white vote, North and South, being careful not to admit to this strategy.

So complex are the ideological, economic, and sectional interests at conflict and in process of accommodation in each party that charges such as these have a ring of authenticity regardless of the door at which they are laid. In contrast to the above story is a pamphlet which was published by the Young Republicans at the national committee in 1960. Its purpose was to make plausible the charge of Democratic hypocrisy on the issue of civil rights. The cover of the document depicted an advertisement in *The Montgomery Advertiser* proclaiming the opportunity to "See and Visit with Sen. Lyndon Johnson and 'Lady Bird' Johnson IN PERSON at the Union Station" in Montgomery. In the lower right and left corners of the advertisement was

---

[4] *Washington Post,* June 25, 1963.

the Democratic rooster with the motto "White Supremacy for the Right." The title of this Republican pamphlet was " 'Civil Rights' up North—White Supremacy Down South . . . Where Do Kennedy-Johnson *Really* Stand?" While piously disclaiming the existence of "something which can be called 'the Negro vote,' " the pamphlet called upon the Massachusetts senator "to repudiate his White Supremist political support" and to call on his Alabama supporters to cast write-in votes rather than vote for him under a white supremacy label which appeared on the Alabama ballot. On the same ballot the Republican motto was "America First G.O.P."

Here, then, is a section of the Republican Party whose motto on the Alabama state ballot was "America First," with all the connotations of the Fascist-type America First Movement of the 1930's and 1940's, admonishing the son of one of the leading Democratic sympathizers of the America First Movement to disavow his state party supporters because of their use of the white supremacy motto. And this civil rights pamphlet appeared at a time when presidential candidate Nixon was disavowing vice-presidential candidate Lodge's promise of a Negro in the cabinet and was refusing to make a speech in Harlem on grounds that he did not wish to seem to pander to the vote of any ethnic or religious group. It also appeared in the year in which the Republican presidential candidate received 49 per cent of the popular vote in the South and scheduled major appearances in North and South Carolina, Louisiana, and Texas.

One may well ask, is there a white man's party? Are there two white men's parties? Or, are there, perhaps, two very mixed-up parties?

Each of the national committees at least purports to be interested in cultivating the vote of minority ethnic and religious groups. By personal ability and abrasive honesty, the brilliant Negro newspaperman Louis Martin, as deputy chairman of the Democratic National Committee, made himself a man of power during the Kennedy administration. His specialty is understanding, interpreting, and corralling the Negro vote. In July, 1962, Clay J. Claiborne of Atlantic City, New Jersey, was appointed special assistant to Chairman Miller at the Republican National Committee, a position which had been filled by Valores J. "Val" Washington of Chicago for some fourteen years.

As more and more minority representatives come under the political tent in presidential election years, it becomes increasingly difficult to compare the magnitude of importance attached to the Negro vote as against that of the Poles, the Czechs, and the Ukraines, to mention but three. They, too, become the object of high-pressured wooing, with the especially developed movies and pamphlets, not to mention stock phrases celebrating patron saints' days and observing the anniversaries of national heroes and important military victories, shoe-horned into political speeches as suited to the occasion and the audience.

Thus does each party seek the Negro vote and each seek the Southern vote while each also seeks that elusive key to victory, the independent or moderate vote. When the chips are down in campaign time and when funds must be budgeted to competitive programs and purposes, the priorities become clear. Likewise, when the administration skews its legislative program to placate one or another interest in anticipation of an election year, the priorities become clear. The Republican Party in 1964, as in 1960, is strongly pressed by some of its members to weigh the scales in favor of the Southern vote, while trying to hold on to at least a minimum, stable core of the Negro vote. The Democrats are going all out for the Negro vote and hope to hold onto the South.

Minorities at the National Committees

At the Republican National Convention of 1884, John R. Lynch of Mississippi, a Negro, was elected temporary chairman.[5] Short of Louis Martin's present position as deputy chairman of the DNC, this is probably the highest office any Negro has occupied in either party.

The Democratic appeal to the Negro has been largely economic. In the North, as the lowest socioeconomic group, the welfare policies of the New Deal attracted large numbers of Negro voters to Democratic standards. During World War II more arrived in Northern urban ghettos from Southern rural ghettos, finding that for the first time they were not denied the vote but, on the contrary, urged by Democratic ward politicians, with money and drinks at hand, to keep the machines in power. By the end of World War II lower-class Democratic Negroes were outvoting middle-class Republican Negroes in every big Northern city (and some Southern cities, such as Memphis) except Philadelphia, where the Republicans held a majority of the Negro vote until 1949.

The Democratic alliance with the big industrial unions serves as one link to the Negro vote. Auto workers', steel workers', machinists',

[5] *Republican Proceedings 1884*, p. 6.

rubber workers', and oil workers' unions made special efforts at registration and campaign times to gather in the lower socioeconomic groups through factory and urban tenement districts; many of these voters appealed to on economic grounds are Negroes, Latin Americans, and recent Eastern or Southern European immigrants. The Democratic National Committee uses Negroes wherever possible in these drives.

The Democrats, like the Republicans, want to woo the Negroes pointedly, but not condescendingly and not so feverishly that non-Negro support will be alienated. In late 1959 Arthur Chapin managed for the DNC a gathering of Negro leaders in Washington where civil rights speeches were given and potential candidates John F. Kennedy, Stuart Symington, and Hubert Humphrey spoke their pieces; the meeting carried the euphemistic title Party Relations Conference.

The nationalities divisions at the two committees are, incidentally, to be distinguished from the effort to garner the Negro vote. They are letterhead groups of ethnic leaders—Poles, Ukrainians, Latin Americans, and various Central Europeans mainly. These divisions are hardly more than publicity channels which are kept open during the off years and used as sources of contacts to and recruits from ethnic organizations during campaigns.

The Republican interest in the Negro vote was regularized in November, 1945, in the National Council of Negro Republicans, which operated out of Philadelphia and acted, in effect, as a satellite organization of the Republican National Committee. The next year, when Herbert Brownell was selected as chairman of the RNC, he invited a Willkie Republican, former Chicago *Defender* staff man, and intimate of Governor Green of Illinois to establish a minorities division. This man was Val Washington, the Indiana University–educated former editor and publisher of the Gary *Sun* and general manager of the Chicago *Defender,* whose disposition was to rely on Negro fraternities, sororities, and fraternal organizations as avenues for communication with Negroes. He insists that, since Negroes have no country clubs or equivalent clubs to which leadership can gravitate, fraternities and sororities provide the best index to Negro leadership. Clay Claiborne's newspaper and Negro fraternal group experience suggests the lasting imprint of Washington's thesis on the Republican National Committee. In the 1960 election Washington sought permission to enlarge his program to go into Negro churches, but he was prevented because of the fear that such an approach, directed almost exclusively to Protestant churches, might be interpreted as evidence of bigotry.

According to Washington's perceptions, the average Negro is a conservative at heart.

> He never had anything. What he's put together, he wants to hold on to. As his grandfather used to say, he had to stretch beans into beans and meat. Negroes don't have as many outlets for their money. The activities of the Negro center around the home. This is why Negroes maintain nice homes on jobs which would not bring such homes to whites.

But, conservative as he may be, "the minute he gets his belly full, the Negro is interested in Civil Rights."

It is readily apparent that effective as this approach might be toward garnering middle-class Negro votes in a segregated society, it falls short of anticipating or exploiting the age of CORE (Congress of Racial Equality), SCLC (Southern Christian Leadership Council), and SNCC (Student Nonviolent Coordinating Committee). Although the Johnson administration is furiously attempting to keep abreast, if not ahead, of the demands of the newly emergent militant civil rights activists, the Republicans can hardly hope to steal a march merely by insisting that the Democratic efforts are a fraud and a delusion.

RNC'S Operation Dixie

The *Jackson* (Mississippi) *Clarion Ledger,* for May 16, 1962, carried a story under the caption, "Congressman Scheduled for Speech." It announced an address by former Rep. John H. Rousselot (R., Calif.) who was to speak at the Heidelberg Hotel "under the auspices of The John Birch Society." Although announcing that "leaders in both parties have shown interest in having a big turnout for" the event, the story went on to stress that "Wirt Yerger, Mississippi state chairman of the Republican party, urges all conservative patriots to attend this address."

In the same month *The New York Times*[6] carried a letter from I. Lee Potter, former Virginia state Republican chairman and director of the RNC's Operation Dixie. Potter responded to a question which *The Times* had posed editorially: "Can the Southern states' righters be convinced that the Republicans are any less desegregation-minded

[6] May 2, 1963.

than the Kennedy Administration?" A second question posed the problem of simultaneously appealing to Southern segregationists and Northern urban liberals. Potter attributed proven Republican gains in the South to economic conservatism and advocacy of a halt to Federal expansion "with its eroding effects on the rights of the individual and the states." "The issue of civil rights—a moot question, now—had nothing to do with our gains."

Virginius Dabney, writing in May, 1963, for *Harper's Magazine,* expressed his amazement that "we Southerners are now only a few years away from a genuine two-party system," the result of which *could* be "a more liberal political orientation than the South has ever known."[7] Dabney stressed the tremendous upsurge in Republican voting for Republican congressional candidates and presidential nominees in the South. He also stressed the possibility that the repeated near success of very conservative Republican candidates could push the so-called liberal Democratic incumbents in the South in the conservative direction.

Many are the hardy politicians who have adhered to the Republican cause in the South, in large part from the conviction that a strong two-party system could be the salvation of the former Confederate states and their immediate neighbors. The problem is, however, whether the states' rights position and segregation, so neatly combined by Gov. George Wallace of Alabama on the occasion of the re-integration of the University of Alabama in June, 1963, or so crudely manipulated by Gov. Ross Barnett of Mississippi in October, 1962, can be separated; whether in the South conservatism can be divorced from racism. If not, we face the spectacle of segregationist Republicans attempting to outdo segregationist Democrats for the immediate decades and of each reinforcing the throwback tendencies of Southern politicians and voters.

There is an irony to this for the conservative Republican whose leader is Barry Goldwater, for it is precisely Goldwater's vaunted promise to repeal laws rather than enact new ones which is needed to sweep away the encrustation of black-code and Jim Crow laws which constitute an anachronism and an incitement to violence in the contemporary South.

The will to win and the indifference to issues which characterize our parties could bring about a Republican hegemony in a segregation-

[7] "What the GOP is Doing in the South," *Harper's Magazine,* May, 1963, pp. 84 ff.

ist South, reacting against the Northern domination of the Democratic Party. Or it might bring, by accident or design, a situation in which Southerners were presented with a choice between two significantly different parties and slates of candidates. The former is more likely than the latter. Chairman Miller in November, 1962, suggested it would be "ridiculous" for Republicans to attempt to discriminate between "segregationist" and nonsegregationist candidates in the South.[8] The response of a youthful group of liberal Republicans to Operation Dixie was expressed in *Advance* in November, 1962, under the sub-caption "Potter's Field":

> Before Mr. Potter begins the 1964 campaign, for instance, it would be well if the party would face the facts of the 1962 election: 1) that the Republican campaign machinery is disproportionately geared to the right-wing, from the petty and parochial Congressional Committee Newsletter to "Operation Dixie"; 2) that the Republican campaign in 1962 was an overall failure in the Senate, where the official bias toward the right wing—particularly in the South—was most pronounced; 3) that the Southern House victories and Senate improvements, though significant, were not as auspicious as Messrs. Potter and Goldwater would have us believe.

ENGAGING THE ACADEMIC COMMUNITY: TWO APPROACHES

In recent years both national committees have made special efforts to engage the faculties and resources of colleges and universities in ways which will be partisanly helpful.

In a free society there is always some intercourse between the institutions of higher learning and the political parties. The universities recruit and develop party leaders in a general way and sometimes quite directly, through special programs of political education. The universities are to some extent hothouses for social and political thought, keeping ideas alive until the soil and weather in the larger communities are prepared for them. For many reasons American universities have not been so politically innovative as some would like, but there is no denying the importance of higher education in con-

---

[8] "Miller Hits G.O.P. Liberals On Southern Tactics Demand," D. S. Broder, *Washington Star*, November 27, 1962.

tributing to political leadership and to the general political dialogue in which parties play a significant part.

Both national committees have recently become more conscious of their relations with the academic world. In the space age education has high positive value; there appears to be an increasing appreciation of higher education, and both parties want it to be part of their image that they are concerned with the things the voters care about.

A second reason, related to the first reason, for the parties' interest in the academic community is the growing size and importance of college enrollments and faculties. A large percentage of the future electorate is in college or will go to college; college teachers are, collectively, among the most influential opinion leaders in our society. Therefore, to improve the parties' reputation among college students and teachers is also to influence the attitudes and opinions of future students and teachers. Such was the thinking behind the creation of the Arts and Sciences Division of the Republican National Committee:

> Anti-intellectualism is a harmful image for a party to project in an era in which education and science have become paramount issues of public policy and loom prominently in the minds of the American voters. It is especially harmful because the academic community alone is such a large one; in the 2,011 institutions of higher education in the United States, the students number 3,402,297 and the faculty (full and part time) over 310,000.[9]

The parties have a third reason for improving their communications with academia. The empirical study of social science and its stepchild, applied social science, have things to say to political leaders. The most spectacular contribution of social science to practical politics is the opinion poll, now so widely accepted that we forget how young it is and how it almost died of precocity in 1948. But in other ways, too, social science has contributed to the welfare of political parties—for example, in the study of voter motivation and perception and of the organization and management of volunteer groups.

The Republican and Democratic National Committees' headquarters have taken different ways to engage the academic world. The Democrats, as we have learned to expect in the comparisons which

[9] Staff memorandum to A. B. Hermann, executive director of the Republican National Committee, December 15, 1959.

emerge in this book, have done so piecemeal on an *ad hoc* basis, fitting man and programs to the needs—or merely whims—of the moment. The Republicans have been systematic. These approaches are not only reflections on a basic difference in political styles, but also responses to the common but erroneous notion that college professors are mainly Democrats. The truth is that in 1956 the Republicans needed to demonstrate their interest in eggheads; the Democrats did not.

Fifty per cent or more of the college professors in the United States vote Republican, but most of these professors are to be found in the schools of law, business, engineering, and medicine and in the professional schools and undergraduate departments which fall outside the humanities and the social sciences. Numerous reasons can be adduced (or perhaps more accurately, conjectured) to explain this. One view is related to psychological studies showing that groups which ascribe to themselves, or perceive that society ascribes to them, low prestige are anticonservative in their politics. Thus veterinarians and dentists tend to be more liberal in their voting behavior than do doctors of medicine. Sociologists attribute similar professional self-pity to college professors and, while holding that it is unwarranted, suggests it may in large part account for the anticonservative reputation which the group has earned.[10] This reputation, we would suggest, has not been earned by the academic community as a whole, but it has been earned *for* the academic community by that portion of it which has, since the New Deal, played the most prominent and vocal part in politics, namely, social scientists.

If the Republican Party was "intellectually bankrupt"[11] in 1956, it was because the bulk of college professors associated with the so-called policy sciences were hostile to business values, alienated by the business orientation of the Republican Party, welcomed the idea of improving society by governmental action, and resented what they perceived to be the tendency of businessmen and the Republican Party to undervalue them, if not to be outright suspicious of them. Republican stalwarts and their business friends quite accurately associated vigorous political action by college professors with the New Deal and the Democratic Party. Also, quite accurately, they attributed to college

[10] Seymour Martin Lipset, *Political Man* (Garden City, N.Y.: Doubleday & Co., 1960), chap. 10, especially pp. 320–326.
[11] The phrase was used by Robert Humphreys, RNC campaign director, in a speech to the Montgomery County (Maryland) Republican Women's Club.

professors in the social sciences a tendency to be more innovative and more willing to tinker with social institutions. In other words, regardless of how many college professors quietly cast their votes for Republican candidates, regardless of the educational attainment and the IQ of Republican candidates, officeholders, and party officials, the image of the Republican Party bordered on anti-intellectualism. A

'I Wonder When He'll Stop Stealing My Thunder?'.

Cartoon by Gib Crockett. Reprinted with permission of *The Washington Star*.

systematic and well-publicized effort to get Republican eggheads seemed to be in order.

The Democratic National Committee turns to its intellectuals when it wants help with particular problems. Political sociologist Lewis Dexter was public-opinion and elections analyst at the DNC from January through November, 1952; he prepared monthly newsletters for general distribution on "What the Polls are Saying," as well as special reports on the polls for internal use.[12] Eggheads were engaged by the Democratic Advisory Council and by the Committee on Political Organization (a Paul Butler creation to exchange organizational know-how among the states), because they had special knowledge in substantive policy areas or because they had some notions about political motivation and voter psychology or because they had skills of voting measurement relevant to campaign strategy.

The inventors of the celebrated "people predictor" are cases in point. In 1959 Prof. Ithiel Pool of the Massachusetts Institute of Technology, Robert Abelson of Yale, and William McPhee of Columbia, Democrats by conviction and voting habit, proposed to some New York liberal Democrats and, through them, to the Advisory Council that selected historical poll data be processed by high-speed computers to seek statistical trends and tendencies which might suggest elements of the 1960 campaign strategy. The Kennedy campaign organization actually used the people predictor in 1960.[13]

For the analysis and translation into politicians' language of regular poll data, the Democrats brought Prof. George Belknap of the University of California to the national committee in 1959. Belknap was given the euphemistic title consultant in voting analysis. He issued a series of mimeographed memoranda interpreting and commenting on poll data. After the convention he associated to some extent with the Louis Harris pollsters who were part of the preconvention Kennedy organization, but here again the integration of regular committee staff and candidate organization staff was less than successful, and Belknap was used little in the campaign except for esoteric studies of crowd measurement.[14]

[12] Lewis A. Dexter, "The Use of Public Opinion Polls by Political Party Organizations," *Public Opinion Quarterly*, XVIII (1954), 53–61.

[13] See Ithiel de Sola Pool and Robert Abelson, "The Simulmatics Project," *Public Opinion Quarterly*, XXV (1961), 167–183. "People predictor" was Roscoe Drummond's name for this project. *New York Herald Tribune*, December 19, 1960.

[14] For this aspect of the crowdsmanship contests during the Nixon-Kennedy campaign, see *New York Times*, October 7, 1960.

Since 1958 both national committees have had political scientists as full-time professional staffers under a program sponsored jointly by the committees and the National Center for Education in Politics. Each year two professors, one a Republican and one a Democrat, take leave from their colleges to serve as faculty fellows at their national party headquarters. The difference in the parties' attitudes toward and use of eggheads can be seen in the contrasting ways the faculty fellows are used. At the Democratic Committee the professor is just another hand, fitting in wherever his interests and talents fit; some have worked in political organization, some in publicity, some in research, and some even in fund-raising. At the Republican Committee the faculty fellows, after the first, were placed in charge of a regular program to identify and make available for work Republican academic talent for local, state, and national organizational and campaign work.

The development of the Republican National Committee's Arts and Sciences Division is an interesting story and may be briefly told for what it says about the self-image of the RNC, as well as for purely descriptive purposes.

The Arts and Sciences Division is rooted in the 1956 presidential campaign, when a group under the leadership of M. Robert Rogers, associated with Washington's "good music station," WMAL, founded the Committee of Arts and Sciences for Eisenhower (CASE). Harry Carmen, dean emeritus of Columbia College, and Helen Hayes were recruited as co-chairmen, and a letterhead organization set up. Out of Rogers' office in Washington, D.C., CASE engaged in a variety of activities calculated to broadcast the impression that artists, scientists, actors, and college professors in large numbers were in the Eisenhower camp. One of the authors spent the summer of 1956 in Washington and, on returning to California, helped establish northern and southern California chapters of CASE.

Immediately after the 1956 campaign, Sherman Adams indicated that a permanent role for CASE would be found. However, the organization languished. In February, 1958, a plan for reactivating CASE was presented to Robert Humphreys at the Republican National Committee, and a memorandum on the desirability of reactivating CASE was sent to Malcolm Moos and Gabriel Hauge on the White House Staff. In March, Moos directed to Sherman Adams and Gabriel Hauge a memorandum reviewing the purpose of CASE during the 1956 campaign but suggesting a different future role:

Today we seek to recruit a talented task force that will

work steadily and at a serious level toward three ends: 1)
to counteract the propaganda mills in and around the
Democratic party; 2) to generate ideas useful to this Administration and to the Republican party; and 3) to make
available for Government and Party service the skills and
talents of persons in the arts, science, and education from
all parts of the nation. It is eminently desirable, of course,
to keep prominent actors on our rolls and to attract more.
But initially the reincarnated CASE should be careful not
to be labelled as a glamour guild, for nothing could do
more to disenchant the many serious-minded people who
feel that a sober effort such as CASE envisages is long
overdue.

The Moos memorandum also suggested ideas for the organizational
structure and the functioning of a proposed council of artists, scientists, and educators. No action was taken on these suggestions, however.

In his year at the RNC, Prof. Philip Wilder of Wabash College
confirmed and intensified staff interest in an operation directed at
intellectuals. Toward the end of his tenure, he set in motion plans for
a meeting of political scientists, which was held on January 14, 1959.
Those present included Malcolm Moos and Robert Merriam from the
White House staff; Charles McWhorter of the vice-president's staff;
Bernard Lamb, field director of the Congressional Committee staff;
Malcolm Smith (of southern California CASE) and Steven Horn,
congressional staff members from the Senate and House side, respectively; and staff members from Georgetown University, the School for
Advanced International Studies, the University of Maryland, Brook-
ings Institution, and, of course, the Republican National Committee.

Assessment of the Republican Party's repute with political scientists was frank. One participant estimated that 80 per cent of political
scientists in the country were Democrats. Discussion moved from broad
evaluation of relationships to a review of what the two groups—the
party and political scientists—could do for each other. One thought
was that the political scientists could help Republican officeholders
publish more frequently, thus getting their names in the mass media
and repudiating the impression that they are inarticulate. They might
also produce objective analyses in various policy fields for the guidance
of Senate and House members. They could be used as researchers and
speakers in campaigns.

Later that month, at the Des Moines meeting of the RNC, Alcorn mentioned the desirability of a program to attract college professors, and in early March an additional meeting of political scientists was held, this time with Sen. Clifford Case of New Jersey and Rep. Fred Schwengel of Iowa joining Meade Alcorn to assure the participants of the party's seriousness of purpose. However, by this time another and, as it proved to be, competing project for improving the intellectual image of the party was under way, and the staff which might have been devoted to establishing an organization equivalent to CASE was siphoned off to the so-called Committee on Program and Progress (see below).

Arthur L. Peterson of Wisconsin State College became the third Republican National Committee faculty fellow in early 1960. Peterson's predecessor, meanwhile, remained at the RNC to help launch the Arts and Sciences Division, established as a regular committee activity in January, 1960. The role of college teachers as opinion-formers was stressed, and a program was outlined for identifying and recruiting the help of Republican-inclined college teachers across the country.

The early months of the effort were frustratingly clerical. A war book was prepared, listing by congressional district all institutions of higher learning in the United States. Starting with twenty names, the Arts and Sciences Division by June, 1960, when the project was turned over to Peterson, had eighteen hundred names of college professors who were Republican or who had indicated their willingness to work for Republican candidates in 1960. These were compiled through correspondence, visits to campuses, and attendance at professional association meetings. Simple-minded as the activity of collecting names of friendly and willing-to-work college professors may be, it proved a strenuous and time-consuming activity and one which soon received attention from the press.

The National Review (January 30, 1960) deigned to ridicule the program, *The Washington Star* (January 16, 1960), *New York Herald Tribune* (January 21), and *Chicago Sun-Times* (January 24) editorialized on the program, and *The Washington Star* and *Louisville Courier-Journal* carried political cartoons depicting worried Democrats watching the program. In August, 1960, Congressman Schwengel reported that

. . . the division has expanded its operation, and has become an integral part of the 1960 campaign operation.

The response has been extraordinarily good. From 645 colleges and universities the names of 4,200 friendly faculty members have poured in.

As newspapermen analyze the several score of academic people who are active in the Kennedy campaign, it is interesting to note by way of contrast, that over 4,000 academic leaders stand ready and waiting for their marching orders to contribute their specialized knowledge, experience, and skills to the Republican campaign at the State, congressional and national levels.

Already hundreds have asked for specific assignments and hundreds are actively engaged in campaigns across the country.[15]

Prof. Earl Nehring of the University of Kansas, the 1961 RNC faculty fellow, reported to Chairman William E. Miller in July, 1961, that the Arts and Sciences roster included about eight thousand names from every state and from more than one thousand colleges and universities. "Copies of pertinent sections of the roster have been distributed to all Republican Senators, Congressmen, State Chairmen and National Committee members." In May, 1961, the Arts and Sciences Division published the first issue of *Republican Report,* which was to serve as a means of contact and liaison with Republican scholars. This publication was continued and enlarged during the tenure of Prof. Robert Huckshorn, 1962–1963 director of the Arts and Science Division, and it was he who introduced the current emphasis on establishing Arts and Sciences groups associated with each state party headquarters, thereby enhancing the prospect of effective use of the man power available. By January, 1964, Prof. John Kessel, then the faculty fellow, was able to report the establishment of seventeen such state-wide groups which "are already preparing position papers, writing speeches, initiating letters-to-the-editor, and performing organization work for the headquarters and candidates."

[15] *Congressional Record,* August 25, 1960.

9
Financing the National Committees

Hobbes once likened money to the life blood of a nation and spoke of tax collectors as the arteries through which the nation's life blood flows. Money is the *sine qua non* to the existence of political parties and to the performance of the vital function of effecting peaceful changes of government in the United States. And tax collectors are not the arteries through which the funds supporting this basic public function flow. Indeed, until 1964 legislation providing for presidential transition and inauguration costs was passed, the president-elect had to perform as a quasi-public official in the time between election and inauguration without the support of public funds, and the inauguration itself was treated as an affair which should be privately supported.

Like all other activities, fund-raising was episodic for the first seventy-five years of national party committee existence, determined by the four-year major cycle and the two-year minor cycle. Even now much of the money-raising is conducted on a crash basis—especially at the Democratic Committee

—with both the intensity of the money hunt and the sources tapped depending on the phases of the political moon.

Immediately after the presidential elections, both parties give thought to paying off their debts, a task which the winning party finds easier than the losing. The favorite and most lucrative devices are employed for debt liquidation: overpriced dinners and other get-togethers variously called victory dinners, appreciation dinners, or, for the losing party, sloganized look-ahead-to-the-next-time affairs. The victors have some *quids* to give for the *quos* of contributors, but, to avoid the suggestion of thoroughgoing impropriety (although some impropriety always accompanies large-scale political financing), we must note that the *quid* may be nothing more than the elation of victory or a handshake from the new president. The defeated party customarily finds debt paying harder and is thrown back on the individuals and groups that make up its core.

The Republicans, for two simple reasons, can ordinarily raise more money than the Democrats: potential Republican givers have more money, and Republicans understand better the how and why of fund-raising. In 1960, however, victory for the Democrats more than offset the general Republican advantage in money-raising. The Democrats had a record debt of about $3,500,000 after the 1960 campaign; by February, 1963, this had been reduced to approximately $500,000, although the much smaller Republican debt of $750,000 had decreased only to $225,000 by January, 1964.[1] In the meantime each party had raised something like $500,000 for the 1962 congressional campaign. Staff members at the Republican National Committee worry about the significance, if any, of the fact that it is taking longer to retire the 1960 campaign debt—in a period of relative prosperity—than it took to retire the 1936 campaign debt in the days of the Depression.

The mid-term congressional campaign is the high point of the two-year curve of fund-raising activity, and the party feasts in January and February of the even-numbered years are always occasions for predictions of upcoming victory, the crowds and the receipts being reasonably good indications of party morale and confidence. The Democrats in 1962, like the Republicans in 1954, found contributions and enthusiasm higher than in the previous twelve years. In campaign years direct solicitation by the chairman, the treasurer, Finance Committee officers, candidates, and campaign managers accounts for a large portion of the increased income. The annual fund-raising dinners

[1] *New York Times,* January 16, 1964.

are held and multiplied, and mass appeals may also be intensified.

Big money cannot yet be raised through broadly based mass appeals. Campaign money has to come, at the national level, in sizable chunks. During noncampaign years, however, a growing band of middle-sized and small givers has recently provided an important share of national committee income. Both parties now have sustaining-membership plans, allowing contributors to give $10 to $100 a year through a pledge system akin to that used by their church or local community chest. These sources, plus the by now well-established state assessments employed by both parties, manage to keep the committees in business, if not out of debt, during the slack year following the presidential election and the not quite so slack year following the mid-term elections.

An understanding of national party finance requires some knowledge of the history of relations among the two Hill campaign committees and the national committee downtown. The congressional campaign committees came into existence in 1866 during the fight between Pres. Andrew Johnson and the Radical Republicans in Congress; the organization of an anti-Johnson Republican campaign committee in the House begat a counterorganization of pro-Johnson Democrats. Thus each congressional committee found itself at the outset in opposition to its own national committee.

We must be careful here not to read more into the word "organization" than we can accurately read into history itself. The congressional committee of pre–World War I, like the national committees themselves (the Senate campaign committees were not created until 1916, after the passage of the Seventeenth Amendment), were hardly more than mutual aid societies for incumbent congressmen who shared ideas, campaign strategies, and some money every two years.

Money seems to be the key to the relationships—money and personalities more than issues. The three committees get along well when their chairmen and career staffers trust one another (which means when they share similar backgrounds and perspectives) and when the national committees agree to subsidize the Hill committees.

After World War I a measure of cooperation and integration was achieved among the national and Hill committees in both parties. What little record remains indicates that after the Congressional elections of 1922 the entente among the Democratic committees disintegrated to be only partially and intermittently regained during the early New Deal days. The Republican committees, however, achieved rather more understanding, including a share-the-money arrangement which lasted until the two Hill committees, revolting against the Hoover leadership of the national committee in the person of Chairman Everett Sanders, determined to run their own show with a $400,000 budget and publicity and research bureaus. In 1938 Chairman Hamilton re-established a financial agreement which, with some modifications, prevails to this day. The Democrats, ever more quarrelsome and untidy than the Republicans, continue to meet each election—if not each new week—with whatever arrangements seem best suited to the accommodations, conflicts, and bank balance of the moment.

ORGANIZATION OF FUND-RAISING

The Republicans approach the problem of national party financing with businesslike matter-of-factness. For more than twenty-five years, professional advice and frequently overlapping personnel have characterized the services provided to the Republican National Finance Committee by the fund-raising and public-relations firm Ketchum, Incorporated, of Pittsburgh. In an interview McClean Work, associate of the Ketchum firm and former director of the Republican Finance Committee, related that in 1936, after Landon's crushing defeat,

> Mr. Ketchum went to Washington, uninvited, to a meeting of the Republican National Committee, and made the radical suggestion that the Party go out and raise its money just like money was raised for other worthy causes. More in desperation than in faith, his proposal was accepted, and that was the beginning of a new era in fundraising in American politics.

Another ex-director of the Republican Finance Committee, Frank J. Kovac, compared its activities to a united appeal. "It owes its existence to an agreement between the chairmen of the three committees, and a formula is followed for distributing the funds between the three based on the budgets submitted."

The Republican Finance Committee was formed by the national committee with the consent and cooperation of the Hill committees, but it is an independent organization, ostensibly not a "party" committee within the terms of the Hatch Act reporting requirements. An attempt is made to secure members from the principal money-raising states. In 1956, for example, the chairman of the Finance Committee was John Clifford Folger, investment banker of Washington, D.C., and the committee included representatives from California, Connecticut, Illinois, Iowa, Massachusetts, Michigan, Minnesota, New York, Ohio, Pennsylvania, Virginia, Washington, and West Virginia. Chairmen of state finance committees are ordinarily added to or associated with the National Finance Committee. The state finance committees, in turn, work closely with the state "political" committees, determining, on the basis of the national quota plus state needs, the amount of money to be raised and the allocations to be made.

A regular annual budget-making process seems to be followed by the Republican Finance Committee—at least in every campaign year. A budget subcommittee of the Finance Committee is charged with handling negotiations among the three national committees, reviewing plans and figures. The original precampaign total for the three committees was $7,800,000 in 1960, although it subsequently rose to $8,300,000.[2] In 1961 the total request fell to $2,500,000, of which $500,000 was earmarked for debt liquidation.

Despite great care and considerable good will, there is often friction between the Republican National and Hill committees, friction which cannot be assuaged by the mere process of joint participation in budgeting and fund-raising. Following the Nixon defeat, the joint budget committee met on December 8, 1960. The Hill committees had on hand six months' operating funds. The national committee had nothing; its monthly operating deficit amounted to $16,000 to $20,000, not counting campaign debt retirement. In the face of affluence on the Hill, the committee downtown groveled to meet its payroll. Such a condition does not engender satisfaction on either side. National committee staff resented the contrast of poverty and affluence; Congressional and Senatorial Campaign Committee staff did not see why their planned operations should be curtailed to bail out the national committee, especially when the only national offices the party could hope to win, short of 1964 and probably 1968, were House and Senate seats.

The Democratic national finance machinery is decentralized, with

---

[2] We hope it is unnecessary to point out that these figures are useful only to indicate the general magnitude of precampaign thinking, to comply with the letter of the Hatch Act limitations of a $9,000,000 total for the three committees. Campaign financing is a jungle of confusion, mistakes, multiple reporting, guesswork, and a smattering of perjury. For the best studies, see Alexander Heard, *The Costs of Democracy* (Chapel Hill, N.C.: University of North Carolina Press, 1960), and the useful monographs published by the Citizens' Research Foundation, especially two by the director of the CRF, Dr. Herbert E. Alexander, *Money, Politics, and Public Reporting* (Princeton, N.J.: Citizens' Research Foundation, 1960), and *Financing the 1960 Election* (Princeton, N.J.: Citizens' Research Foundation, 1962).

each committee doing what it damned well pleases. Sometimes, of course, it pleases to join with the other two committees in arrangements to cover a single campaign or the division of labor, and payment for labor, during noncampaign periods. Some measure of financial coordination is forced on the national committees of both parties, especially in presidential years, by the Hatch Act limitation of $3,000,000 total expenditure a committee. But this may be only a minimal paper coordination, and the national committee may protect itself as easily by establishing an *ad hoc* auxiliary committee.

The Democratic Hill committees do not provide as extensive services as do the Republican congressional and senatorial committees. The regular staff of the Democratic Congressional Campaign Committee consists of only two professional and two clerical persons; during campaigns field men are used as money is available. In both parties most of the money spent by the Hill committees is parceled out to individual candidates by direct grants, and it is this difference which distinguishes the Hill committees most sharply from the national committees. The Hill committees exist primarily to help finance state and local party activity (one should say, more accurately, candidate activity); the national committees exist to direct and administer what there is of national party activity and are financed largely by state and local party interests.

The Finance Division of the Democratic National Committee is headed by the treasurer, who is an elected officer of the whole committee, though in fact the nominee of the president or, more often, the national chairman in consultation with the president or titular leader. The treasurer of the committee is ordinarily not a paid, full-time staff official, although the present treasurer, Richard Maguire, is such. Typically the administration of the Democratic National Committee Finance Division is in the hands of the comptroller (more-or-less chief bookkeeper, forced on the committee by the reporting provisions of the Hatch Act) and an assistant to the chairman (and/or treasurer), who may have the title of finance director. These persons work closely with the chairman and treasurer in policy matters and in contacting big contributors. They serve as the staff core for the fund-raising dinners relied on so heavily by the Democrats. They are in charge of direct-mail solicitations; they oversee the operation of the state quota system and such occasional local drives as Dollars for Democrats. In a noncampaign period, eight to twelve persons will be employed by the Finance Division of the Democratic National Committee.

Even in the national committee itself, there is no such self-conscious and well-articulated finance organization as that shared by the three Republican committees. *Ad hoc* finance committees, consisting of members from all or major states, are established as precampaign planning or postcampaign debts require. These committees ordinarily perform indifferently for a while and soon quietly dissolve of their own inertness and without formal action. Typical is the "Permanent" National Finance Committee created by vote of the Democratic National Committee in January, 1960; many of its members are still active fundraisers (some, of course, never were active fund-raisers at all) and may be handled by Bailey, Maguire, or the comptroller. But all such dealing breaks down sooner rather than later into bilateral negotiations or, at most, understandings that can be handled by a conference telephone call. The existence on paper of such finance committees provides the appearance of formality and, at times, the excuse and opening remark for a phone call or letter.

A tinge of more formal organization—related to Paul Butler's concern for greater national party responsibility—colored the committee fund-raising activities from 1956 to 1960. The Advisory Committe on Fundraising Techniques was formed, with subcommittees on special projects and small gifts; these groups met as committee and subcommittees from time to time, but without any apparent organizational carry-over after the 1960 convention. In general, money-raising procedures at the Democratic National Committee remain informal and largely oral.

SOURCES AND DEVICES OF
NATIONAL COMMITTEE FINANCING

Most of the financial support for the national committees comes directly or indirectly from individuals and party groups that are also active money-givers and money-raisers for state parties and candidates. The only significant exceptions are contributions which come from national interest groups which find uneasy alliance with what may be loosely called the two national parties. These interest groups represent, in a general way, the labor-liberal constellations on the Democratic side and the organized business community on the Republican. Since both corporations and unions are prevented by law from direct contributions to party committees, this "national money" flows through individuals and complex arrangements of ticket purchasing and "independent political education" endeavors. The Republicans get large gifts from corporation executives who voluntarily contribute bonuses given to them by boards of directors; the Democrats get similar individual contributions from union officials. Political action committees, independent committees for candidates, registration drives, literature, and supplies are underwritten by national organizations in more-or-less overt collusion with party and campaign officials. Much money from these sources is funneled up through the state quota system and through the purchase of tickets and blocs of tickets to overpriced dinners and rallies.

State Quota Systems

The basic device of financing for both national party committees is a system of quotas allocated to each state committee as its fair share of the operating costs of the national party activity. The origins of the quota system go back to the beginnings of the committees when presidential campaign assessments were made on state party groups. The regularization of the quota system as support for annual ongoing costs of the committees was begun with the innovations of Republican Chairman Hamilton's period, 1937–1940. The Democrats, in their less systematic way—and also enjoying the advantages of the in-party— did not establish formal quotas until 1953. Estranged from the big-city regulars, surrounded by Stevensonian amateurs (being one himself), groping with a $1,000,000 debt, Stephen Mitchell borrowed the quota system from the Republicans. Democratic use of the state quota system seems to have survived both the return of the old pros to the committee and of a Democrat to the White House.

The quotas in both parties are based on a formula of fairness which recognizes state size, wealth, and party strength. The Democratic formula in 1960 was based on each state's average of the following factors (as a percentage of total DNC budget): electoral college vote; Democrats in the House of Representatives as a percentage of all Democratic congressmen; total state population as a percentage of national population; the state's estimated expendable personal income as a percentage of the national total. Republicans employ a similar formula. The Republicans do not disclose state quotas or receipts by states. The Democrats do—or did during the Mitchell-Butler period. As of January, 1960, the Democratic yearly quotas had a range from $650 for the Canal Zone and Virgin Islands to $106,000 for New York. Many anomalies existed—Kentucky's quota was the same as Massachusetts's and Ohio's was considerably more than California's—

giving rise to state complaints and recalcitrance. The latest report on Democratic state quota performance, issued May 2, 1960, showed only six states and territories paid up from 1957–1960; they were the District of Columbia, Maryland, New Jersey, South Dakota, Virgin Islands, and Wyoming. Rhode Island, Illinois, New York, and Minnesota were among those badly delinquent.

No significant patterns can be made of the various states' responses to the 1957–1960 Democratic quotas except that personalities and personal relations were critical. New York and Illinois were slackers because the key leaders in these strong organization states disliked Butler and all his works; District of Columbia and Maryland quotas were met by stateless liberals—stateless because they lived either in the District or in nearby Montgomery County (constantly feuding with the Baltimore-based state organization) and their $100 dinner tickets were credited to the District and Maryland quotas. A number of state quotas were raised (or, in some cases, blocked) largely through the efforts of single individuals: Arkansas had a good record mainly because of the work of DNC field man Harold Jinks, an Arkansan; Dennis Jensen, a young South Dakotan and former state executive director there, became national finance director in 1959; Pennsylvania's record was better than its big-organization sister states of New York and Illinois only because Matt McCloskey's self-image and reputation were partially at stake in his own state's quota.

The use of quotas by the national committees of both parties is more accurately thought of as a system rather than a device of fundraising. Income from all fund-raising events conducted at the state level and from most national activities is credited to the state quota; thus income from tickets purchased in Michigan for the $100-a-plate dinner in Washington and even tickets purchased by Michiganders in Washington was credited to the Michigan quota. The general rule is that the national committees do not question or care about the intrastate sources of a state's payments on its quota.

The quota system appears to have worked tolerably well for both parties. There is mounting evidence, however, that the Republicans are increasingly reluctant to depend on it. One of the first moves of Hamilton W. Wright, upon taking over the directorship of the Republican Finance Committee in 1963, was to hire an Ohio management consulting firm to help frame a direct-mail solicitation program, freeing the party of predominant dependence on the fulfillment of state quotas. The significant contribution of William Warner to the RNC in the years following his accession to the position of executive director under William Miller was the launching of a direct-mail, small-contributions campaign which brought in funds in amounts which, in the eyes of the staff, made the difference between keeping the RNC doors open or closing them. He raised $650,000 in 1962 and $1,107,000 in 1963 through such appeals. The problem, especially in a campaign year, may not be so much one of collecting the quota from each state, as collecting it in a timely fashion. The national committees employ credit to a maximum extent, but it is necessary to have a certain amount of money in the bank in order to operate effectively. If in a campaign year this money is in the bank in March or April, its value toward planning an effective campaign is vastly greater than if it goes into the bank in September or October.

Direct Personal Solicitation

In theory the Republican National Committee members, officers, and staff are not expected to make any *special* fund-raising calls for the national committee alone. National committee members and officials are expected to cooperate to the limit of their abilities in soliciting funds for the united Republican appeals. Where there is no working union of Republican finance committees, individuals may be asked to give and get contributions for the national committee. Some spontaneous giving and getting takes place out of the united framework of interlapping national, state, and local finance committees. The Republican National Finance Committee has a status-appeal program, Republican Associates, which grants some trivial perquisites and a membership card to anyone contributing $1,000 or more. In an effort to avoid crossing state finance chairmen, the National Finance Committee abstains from the Associates program in states like Pennsylvania, where local party officials object to direct national fund-raising that competes with their own. Such fastidiousness can cost the national party thousands of dollars a year in contributions (probably $50,000 in Pennsylvania alone), but is a practical tribute to the true source of power in the American party structure. Cross the state organization, and it may be careless about meeting its quota.

Nevertheless, special personal appeal for large gifts or loans must sometimes be made in both parties by the chairman, the treasurer, or someone associated with the campaign of the moment. Not the best-laid plans of God and fund-raisers can change the basically spontaneous and *ad hoc* nature of American party organization and campaigning.

An important difference between Republican and Democratic party leaders is that Democrats are relatively undisturbed by—and often seem to thrive on—the *ad hoc*ness of politics. Republicans embrace order; they try to impress it on the anarchy of politics. Democrats resist order or accept it only as a last resort. This difference may be, in part, no more than the prodigality of the majority party willing and able to waste some of its margin, and the frugality of the minority party aware that organization may compensate for numbers. Or it may be, as some have suggested, a psychological and temperamental difference between those who are attracted to one party and those attracted to the other.

However that may be, tapping the wealthy contributor is a game played by all comers in the Democratic Party. Some Democrats play it with zest, others reluctantly. Some seek and give out of principle; probably more give out of general or specific self-interest. Some do it gently, some without a trace of subtlety; some do it, in the words of Oscar Wilde, "with a bitter look, some with a flattering word."

Alexander found that 45 per cent of all reported individual contributions made to the Democratic National Committee in 1960 came in gifts of $500 or more; 52 per cent of all Republican National Committee individual contributions were in that category. In all, about four thousand persons contributed $500 or more in that year to a total of seventy national-level committees. Ninety-five persons—sixty Republicans and thirty-five Democrats—contributed a total of $10,000 or more each to their parties in 1960.[3]

In noncampaign years money received by the Democratic Committee from large gifts will be credited to the state quota of the contributor's state if such an attribution is requested. Despite this recognition of the state party, conflict and jealousy are usual consequences of national raiding of state sources of big donations. The national committee contributors tend to be dissident, reform, or "national" Democrats in conflict with their state and local organizations, as, to give just two examples, were the New York City Stevenson supporters who underwrote the Advisory Council from 1956 to 1960 and the anti-Johnson Texas friends of National Committeewoman Mrs. R. D. "Frankie" Randolph of Houston.

Dinners and Other Overpriced Events

The Democrats originated the $100-a-plate dinner. Credit belongs

[3] Alexander, *Financing the 1960 Election, op. cit.,* pp. 57–59.

to Matthew McCloskey, millionaire building contractor and Democratic national treasurer from 1955 to 1962. In 1935 McCloskey suggested the plan to David L. Lawrence, then Pennsylvania state chairman. Lawrence says that "when he broached the idea to me that you could get people to pay $100 a plate for dinner, I thought he should have his head examined."[4] But the first dinner was successful, and the device has since been used increasingly at all levels by both parties. A newspaper count of overpriced political fund-raising events in 1960 revealed 213 dinners, luncheons, breakfasts, and cocktail parties at all levels; many more were held and not reported in the newspapers scanned. Alexander cites a *New York Times* estimate that more than $3,000,000 was raised at New York City events alone.[5]

Overpriced party galas are pegged at what the traffic will bear. Five-dollar bean suppers are common in rural areas; $1,000-a-plate dinners with the president have lately enriched the Democrats in Washington and elsewhere.[6] The most successful overpriced fund-raising event ever conducted—actually a national system of events—was the 1956 Salute to Eisenhower extravaganza, linked by closed-circuit television, grossing over $5,000,000 for the Republican National Finance Committee. The most lucrative single event to date was probably the Democratic National Committee's Dinner and Gala on January 18, 1963, where, to the cries of Republican leaders and New Frontier bureaucrats who were encouraged to buy "voluntary" $100 tickets, a total of approximately $1,200,000 was realized.

McCloskey's innovation has proved to be a great bonanza for both sides of the political street since 1935. For the contributor there is a social occasion, snob appeal, and often an opportunity to tag the contribution as an organization or business expense. For the national committees, there is money!

Mass Solicitations

For many years the national party committees have been lured by the promise of big money in little sums. They are, at the same time, frustrated by the costs of collecting small contributions from many people. Many experiments have been made. Only two devices have been found to be at all useful.

One, now seemingly established in both parties, is the idea of the

[4] *New York Times,* June 10, 1962.

[5] Alexander, *Financing the 1960 Election, op. cit.,* p. 56.

[6] See *Washington Star,* January 19, 1963 (over $500,000 grossed), and *New York Times,* May 17, 1962 ($400,000 grossed).

sustaining membership, solicited by mail and processed by mass (electronic) methods. The germ of the sustaining-membership idea is found at least as far back as the early 1920's in the Democratic Victory clubs started by Chairman Cordell Hull and featuring local groups of ten or more members who each paid $5 into the party treasury.[7] The modern form of sustaining memberships seems to have been instituted by the Hamilton-Ketchum team at the Republican National Committee in 1937. The following year a total of $202,343.72 was reported as receipts from 6,367 sustaining members.[8] The Hamilton program lapsed after 1940.

Democratic Chairman Butler revived the idea of sustaining memberships in 1956. In 1959, of a total spendable income of about $750,-000, the Democratic National Committee realized $221,000 from the sustaining memberships; about twenty thousand persons contributed to this program during that year. In 1960 sustaining-membership income was estimated at about $600,000. Since January, 1961, the Democratic sustaining-membership program has been kept but not emphasized. The plain truth is that, with a President in the White House, the Democrats have other sources of money that are easier to get and in greater supply.

In early 1962, lending support to the notion that the sustaining-membership idea is still primarily an out-party device, the Republican National Committee launched its own Sustaining Program for Republican Party Headquarters. The basic pitch letter is signed by the national chairman, the two Hill committee chairmen, and the chairman of the Finance Committee; to underscore the integration of the Republican National Committee sustaining-membership program with the united finance system, another letter to potential contributors, signed by Senatorial Campaign Committee Chairman Morton (elected to the Senate chairmanship in 1962 after resigning the national chairmanship in 1961), points out that "extra money will be needed in campaign years and . . . this contribution in no way relieves me of my responsibility to local and state organizations or to special contributions in presidential and congressional years." About $700,000 was received from the new sustaining program between March and the end of December, 1962. Over $1,000,000 was realized from the pro-

[7] Hull, *op. cit.*, I, 114.

[8] Karl Lamb, "John Hamilton and the Revitalization of the Republican Party, 1936–40," *Papers of the Michigan Academy of Science, Arts, and Letters,* XLV (1960), 239, citing Republican National Committee publicity release, November 29, 1938.

gram in 1963; that constituted about one-half the combined budgets of the three national-level Republican committees.

The second mass solicitation device used by the national party committees is the door-to-door campaign. The Democrats have shown more interest in doorstep finance drives than have the Republicans. Only in 1958 did the Republican National Committee sponsor its Neighbor to Neighbor Drive as an official national project. The Democrats have undertaken five national Dollars for Democrats drives from 1956 through 1960; in 1961 and 1962 the national committee cooperated with state organizations, gave advice and counsel on the drives, but placed little emphasis on the program.

The receipts from the five Dollars for Democrats drives and the one Republican small-gifts drive were shared with state and local party committees—among the Democrats one-third each. Mrs. Julia Kirlan of the Republican National Committee finance staff reported that the GOP's Neighbor to Neighbor Drive grossed $1,000,000 in 1958; assuming an equal three-way split, about $333,000 came to the national committee. For a number of reasons, the receipts from local drives sometimes get stuck in the pipeline from precinct to national committee, and the Washington headquarters may be fortunate to get 25 to 30 per cent of the gross. The national receipts from the 1956 and 1957 Dollars for Democrats Drive were each about $50,000; in 1958 slightly more than $100,000 was realized by the Democratic National Committee; in 1959, $110,000; and in 1960, $120,000.

Many arguments are made, on normative grounds having to do with the evils of large contributions and the virtues of small, as well as organizational grounds having to do with stimulating precinct work, for the continuation and encouragement of small-gift drives for political parties.[9] The potential is admittedly great. Big money in little sums will continue to be sought, especially by the Democrats when they are the out-party. But, given the primitiveness of party organization in America, the lack of communication and sanctions, the absence of emotional appeal and tax incentives for the giver, plus the likelihood that other and easier (if less theoretically pure) money-raising techniques are available to the parties—given all these facts, the national

[9] See Bernard Hennessy, *Dollars for Democrats 1959* ("Eagleton Cases in Practical Politics" [New York: McGraw-Hill, 1960]), for the objectives, procedures, and problems of a national door-to-door search for "clean" political money.

committees cannot hope to be supported soon, or perhaps ever, entirely by small contributors.

Contributions from Federal Employees

In January, 1963, *The Washington Post* felt compelled to cluck its editorial tongue at the "Hatch Act Eclipse."

> However one looks at it, the pressure that has been applied to Government employees to buy tickets for the Democratic fund-raising affair tonight is a shabby business. The Hatch Act tells Federal employees that they may not participate in partisan activities [*sic;* this is not so]. The Civil Service System holds out to them assurance that they will be compensated and promoted on the basis of merit. Yet many of them are being pressured to give $100 to the Democratic cause—in installments if they cannot afford to buy a ticket to the gala outright—by their supervising officials who should be the first to respect the spirit and letter of the law.[10]

Nearly two years earlier, *The Post* had carried a story, "FBI Probes Charges of Hatch Act Violation," the burden of which was that the Justice Department had begun an investigation "to ascertain whether the Hatch Act may have been violated by certain Eisenhower Administration employees during the last election campaign."[11] FBI agents were interviewing Post Office Department and NLRB employees who said their superiors had pressured them into buying tickets for a Republican fund-raising dinner. *The Post* concluded the story with the following paragraphs, bracketed here, as in the original:

> [Although denied emphatically by both Democratic and Republican sources, it is an ill-kept secret that Republicans claim tangible evidence of serious violations of the Hatch Act by some ranking Democrats in the Post Office Department.
>
> [It is understood that several weeks ago when leading Republicans on Capitol Hill thought they had pinned down

[10] *Washington Post,* January 18, 1963.
[11] *Ibid.,* June 22, 1961.

suspicions with affidavits, they went to the White House
to arrange a "gentleman's agreement."

[Under the reported agreement, the Republicans were to
stay mum about Democratic shenanigans if the Democrats
conveniently forgot about similar activities under the Eisenhower Administration.]

President Kennedy reduced *The Post*'s 1963 editorial to proper
perspective by naming Jerry Kluttz, whose bylined stories of pressures
on civil servants to purchase tickets were featured in *The Post,* as "the
man who sold the most tickets tonight."[12] Having made light of the
Hatch Act implications, the President twitted the purchasers of tickets.
He recalled that the $100-a-plate dinner had been invented some thirty
years earlier. "We have revolutionized that by removing the dinner,"
the President told his audience, "but we are hanging on to the $100.
The day will come when we will let you go."

If one chose to pontificate, he might use this presidential flip-
pancy as a text on political and statutory morality and the obligation of
the citizen to obey the law and of the president to set an example of
rectitude. The simple truth is that the standard expressed or implied in
the Hatch Act is one which neither party is prepared to meet, and it
is inconsistent with the structure, processes, and proclivities of the two
parties in the United States. Thus they honor it by evading it and
express good-humored contempt for it by condoning mutual violations.
Illogically, we seem to have defined evasion or violation of the law to
be conditions for the continued existence of the two major parties and
whatever measure of party government they provide us.

The fact of the matter is that neither party is unduly fastidious
about the source or method of raising the funds which are the condition of survival and effective performance; indeed, more than funds
is involved, as credit cards, executives, company and union automobiles,
public-relations accounts, and other essentials to performance in our
society are lent, surreptitiously and in violation of the unbending spirit,
if not the foolish words, of the corrupt practices acts.

A most likely object of pressure for political contribution is that
body of civil servants who, whatever the protestations of the party
in power about the neutrality of government employees, owe their jobs
in some measure to political pressure, influence, or condonation. The

[12] *Ibid.,* January 19, 1963.

political chameleons are those most susceptible to outright pressure. These are the GS-12 and above civil servants, whose political affiliations are changed or muted with changes of administration. A new administration is likely, with tongue in cheek, to mistake political muteness for political mutation when it comes to exacting political contributions.

The Washington Post may have established its moral rectitude with the editorial of January, 1963, but it did not get to the point. The point was that the Kennedy administration violated the Hatch Act no more certainly than did the Eisenhower, Truman, and Roosevelt administrations before it (the original Hatch Act being, at least in part, political spite against F.D.R.). They merely violated it more methodically and more effectively. If exacting political tribute from civil servants is to be treated as akin to robbing banks, it is legitimate to draw an analogy between the two. And, although an amateurish or bungled bank robbery may be no less illegal than a smooth, professional job, it is not logical to condemn a smooth job while tolerating the bungled one. Until we find ways of making political money honest, respected, and available in sufficient amounts, we can expect that those who dance will, to some extent, pay the piper.

TRENDS AND PROSPECTS FOR FINANCING

Our review of national committee financing leads us to believe that future developments depend on three factors: (1) the rate of growth and cooperation among the national and Hill committee activities in both parties; (2) the continued availability of present sources of income for the parties; and (3) new legislation to regulate or subsidize party financing.

The trend clearly is toward greater national party organization and activity. Reflecting general sociopolitical forces in America and to some degree characterized by a conscious drive toward greater party centralization and responsibility, the national committees seem fated to play an increasingly important role in American politics. We expect that the national leaders and their institutions, with a good deal of fumbling and indecision, will develop, as the times require, greater coordination and unification. This means, among other things, that the financing of national party activity must be further regularized. The united finance system of the Republicans should continue to be supported and perfected by the officers and members of the national and Hill committees. No serious obstacle would seem to prevent the Democrats from establishing a similarly unified finance structure, although delay until the Democrats are again the out-party might make such unification impossible.[13]

We expect, second, that all the currently used fund-raising techniques will continue to be available to the national committees. Despite occasional grumbling, those who now support the parties out of gratitude, anticipation, habit, principle—and, one must confess, on some occasions out of subtle coercion—will continue to do so. Overpriced events promise to remain important sources of funds. Sustaining-membership programs may contain the greatest promise, and we urge them upon the parties for reasons of internal stability and *esprit de corps* as well as for wider considerations of public policy. The state quota system is by now widely agreed to in principle; its increased success depends on many developments, small and large, out of which may gradually evolve an American party system of unity, cohesion, and responsibility.

A thorough consideration of the final element upon which the future of national committee financing depends—new legislation to regulate or subsidize party activity—would be too complex to be undertaken here.[14] We find much understanding and good sense in the recent report of the President's Commission on Campaign Costs.[15] What we take to be a principal recommendation of the President's Commission, namely, that eligibility for the tax credit be given only to contributors to the national committees or other party groups designated by the national committees, strikes us as being a reform for which the American public and Congress may be ready. This provision, if passed, might have startling significance for the creation of more responsible parties in the United States; it might provide a sanction of great power to the national committees. We hardly think that the congressional party leaders are yet in the mood to allow such a change in our party system. We think, wishfully, that they should be farsighted and daring enough to do so.

---

[13] As we have noted, innovations at the national committees have tended to come during out-party periods. However, a thoughtful attempt at reform by a strong and popular president could accomplish much.

[14] For a well-argued brief in support of direct federal contributions to political campaigns, see Phillip M. Stern, "A Cure for Political Fundraising," *Harper's Magazine* (May 1962), pp. 59–63.

[15] *Financing Presidential Campaigns, Report of the President's Commission on Campaign Costs* (Washington, D.C.: Government Printing Office, 1962).

10

The Republican National Committee and "Party Policy," 1920–1963

Political parties are popularly regarded as vehicles for providing the electorate with alternative candidates and alternative policies from which to make a choice. The parties are supposed to stand for something; in the minds of their more vehement adherents, they are supposed to, and do, stand for something which is enduring and is right. But who shall proclaim what the party stands for at any given time? It might, for example, seem obvious to the casual student of American politics that the most recent presidential candidate of the out-party is, as titular leader, the national spokesman for the party.

But, of course, Rep. William Miller, Republican national chairman, proclaimed in Los Angeles in October, 1961, that Richard M. Nixon was not the titular head of the party and that Eisenhower came closer than anyone to filling that position. When former President Eisenhower some months later, in June, 1962, convened a meeting at his Gettysburg farm, he said things which caused elected Republican policy-makers on the Hill to blanch with impotent fury. Who speaks for

191

the party, an ex-president with no prospect of future elective office-holding or those who hold their positions of national office as a result of an electoral mandate? Or, perhaps, does a bureaucratic entity called the national committee, which performs essential functions for the party and is probably regarded by the rank-and-file voter (although certainly not by the county chairman or the candidate for office) as the national party headquarters?

These are rhetorical questions, for it is not the purpose of this and the next chapter to attempt a direct answer to them. Various groups at various times attempt to speak for their party. It may be a women's federation attempting to reduce party principles to a few clarion statements which can be mimeographed on the back of a post card. It may be an effort of the congressional delegation, resulting in the kind of statement which was published in June, 1962, by the Joint Committee on Republican Principles, co-chaired by Rep. Melvin R. Laird of Wisconsin and Sen. Bourke B. Hickenlooper of Iowa; this effort was developed in cooperation with the Republican National Committee, which loaned its research director, William Prendergast, to serve as executive secretary of the *ad hoc* Joint Committee. With a periodicity which is becoming noticeable, the national committees would appear to sense the desirability of engaging in off-year platform drafting.

Both national committees in recent years have tried to formulate party positions on the major issues. This process is complicated by a number of factors. First, and perhaps foremost, is that both national committees must attempt to define and identify what they consider to be the major issues of the time. They then must try to outline party positions on these issues, carefully balancing a number of political considerations. Moreover, the national committees must consider both the political philosophy and tradition of their respective parties and the practical politics of appealing to voters to win elections. This need to win elections, of course, implies constant sensitivity and awareness by the national committees to rapidly changing economic, social, and political conditions. In fact, the rapid rate of political and social change in the twentieth-century United States poses one of the major problems for the national committees or party conventions in outlining positions on major issues. Frequently platforms adopted by the parties at their national conventions need to be drastically revised and redefined during the four years between conventions.

REPUBLICAN ADVISORY COMMITTEES, 1920–1944

Three committees were established by the Republican Party between 1920 and 1944 to consider policies and programs before the adoption of platforms at the national conventions. At the time each committee was created, the Republican Party was the minority party, although in 1920 the Republicans had control of Congress.

Generally speaking, in all the three cases the Republicans had no current record of legislative and executive accomplishments.

The purpose of the pre-convention studies was to do the basic investigation, research and analysis work and provide the Convention with factual reports and recommendations on policy to be used in drafting the Party platform.[1]

This was the general purpose outlined for the three committees created by the Republican Party. The names of these committees were the Republican Advisory Committee on Policies and Platforms, established in 1919 and headed by Will Hays; the Republican Program Committee of 1938–1940, headed by Glenn Frank; and the Republican Post-War Advisory Council which had only one important and dramatic meeting—at Mackinac Island, Michigan, in 1943.

Chairman Will H. Hays, under authority granted by the Republican National Committee in December, 1919, appointed the Advisory Committee on Policies and Platform.[2] It consisted of twelve members of the Republican National Committee and a large number of other Republican leaders, including former Pres. William H. Taft, Charles Evans Hughes, and twenty-three senators and representatives in Congress. The Advisory Committee was to

. . . investigate the existing needs and conditions affecting specific problems that would have to be considered by the National Convention; to gather facts and data; to invite a full expression of opinions of leading Republicans and to submit its recommendations and the material it collected,

[1] "Pre-National Convention Research and Study Programs on Republican Party Policy, 1920–1944" (Research Division, Republican National Committee, October 1959), p. 1.
[2] *New York Times,* February 5, 1920; *Republican Campaign Textbook 1920* (New York: Republican National Committee, 1920), pp. 482–485.

in convenient form, to the Resolutions Committee of the National Convention.[3]

The full committee of 173 members from every part of the nation organized into eighteen subcommittees. Ogden Mills, a well-known member of the New York State Legislature, was chairman of the fifteen-man Executive Committee.

Despite the long and impressive list of issues scheduled for study, the Advisory Committee failed to consider perhaps the most important issue of the day—ratification of the League of National Covenant. One hundred thousand questionnaires were sent to selected "men and women of all sections of the country" and, although according to the committee the questionnaire was designed to sample grass-roots opinion, some felt it was aimed more at influencing opinion.

The 1920 Advisory Committee on Policies and Platform set a pattern for later Republican committees. It reflected an ambitious attempt on the part of Republican leaders to formulate positions and establish policies to guide the next convention.

Like the stock market and the American economy, the Republican Party suffered severe setbacks and reversals during the 1930's. The Glenn Frank Committee, known as the Republican Program Committee 1937–1940, was an attempt to improve the fortunes of the Republican Party. It had hit a low in 1936 when Alf Landon carried only Maine and Vermont. Former Pres. Herbert Hoover suggested a mid-term national convention. Republican National Chairman John Hamilton urged action on Hoover's proposal and on November 5, 1937, the Republican Program Committee was created. Dr. Glenn Frank, former president of the University of Wisconsin, was named chairman of the 200-member Program Committee. He outlined the purposes of the committee as to provide "an utterly honest and objective audit of the New Deal; to restate and reinterpret" the Republican philosophy; and to "create a comprehensive report of policy."[4]

The Program Committee organized into nine regional groupings, with a chairman and assisting officers in each region. In the first year of the Program Committee's activities, over fifty regional subcommittees were set to work. Preliminary reports of the regional subcommittees were made at a five-day meeting of the full Program Committee in August, 1938. One of the reports was written by Dr.

[3] *Ibid.*, pp. 483–484.
[4] *New York Times*, March 1, 1938.

Ralph J. Bunche, who was then teaching at Howard University. His 133-page report was titled "Needs of the Negro."

The full report of the Program Committee, *A Program For a Dynamic America, A Statement of Republican Principles,* was submitted to the Republican National Committee on February 16, 1940. The Frank report was given wide publicity, and it was printed in a 116-page booklet. It was also submitted to the 1940 Republic National Convention, but a later staff evaluation concluded that "upon examining the 1940 Republican Platform, [it is evident] that little attention was paid to the Program Committee's report."[5]

It was the struggle between the Willkie internationalists and the old-guard isolationists which led to the creation of the Republican Post-War Advisory Council on June 1, 1943. Chairman Harrison Spangler appointed the Advisory Council which consisted of about fifty Republican senators, representatives, governors, and members of the Republican National Committee. The Republican Post-War Advisory Council received authority from the RNC but was independent of it. The purpose of the Advisory Council was to develop "a realistic peacetime program for American progress."

Only one meeting of the Post-War Advisory Council was held— on Mackinac Island, Michigan, September, 1943. Thereafter eight study committees were organized. Reports from four of the eight committees were presented to the Republican Platform Committee in 1944, and it is said that Sen. Arthur Vandenberg's report, on behalf of the Foreign Policy Committee, was influential in drafting the platform and in developing his own internationalism.

THE "PERCY COMMITTEE"

In the 1958 election the Republican Party suffered a severe defeat, losing forty-eight seats in the House of Representatives. Not since 1937 had there been fewer Republicans in the House or fewer Republican governors or fewer Republicans in state legislatures than there were in early 1959.

It is probably true of political parties as of individuals that they become most introspective following failure. In December, 1958, a group of Republicans met at the White House with President Eisenhower to conduct a post-mortem on the November disaster. The group included Meade Alcorn, chairman of the Republican National Com-

---

[5] "Pre-National Convention . . .," *op. cit.,* p. 6.

mittee, and a young Chicago businessman, Charles Percy, president of
the Bell and Howell Company.

During the White House meeting the group heard a chalk talk
which subsequently was to be presented to the Republican National
Committee members when they met in Des Moines, Iowa, on January
22, 1959. In the course of the talk the public opinion pollster who
presented it suggested, among other things, that "the Republican Party
is attracting the older people much more than the younger people.
This, of course, is a very bad age profile because old people die whereas
young people live to vote another day." The presentation also stressed
the need to improve Republican salesmanship, presenting the Republican problem in terms which suggested that it was merely a matter
of making the party more marketable.

Of course, the answer to the suggestion that old people die
whereas young people live to vote again is that, if the problem of the
Republican Party is merely that of the age group which supports it,
young people can be counted on to grow old and, presumably, as old
people, to vote Republican. And the answer to the suggestion of the
marketability of the party is: What is the nature of the product which
is to be sold? The story possibly is apocryphal, but it appears that
Charles Percy raised the latter question during the White House
meeting, suggesting that the problem of the Republican Party was
not so much a problem of marketing as a problem of identity, of
finding out what the party stands for and attempting to persuade the
American people that what the Republican Party stands for is a set
of principles and a way of going about attacking common problems
which warrant their support.

There is evidence that at approximately this time and independently from consideration of the electoral results of November, President
Eisenhower was thinking in terms of national goals. (He subsequently
created the Commission on National Goals.) The result of the White
House meeting was a presidential request to Meade Alcorn that he
form a committee to define the goals of the Republican Party. Alcorn
took the occasion of the January, 1959, Republican National Committee meeting in Des Moines to recommend creation of the Republican Committee on Program and Progress.

The timeliness of the endeavor became evident as the national
news media reacted to it during 1959. In April, 1959, each member
of the Committee on Program and Progress and its executive received

a letter from W. D. Maxwell, editor of the *Chicago Tribune*, enclosing "First Principles," the first of a series of editorials to appear in the *Chicago Tribune*. This series ultimately was completed in twenty episodes which constituted the *Chicago Tribune*'s contribution to the thinking of the Republican Committee on Program and Progress.

Chairman Meade Alcorn proceeded in late January and throughout February to compose the policy committee. Its membership was broadly representative of the Republican Party. The Percy Committee's subsequent relations with elected Republican office holders in Congress were enhanced by the presence on it of Rep. Charles A. Halleck of Indiana and Sen. Everett McKinley Dirksen of Illinois, the minority leaders respectively of the House and the Senate. Other committee members included officeholders on the state level, such as Gov. Cecil Underwood of West Virginia; Benjamin S. Adamowski, state's attorney for Cook County; and Robert A. Taft, Jr., then a member of the Ohio state legislature. The group included lawyers, doctors, businessmen, college professors, experts in communications, farmers, labor union leaders, former members of the Eisenhower administration, and representatives of various faiths and races in the United States. As chairman of the committee, Meade Alcorn selected Charles H. Percy of Chicago, the young industrialist who had largely been responsible for its origin.

The committee's charter developed in the course of numerous and lengthy consultations with Chairman Alcorn. Two paragraphs are perhaps worthy of quotation from the charter which Alcorn delivered to the Committee on Program and Progress:

> How can the fundamental principles of the Republican Party be applied to the social, economic, and international problems of today and of the reasonably foreseeable future so as to strengthen our free society and achieve the fullest life and the greatest opportunity for the American people?
>
> You will have to anticipate as realistically as you can the course and pace of social, technological, and economic change as they affect the areas of political activity. You will seek to apply the basic principles of Republicanism to these findings in such a manner as to provide guideposts to the solution of contemporary and emerging problems with which we will continue to be confronted. You will seek to provide not only guideposts which will help our

party along the road to victory in 1960 but guideposts which
we can follow towards success in the years beyond.

Much of the month of February was taken up with considerations
of how to organize the committee. The tendency of the Republican
National Committee staff was to assume that the policy committee
should be split up in much the manner that congressional committees
are, with subcommittees on such topics as agriculture, labor, banking,
urban affairs, civil rights, medical care, and so on. Another view-
point was that to create a subcommittee on agriculture would be to
invite—indeed, to make inevitable—its composition by the farmers
and ranchers on the Program and Progress Committee. To create a
subcommittee on labor would make inevitable its domination by the
labor leaders; to create a subcommittee on banking would be to
tie it to the bankers and financiers. It might be desirable somehow
or other to arrive at an organizational format which would link labor
leaders with industrialists in the definition of broad economic policy
goals affecting both and to link both with the farmers. It might be
desirable that some format broader than civil rights be identified for
the purpose of associating the Republican Party with the pursuit of
goals which have as their focus human beings rather than abstract
principles. All agreed that it was essential that the Republican Party
appear to be concerned with the future and with the impact of science
and technology on American society. Finally, it appeared desirable
that the party be concerned as much with peace as with national
security.

The result of a week of staff discussion was a decision to form
four task forces. The four task forces and the description of their
jurisdiction are as follows:

1. *The Impact of Science and Technology.* How scientific
   and technological development can be harnessed to enlarge the opportunities of youth, and personal freedom
   for the American people; how government may encourage scientific and technological development without
   distorting or stifling it; and the problem of social and
   political lag.

2. *National Security and Peace.* This task force explored
   the entire field of public policy as it relates to the goal
   of national survival in a world at peace.

3. *Human Rights and Needs.* The concern of this task
force ranged from civil rights to the problems of
urbanism, education, health, and social insurance.

4. *Economic Opportunity and Progress.* Avoiding radical
fluctuations in the level of economic activity, and maintaining an adequate rate of economic growth to accommodate a steadily increasing working force.

Charles Ducommun, president of Ducommun Metals, Los Angeles,
accepted the chairmanship of the first task force. Dr. Albert Jacobs,
president of Trinity College, acted as chairman of the second. The
third and fourth were headed by Bertha Adkins, under secretary of
Health, Education, and Welfare, and Dr. Gabriel Hauge, chairman
of the Finance Committee and member of the board of the Manu-
facturers Trust Company. Miss Adkins had formerly been assistant
chairman of the RNC, and Dr. Hauge had formerly been an economic
adviser to President Eisenhower.

It was a source of some amusement and satisfaction to those who
organized the Percy Committee that, within a week following the
announcement of its organization, Democratic Chairman Butler announced the establishment of the Advisory Committee on Science and
Technology to the Democratic Advisory Council. The Republicans
felt they had stolen a march on the Advisory Council, a skilled and
imaginative group.

At a conversation the day before the first formal meeting of the
Percy Committee, March 12, 1959, it became apparent that Meade
Alcorn regarded it as an opportunity for improving the Republican
image, but also as a potential source of increased factionalism, whereas
Charles Percy saw it as an opportunity to liberalize the Republican
Party. To improve the Republican image, the chief suggestion that
Mr. Percy put forward at the meeting was the desirability of adopting
a more catchy title than Republican Committee on Program and
Progress, but this suggestion was shelved for fear of giving additional
opportunity for such Democratic attacks as the brilliant lampoon
which had just appeared in the *Democratic Digest* (see p. 201).

At its full meeting Friday and Saturday, March 13 and 14, 1959,
the Program and Progress Committee heard from Alcorn, Vice-
President Nixon, congressional leaders, and from one another. Nixon
informally admonished the group that it must do more than write

an advertisement or attempt to put a new face on the same old product if it was to contribute to the nation and to the party.

Most of the advice offered by Republicans from the Hill could be summarized in the phrase, "fold up your tents and go home before you do a great deal of harm." Indeed, Senator Goldwater insisted on addressing the Percy Committee Saturday morning, March 14, at 9 A.M., with a slide presentation designed to show that, although two of the most significant Republican victories in 1958 had been his in Arizona and Governor Rockefeller's in New York, the latter really represented a Republican failure and the former constituted the Republican wave of the future.

The views of the members themselves ranged from those who wanted to create a report consisting of slogans which might almost literally be put on a post card, to those who wanted the Percy Committee to arrive at a report which would simultaneously recognize the crucial issues of the day, identify the Republican Party with concern for them, and distinguish the Republican Party from the Democratic Party.

At the Republican National Committee headquarters in Washington, a small staff was assembled for the Percy Committee. The staff collected and sent out to the task force members numerous books, articles, and government documents which might be helpful to them in their work. The headquarters staff also sent out, on Percy's behalf, over eleven thousand letters directed to college presidents; professors; community leaders; businessmen; and every 1958 Republican candidate for Congress, governor, and selected state-wide public office. These letters induced an avalanche of communications by mail and telephone and scores of personal visits. The analysis of these responses occupied the full time of two staff members for a two-month period and was made available to the full membership of the Percy Committee.

By early July the task forces had completed the drafts of their tentative reports. During the last days of April, the full Program and Progress Committee met in Highland Park, Illinois. The third and last meeting of the full Committee was to be held in Denver, July 16 to 19.

Charles Halleck atended the Highland Park meeting. Everett Dirksen was represented at that meeting, as at most task force meetings, by his assistant, Harold Rainville. This was the last meeting to be attended by the brother of Styles Bridges, Ronald Bridges, who soon was to be lost in a boating accident in Maine. Bridges was the only

Cartoon by Leo Hershfield. Reprinted with permission.

member of the Percy Committee also to have been a member of the Republican Policy Committee established by National Chairman John Hamilton in 1936.

The most influential committee member other than Charles Percy was Gabriel Hauge, former economic assistant to President Eisenhower, Harvard economics Ph.D., and former college professor. When Charles Halleck spoke, he was listened to in part because of the position which he held and in part because of the obvious quality of his comments. When Harold Rainville spoke, he was listened to with patience and sometimes tolerance because he represented Everett Dirksen. When Hauge spoke, he was listened to for what he had to say, not for the manner in which he said it and not in consequence of the position which he held.

Following the Highland Park meeting, the four task forces began preparation of their final draft reports, to be circulated to all Percy Committee members in June and to be the subject of a prolonged and concerted effort to arrive at consensus at the final meeting in Denver.

Virtually every member of the Percy Committee attended the four-day Denver meeting. At least a half-day was given to detailed discussion of each draft task force report. This was the final opportunity for each member to precipitate so clear-cut a consensus on any issue as to be reasonably certain of carrying his position into the final report. Four days and nights of talk resulted in a mandate to the chairman and staff to revise the draft reports to accord with the consensus formally recorded in the minutes of the meeting.

The final reports, printed in small type on newspaperweight paper in four pamphlets with drab covers, were released in staggered fashion over two weeks in October (the Khrushchev visit and spirit of Camp David pre-empted the month of September). The reports subsequently appeared as *Decisions for a Better America*.[6]

It is our contention in this book that the image-making activities of the two national committees are and ought to be given special importance. The work of the national committees is very largely publicity and public relations, and, however much an exercise like the Percy Committee may or may not contribute to a clarification of party policy (which is, of course, valuable in its own right), it may be justified by the kinds and amounts of media attention it creates for the party.

[6] Garden City, N.Y.: Doubleday & Co., 1960.

During 1959 press attention to the Percy Committee was not only continuous and widespread, but almost consistently friendly and positive. The composite picture which newsmen drew of the enterprise can be drawn from the press clippings: it was a goal-framing activity, undertaken at the personal behest of President Eisenhower. The Percy Committee frequently was described as a "study group." The impression was conveyed that its function was contemplative and introspective. It was concerned with the problems of the future; it was seeking to re-establish part of the past.

No systematic survey of the press response to the Percy Committee was undertaken by the Republican National Committee staff. However, a randomly assembled collection of newspaper clippings suggests that the $70,000 expenditure on the Percy Committee may have been justified on press coverage alone. Meade Alcorn's proposal of such a committee at the Des Moines meeting of the RNC in January; the announcement of the composition of the Percy Committee and appointment of its chairman in late February; the initial meeting of the Percy Committee in mid-March; successive meetings of the full Program and Progress Committee in Highland Park and Denver, coming in late April and mid-July; and finally the actual release of the reports, scattered over the month of October, 1959, punctuated the calendar year with nationwide AP and UPI wire stories and with sporadic but considerable feature and local stories.

In its March 18, 1959, issue, *Human Events*, at the conservative end of American politics, advised the Percy Committee to readopt an earlier statement of policy which proclaimed that "the major domestic issue today is liberty against socialism." Unable to satisfy the ultraconservatives, the Percy Committee was not likely to satisfy liberal Democrats either. In the *New Republic* of March 7, 1960, Gerald W. Johnson described the Percy Report as being "simply beyond criticism, as far above it as Hansel and Gretel, Cinderella, or any other first-rate fairy tale." But other columnists reviewed the Percy Committee's work sympathetically.

Doris Fleeson, in her May 4, 1959, column, announced that "G.O.P. Charts Comeback Trail." Dealing with the Highland Park meeting, she reported:

> The committee got acquainted with the new national chairman, Senator Morton of Kentucky, and listened to more college professors than most of them had seen since

their college days. The old pro touch was lent by Governor Stratton of Illinois, who dined with them Saturday night at the Percy residence.

She went on to stress the presence on the Percy Committee of the party's leaders in the Senate and House, Senator Dirksen and Representative Halleck:

> This is one of the major differences between the G.O.P. group and the Democratic Advisory Council with which it is being compared, especially now that it has so notably embraced the egghead influence. Speaker Rayburn and Senator Johnson refused to join the Democratic group, and their distaste for its free advice in party matters is extreme.

Syndicated columnists are an unmeasured but important force in the propagation of information, analyses, and views. A reader's only contact with a political enterprise like the Percy Committee may come from the reading of a newspaper column. Headlines are probably all that most readers digested of the Percy Committee's work, but they provided an important (if vague) notion of the sources and nature of the report and the problems with which a major political party must be concerned.

NATIONAL REPUBLICAN POLICY DURING THE KENNEDY YEARS

Eisenhower's concern for the image of the Republican Party led him, as we have just seen, to suggest one of the major efforts of recent times to define party creed. Interestingly, the former President's influence in his party has come to be more vigorously asserted in his retirement than it was during his White House tenure. In June, 1962, the persistence of Eisenhower's concern for party image and his tardy discovery of the Republican National Committee were signaled when a group of Republican leaders, including former Vice-President Nixon and the minority leaders of the House and Senate convened at the All Republican Conference on the Eisenhower farm at Gettysburg.

The meeting was to formalize the creation of the National Republican Citizens Committee, and it signaled Eisenhower's discovery of the Republican National Committee in that Chairman Miller not only was persuaded to go along with the All Republican Conference and Citizens Committee, but the RNC staff performed the logistical work for the Gettysburg Conference.[7]

The Gettysburg Conference was, said the unfriendly *National Review*, the embodiment of an effort upon the part of so-called liberal Republicans to take over the party.

> Where once there was only one Republican National Committee, now there are three. Where once the traditional voice of the minority party was that of its congressional leadership, now there will be a chorus of unity.

It was, said *The National Review*, the "least appealing mess of modern Republicanism since Harold Stassen last ran last."[8]

When the Republicans gathered at Gettysburg, no speaker mentioned the National Citizens Committee, but its launching was announced in the next day's *New York Herald Tribune*. Such was the clamor and furor which attended the Gettysburg meeting that Chairman Miller attempted to "clarify the situation"—a euphemistic phrase much overworked in politics.[9] In a press release of July 9, 1962, he gave the contents of a letter to all Republican National Committee members:

> It is important for all of us clearly to understand the results of the meeting at Gettysburg June 30 where the All Republican Conference held its initial organizational session.

> Members of the Executive Committee of the Republican National Committee were invited along with all our Governors, Congressional Leaders, former Administration Officials and other prominent Republicans. The sizeable turnout and the enthusiasm attending this occasion were noteworthy. It was proved there at General Eisenhower's farm that this new undertaking was very well received.

---

[7] Subsequent news stories stressed Miller's initial reluctance to "add another appendage to the Republican organization setup" and attributed his change of attitude to Eisenhower's popularity. See *Washington Star*, July 12, 1962.

[8] *National Review*, September 25, 1962.

[9] See "G.O.P. Group Clarifies Role," *Washington Star*, July 12, 1962, reporting, among other things, that Chairman Miller had given assurances that the RNCC would "not support any individual candidate for the 1964 party presidential nomination."

The result is, we now have a broadly representative group of influential Republicans eager to be of service to the Party at all levels in all parts of the country and eager to help without in any way transgressing upon the responsibilities of the Party's official leadership [N.B.]. We have here established a mechanism through which the talents of many experts may be concentrated upon current problems. This is a major achievement for our Party.

Before this meeting [N.B.] a National Republican Citizens Committee had been formed by leaders of former citizen and volunteer groups, and General Eisenhower had agreed to become its honorary chairman. Representatives of this new group were therefore included in our All Republican Conference.

All of us are of course mindful of the possibility of confusion when volunteer organizations enter the field normally occupied by full time professionals. We have dealt specifically with this problem. There is a firm agreement that the National Republican Citizens Committee will cooperate closely with established Party agencies. There is firm agreement that this new group will scrupulously avoid wasteful duplication and overlap. . . .

The NRCC shortly took offices in the Commonwealth Building in Washington—allegedly, in large part, to give the former President a worthy Washington headquarters—acquired a full-time executive director who had been in political public-relations and campaign work in California, and a budget.[10] Shortly thereafter it acquired a chairman in the person of a Chicago insurance executive, George Herrmann.[11] Its program, as announced by its executive director, Don C. Frey, in an interview with David S. Broder,

. . . is focused on overcoming the two greatest advantages Democrats normally enjoy on election day: An edge in precinct manpower and the "predisposition" of a majority of American citizens—about fifty-six per cent in most surveys—to vote Democratic.[12]

[10] *Sunday Star* (Washington), November 25, 1962.
[11] *Washington Star*, November 30, 1962.
[12] *Loc. cit.*

Since this is the campaign dogma of just about every Republican organization in Washington and undoubtedly will be the formula adopted by the presidential candidate, it is difficult to see how the new NRCC "will scrupulously avoid wasteful duplication and overlap."

The Broder story announced that the NRCC had subscriptions of "close to $100,000 from 200 contributors on its first direct appeal for support." This is a fact of political life not likely to escape the attention of the congressional party which collectively, through the Senate and the Congressional Campaign Committee, and individually must scrounge for funds for next year's campaign. And it is useful to keep in mind that for a member of the House there is always an election *next year*. Elected in November, he takes or resumes his seat in the House the next January and is up for election in November of the year beyond that. The prospect of diversion of funds undoubtedly influenced congressional attitudes toward the new committee. A UPI story carried in *The Washington Post*, July 17, 1962, stressed this concern on the part of Dirksen and Halleck:

> Top Republican congressional leaders made it clear yester-day that they do not want a newly formed "Republican Citizens Committee" siphoning off money badly needed by regular GOP organizations for campaign purposes.

The two leaders had taken the trouble to fly to Gettysburg for a two-hour session with former President Eisenhower in order to be certain their concern was understood.

The function and behavior of a volunteer organization such as the NRCC will be difficult to keep within the channels established by formal party organization.[13] Indeed, the functions and behavior of such an auxiliary group will often run athwart the mores and prac-tices of the established party organizations; otherwise there would be no reason for the existence of the auxiliary group. *The Washington Post* on July 5, 1962, quoted Eisenhower as follows:

> As for the National Republican Citizens Committee, he said it would be a meeting place for possibly hundreds of thousands of persons "who for one reason or another simply cannot or will not participate in an orthodox Republican organization."

[13] In the first year of the NRCC operation, it carefully exchanged lists of contributors with the RNC in order to avoid duplication of effort and contact.

Other stories reflected the attempt to embue the group with substantive purpose, falling short of policy-making—a thin rail for a body to walk:

The meeting, party officials say, has a twofold purpose: to establish on a permanent basis a larger forum for GOP pronouncements by forming a consultative, but not policy-making body of prominent Republicans in and out of Congress.[14]

Little wonder that the NRCC should be regarded with hostility by professional politicians ("It can drop dead," the Wisconsin national committeeman told a UPI man).[15] The Citizens Committee met in Hershey, Pennsylvania, June 16, 1963, and frustrated the best efforts of newspapermen to attribute to it a candidate-selection function.[16] At the Hershey meeting it spun off an additional organization, the twenty-three-member Critical Issues Council, headed by Milton Eisenhower. The group was heavily weighted to favor Eisenhower administration policies and included five former Eisenhower cabinet members, two top military leaders during his administration, and four of his former economic advisers.[17]

The congressional party, the traditional voice of out-party Republicanism, is not resigned to having given up this function to any presidential party volunteers. Thus, antedating the formation of the National Republican Citizens Committee were numerous congressional Republican efforts to assert and pin down the minority party policy-making role. Senators Kenneth B. Keating and Jacob K. Javits of New York competed with each other for newspaper space and influence in December, 1960, with alternative proposals for filling the Republican policy-defining lacuna to result from the coming inauguration of John F. Kennedy. Keating's proposal foreshadowed the All Republican Conference which was to meet eighteen months later. It was compared by Robert Albright of *The Washington Post* to the Democratic Advisory Council, but Keating "preferred to compare it to the so-called Percy Committee set up by Republicans to formulate party programs in advance of the Republican Convention."[18] Senator Javits suggested a Republican "shadow cabinet," quite similar to the All Republican

---

[14] *Los Angeles Times,* June 24, 1962.
[15] *New York Times,* September 2, 1962.
[16] "G.O.P. 'Citizens' Lack a Candidate," *ibid.,* June 17, 1963.
[17] *Washington Post,* August 5, 1963.
[18] *Ibid.,* December 6, 1960.

Committee in composition and purpose, but Javits emphasized that his group would operate within the framework of the Republican National Committee—a tolerant view for a senator.

At about this time House Minority Leader Halleck was emphatically expressing his understanding of where the GOP policy-making role would lie during the Kennedy administration. The responsible opposition was the congressional Republican party, and, while willing to consult in advance with "official and active Republicans" around the country, it would represent Republican policy positions during the new administration.[19] Shortly after the first anniversary of the Kennedy inauguration, the House and Senate Republicans were hard at work on a policy statement which appeared in the very month of the Gettysburg tent meeting. The report of the 1962 Joint Committee on Republican Principles was released on June 5.[20] The fact that the drafting was done largely by William B. Prendergast, research director of the RNC, who was shortly to become a staff member at the Gettysburg meeting, is indicative of the tenuous nature of coalitions in the party and the national committee's determination to keep, if possible, a finger in every pie.

In the early 1960's Republican state chairmen and governors also attempted to make their influence more keenly felt in national Republican policy. In March, 1963, Ohio Republican State Chairman Ray Bliss, considered by many of his colleagues the logical choice for national chairman (and seemingly loath to campaign for the post) convened the Republican State Chairmen's Conference in Washington. In two days of closed meetings, the chairmen heard presentations on fund-raising; the use of field men, labor and the Republican Party, and the use of party publications and surveys. The lasting results of this meeting are not yet discernible, but the Chairmen's Conference may not be dismissed as wholly ephemeral.

Finally, following the National Governors Conference in Miami in midsummer, 1963, at which meeting a political split developed on the civil rights issue, the Republican governors formed the Republican

19 "Hill Will Set GOP Policy, Halleck Says," *Washington Post*, December 7, 1960.

20 "A Declaration of Republican Principle and Policy, The Report of the 1962 Joint Committee on Republican Principles," Rep. Melvin R. Laird, chairman; Sen. Bourke B. Hickenlooper, co-chairman; William B. Prendergast, executive secretary. Members included Senators Aiken, Bennett, Morton, Keating, and Tower and Representatives Frelinghusen, Lipscomb, May, Goodell, and Bromwell.

Governors Association. Gov. Robert E. Smylie of Idaho called a meeting in Denver for September 14, 1963. The news release on the meeting was put out by the Republican National Committee, and Chairman Miller was reported to "see the Association as a promising vehicle for improving liaison between the Governors and other elements of the party."[21] The release indicated that the Governors Association would "function also as an advisory body to the National Chairman." The participation in the governors' meeting of Chairman Miller, Senate and House Campaign Chairmen Thruston Morton and Bob Wilson, and the State Chairmen's Association head, Ray Bliss, gave promise that the new group might form part of an increasingly articulated structure of Republican organizations.

It is not yet clear where the National Republican Citizens Committee fits into this cluster of Republican professionals, but it is clear that the amateurs and presidential party leaders who ran the 1952 Eisenhower campaign and the 1960 Nixon campaign will seek to extend their influence through 1964 and 1968.

[21] "GOP Governors to Meet in Denver," Republican National Committee press release, August 16, 1963.

11

The Democratic Advisory Council

Before 1956 the Democratic National Committee had no history of systematic attempts to create policy for "the Democratic Party." As one would expect, the DNC chairmanship, staff positions, and publicity organs were used from time to time in the ever-present jockeying within the party for place and preferment. Presidents, presidential hopefuls, national chairmen, and even staff officers made use of issues and policy statements to further their own programs, ideas, or electoral chances.

From 1928 to 1932, for example, the Smith-Raskob faction attempted to get DNC policy statements on tariffs and prohibition. Cordell Hull, a former chairman, opposed such exercises as *ultra vires*. The Democratic National Committee, he said, "has no authority, express or implied, to prescribe issues for the Democratic rank and file of the Nation . . . or to enunciate and proclaim any platform of principles."[1]

Despite Hull's strictures (seconded by the *public* posture of all chairmen as neutrals), the major policy impact of the two national committees has

[1] Hull, *op. cit.*, I, 142.

historically been made in this way. The committees are used as strategic devices within and among the unstable coalitions which form and reform as candidate and party leadership rivalries are played out. The national committees and the agencies of the committees are the conduits and apparatus through which administration policies, opposition policies, and party platforms get enunciated. Those who have control of national committee agencies or offices use them to further their own policy ideas or the ideas of party groups or factions to which they belong. Platforms may be heavily influenced in this way even by national committee staff members who serve the chairmen, the major prospective candidates, and the platform or resolutions committees which labor in advance of the conventions. The national committee staffs and some of the committee members are clearly in a position to make what may be called party policy, bearing in mind the limited impact of platforms alone.

These are the ways in which committee members, especially chairmen, and staff help to shape what may be loosely called party policy. They do so in the context of legislative proposals, campaign issues, publicity flourishes, and platform construction, and they do so in concert or in conflict with all others who care about policy and who have or claim the ability to influence votes. These are the ordinary, everyday, and undoubtedly the most important ways to exert influence, achieving results on policies as they are constantly made and remade.

But now and then there are organized, more-or-less systematic, more-or-less institutionalized, group attempts by national committee agencies to influence, create, or discover party policy on issues which are important or which can be made to appear important for partisan advantage.

Hard-boiled observers of American politics are likely to discount grandstand efforts by groups of politicians to create policy. They complain that only platitudes and generalizations result from such undertakings. Implied in such criticism is the thought that policy-making is at best a bootless task because the heterogeneous coalition that calls itself, at any point in time, the Democratic or the Republican Party cannot agree on anything more specific than "Americanism," or "good government"; at worst, they say, the coalition is apt to be seriously discommoded by the exposure of its policy differences.

The defense of national party policy groups comes mainly from two kinds of person. There are, first, those who care about policy because it is policy; they want to see governmental measures enacted, positions taken, and programs started, maintained, changed, or ended, and they see (perhaps with naïve simplification) a relationship between party pronouncements and governmental policy. Second, there are party leaders and workers who care about the image of the party and who see that image is associated with (though hardly the same thing as) policy stands. Image is a hard-to-define collection of public attitudes and predispositions which are critical for winning elections. Those who want to win elections (even those commonly regarded as uninterested in issues) see that policy pronouncements can have consequences for the party's image, which can in turn have consequences for victory or defeat.

Those who for tactical reasons want the party to have something called policy are likely to have little patience with ideologues and issues-oriented colleagues. The modern image-seekers deal to some extent with policy in the way of Pennsylvania boss Boies Penrose. "Senator," a cub reporter once asked him, "what do you mean when you say your platform is Americanism?" Penrose is supposed to have responded, "I don't know what it is, but it sure gets votes." Nowadays there may be a demand for policy statements more specific than Americanism, but the dynamics of party coalition-making argue for as much generalization as possible. The party thinker may want to say clearly what he has in mind; the party strategist prefers policy that leaves room for interpretation.

When systematic policy-making efforts are tried by the national committees it is inevitable that the specificity-generality conflict should arise. In addition to this are the conflicts between spokesmen for the presidential parties and those for the congressional parties, conflicts which frequently have sectional appearances in both parties (in the Democratic Party, Southern congressional leaders versus Northern presidential leaders; in the Republican Party, Midwestern congressional leaders versus Eastern presidential leaders).

The Democratic Advisory Council (DAC) was the instrument of the non-Southern presidential Democratic Party. It was the voice of the urban intellectual liberal, the creation of the friends and supporters of Adlai Stevenson. Stevenson's own continued interest and encouragement provided much of the drive for the DAC and, indirectly through his friends and acquaintances, almost all of the financial support. Thomas Finletter, a New York lawyer and former secretary of the Air Force, was perhaps the most important figure next to Stevenson in the establishment and nurturance of the Democratic Advisory Council.

The support of Chairman Butler and of former President Truman was indispensable to the creation of the DAC, and it was quick in coming when the Stevenson crowd first suggested such a group immediately after the defeat of 1956.

The idea of an advisory council to engage in policy-making is an old one at the national committees, although nothing so formal as the DAC had ever been attempted by the Democrats. There was knowledge of and some research on the earlier policy groups of the Republican National Committee.

In a more immediate sense the intellectual rationale for the DAC came from renewed interest in the idea of responsible party government, effectively brought to public attention in 1950 with the publication of the American Political Science Association report *Toward A More Responsible Two-Party System*.[2] This report suggested a number of organizational changes and innovations including a national party council of fifty members to be representative of the national committee, the congressional party organization, the state committees, the party's governors, such special party groups as the youth divisions, and persons selected from "the party following at large" (perhaps chosen by the national convention). The proposed party council thus constituted should, according to the APSA report, concern itself with

> . . . the larger problems of party management, preparation of a draft platform every four years, interpretation of the platform in the light of contemporary problems, and a gentle policing of party regularity through commentary on prospective congressional candidates and investigations of "conspicuous departures from general party decisions."[3]

An examination of the statement of purposes of the Democratic Advisory Council will reveal the influence which the APSA's report had on the creation of the DAC.[4] The Advisory Council was created

[2] Published as a supplement to the *American Political Science Review*, XLIV (September 1950). (The report was also published separately in 1950 by Rinehart and Company.)

[3] *Ibid.*, p. 43.

[4] The leaders of the DAC themselves admitted the influence of the APSA report. The executive director, Charles Tyroler II, wrote that the report "is generally believed to have furnished the framework for the Democratic Advisory Council" (letter to B. Hennessy, March 8, 1962). Chairman Butler

to be widely representative of Democratic interests and individuals, "to provide a collective voice for the Democratic Party, representing on a year-round basis the millions of Democrats who may or may not be represented in either House of the Congress."[5] The implication was that the Advisory Council represented *all* Democrats and therefore might be presumed to have special authority to speak for the party, greater authority, for example, than the Democratic members or leaders of Congress, whose constituencies were unevenly distributed over the country.

The DAC's task was to be principally one of issuing authoritative statements on matters of national and international policy. Those statements might be, in part, platform exegesis: "Our Party's platform will be our basic guide. . . ." But all matters fell within the purview of the Council:

> In new situations which may not be dealt with in our platform . . . this Advisory Council will enable our Party—on a national basis—to present new programs to meet problems which arise during the period between conventions.

In short, the Democratic Advisory Council gave itself carte blanche to issue policy statements any time it could get a nearly unanimous agreement among its members. How often it could do that and on what kinds of issues depended on the homogeneity of the views of its members.

The membership of the Advisory Council, when established, was ideologically more homogeneous than its proposers had hoped. As soon as authorization was given for the DAC, Chairman Butler sent invitations to twenty prominent Democrats representing the congressional and state leadership and at-large elements of the party. The response was not good. Of the ten congressional leaders only one— Senator Humphrey—joined at once. Three of the five senators— Lyndon Johnson of Texas, Mike Mansfield of Montana, and George Smathers of Florida—never joined at all; Sen. John F. Kennedy of

---

many times referred to the recommendations of the APSA report and in several ways attempted to implement some of these recommendations from 1954 to 1960; for a cogent discussion of this see Daniel M. Ogden, Jr., "Party Theory and Political Reality Inside the Democratic Party," paper given at the Annual Meeting of the American Political Science Association, New York, September 8–10, 1960.

[5] This quotation and the two following ones are from a Democratic National Committee press release, November 27, 1956.

Massachusetts joined much later, when the 1960 nomination contest approached and the Kennedy strategists felt the need for a liberal image. From the House were invited Speaker Rayburn, Majority Leader John McCormack, Congressional Campaign Committee Chairman Michael J. Kirwan, Chief Whip Carl Albert, and Rep. Edith Green (presumably because a woman and a Westerner); no one of these invitees joined, although Mrs. Green was disposed to join until she talked with Mr. Sam. Rayburn was adamantly opposed to the Advisory Council, more so than Senate Majority Leader Johnson.

Acceptances were received from three of the five invitees in the governors and mayors category. Governors Averell Harriman of New York and G. Mennen Williams of Michigan and Mayor Raymond Tucker of St. Louis joined promptly. Gov. Luther Hodges of North Carolina declined. Gov. Ernest McFarland of Arizona joined after a long delay but resigned within a year; Gov. Stephen McNichols of Colorado was then chosen in McFarland's place. Three of the five at-large invitees also accepted: former President Truman, titular leader Adlai Stevenson, and Sen. Estes Kefauver, the 1960 vice-presidential nominee. John Battle, former governor of Virginia, declined. Mrs. Eleanor Roosevelt declined full membership (believing that her obligations as a newspaper columnist prevented such an attachment), but, as a consultant to the Advisory Council, she became quite closely associated with its work as time went on.

Of the twenty invitees only seven joined at once as full members. Eleven refused outright. As a consequence of these refusals, the DAC had no members representing the congressional leadership. Senator Humphrey (in 1963, as assistant majority leader, still not a member of the Senate Establishment) was very much an outsider in 1956. Estes Kefauver, another Senate outsider, was given membership as the most recent vice-presidential nominee.

Southern representation was likewise scarce, consisting of only three of the fourteen members of the Democratic National Committee's Executive Committee, which constituted the ex officio members of the Advisory Council. From the South were Camille F. Gravel, Jr., national committeeman from Louisiana, and Committeewomen Mrs. Benjamin Bryan Everett of North Carolina and Mrs. Lennard Thomas of Alabama.

The proclaimed hope of the Advisory Council's founders— namely, that it would provide a widely representative leadership group and forum for policy-making—was hardly to be realized as soon as it became apparent that the congressional and Southern wings of the party would exclude themselves (except for the three uninfluential Southern members of the DNC). The liberals who created the DAC seemed genuinely to have hoped that a widely representative group could be created, but they were not especially surprised when Speaker Rayburn led the congressional party and its Southern sympathizers away from any kind of participation—even led them, from time to time, into flare-ups of public opposition. In short, the Democratic conservatives and Southern moderates refused to be associated with the Advisory Council. Their interests were not to be advanced by their becoming a permanent minority in a group led by liberals and dedicated to liberal policy.

The liberals must also have been aware that, had the conservatives joined the Advisory Council, the objective of representativeness would have been achieved, but some of the attention-getting power of the Advisory Council would probably have been lost. Only through the blandest kind of generalization can unanimity or near unanimity be achieved by a representative group of American Democratic Party leaders. But bland generalizations will not command the attention from the mass media that was, in fact, received by the DAC when it began to speak in the clever, acid, reformist language of New Deal–Fair Deal liberalism. So, in failing to achieve representativeness, the Advisory Council was able to achieve enough like-mindedness to permit the issuance of hard-hitting, reasonably specific, criticisms of the Eisenhower administration and proposals for alternative policy.

In the winter of 1959–1960, at the height of its activities during the build-up before the 1960 convention, the Democratic Advisory Council had thirty-one members. Chairman Butler and the other thirteen members of the national committee's Executive Committee constituted the ex officio nucleus of the Advisory Council. The governors of California, Colorado, Florida, Massachusetts, Michigan, Minnesota, and Pennsylvania were members, as was ex-Governor Harriman of New York. Presidential hopefuls Kennedy and Symington had by then joined fellow Senators Humphrey and Kefauver. Truman, Stevenson, and ex-Sen. Herbert Lehman continued as members, along with Mayor Tucker of St. Louis. George Harrison, president of the Railway Clerks Union, had been chosen as the union representative. Mrs. Roosevelt increased her participation, giving generously of her talents, but remained a consultant to the DAC.

From the very first, the Advisory Council established subject matter committees. These committees, consisting for the most part of persons *not* members of the DAC, served the two important functions of providing recognition for additional presidential-wing Democrats and creating quickly a large volume of what might be called raw material for policy memorandums, articles, position papers, and statements. These documents were prepared for Advisory Council approval and release or increasingly, as time went on, issued by the committees themselves "by authority of the Advisory Council."

The first two committees were the Advisory Committee on Foreign Policy, chaired by former Secretary of State Dean Acheson, and the Advisory Committee on Economic Policy, headed by J. Kenneth Galbraith, the Harvard professor. Other committees were developed as opportunity and need allowed. The growth in numbers and importance of the subject matter committees is described by Charles Tyroler, executive director of the Advisory Council:

> At the time of the original announcement of two pamphlet series, we had only two committees and it was thought that everything domestic would come under Galbraith's group, and everything foreign and military under Acheson's. As time went on and we expanded, other committees took on the task of preparing pamphlets.[6]

In addition to the Foreign Policy and Economic Policy committees, there was the Advisory Committee on Labor Policy, headed by Harrison, but never very active (it issued only one statement) although it included the heads of all the big labor unions except the Teamsters; the Committee on Science and Technology, headed by the chairman of Yale's Biophysics Department and boasting three Nobel Prize winners; the Committee on Urban and Suburban Problems, headed by Mayor Richard Lee of New Haven and including the mayors of New York, St. Paul, Philadelphia, Nashville, and South Bend, as well as assorted city planners and intellectuals. In early 1960 five more advisory committees were set up: Civil Rights, chaired by Mrs. Roosevelt; Farm Policy, chaired by Gov. Herschel Loveless of Iowa; Health Policy, under Dr. Michael DeBakey; Natural Resources, led by Oregon National Committeeman C. Girard Davidson; and Social Security, with Arthur J. Altmeyer as chairman.

The objectives of the Democratic Advisory Council and its com-

[6] Letter, March 8, 1962.

mittees were few and simple. They were interested in promoting national, liberal policies for the social problems of the day. This was the substantive end to which their activities tended. Strategically, they were concerned with the enhancement of the Democratic Party image (or that image which is national and liberal in character) and with the maintenance of a critical and relentless fighting opposition to the Eisenhower administration.

For these purposes the Advisory Council and its committees needed a good press. The strategy for a good press was likewise simple—big names talking about important matters. The typical procedure of the DAC and committees was as follows.

The DAC met as a whole two or three times a year. At these meetings it considered draft reports of its committees or of individual members of the Council, to be issued as statements of the DAC or as pamphlets of the committees. The products of Advisory Council and its committees were offered as recommendations for party or governmental policy and as general contributions to the democratic dialogue. The first of the Foreign Policy Committee pamphlets, for example, was introduced with the following note:

These pamphets are recommendations for policy, prepared under the authority and supervision of the Advisory Council. They are in furtherance of the most ancient and the most vigorous tradition of the Democratic Party—to bring about the widest discussion and understanding of public questions, and participation in forming Party Policy.

It is of some interest, reflecting the absence of complete agreement among the Advisory Council members (as one would expect), that the second pamphlet of the Foreign Policy Committee's series added this sentence to the prefatory note: "They do not necessarily reflect the precise views of all members of the Advisory Council." Committee documents were described as "prepared under the authority" of the Advisory Council; pronouncements of the whole Advisory Council were identified as statements by the Democratic Advisory Council. Members of the Advisory Council could dissent in textual notes if they desired, but the procedure was used only rarely, for the most part by the Southern members on civil rights matters.

The typical procedure for the creation of DAC or committee documents was described on the occasion of the release of a foreign policy pamphlet:

The pamphlet has been in preparation for four months. The original draft was written by Mr. Acheson. He submitted it to the members of the Advisory Committee on Foreign Policy, first by mail and then during an all-day meeting of the Committee on January 20. A revised version was then submitted to the Advisory Council, first by mail then during a two-day session of the Council in Washington on February 1 and 2. The final version was then prepared by Mr. Acheson, reflecting the discussions and suggestions.[7]

Advisory Council statements varied in subject from short topical matters—criticism of the Eisenhower space efforts at the time of the launching of the first Russian space satellite—to forty-page omnibus documents one of which ("The Democratic Task During the Next Two Years," issued December 7, 1958) was appropriately nicknamed Butler's state of the union message. The intent of the Advisory Council's managers was to keep in the forefront the political issues which they thought would produce the best pro-Democratic and anti-Republican impressions. There was a constant criticism of the Republican administration, a concentration on the promises of the 1956 Democratic platform (with some updating commentary), and an emphasis on welfare and civil rights programs which were not being stressed in Congress.

The Advisory Council and its subject matter committees published over sixty pamphlets and statements from January, 1957, to June, 1960. A few additional statements were issued by the Advisory Council's Administrative Committee consisting of Butler, Thomas K. Finletter, and former Solicitor General Philip B. Perlman (joined toward the end of the DAC's lifetime by Henry B. Fowler, a Washington lawyer and former director of the Office of Defense Management, and Charles S. Murphy, a former White House counsel under President Truman). In practice very few occasions were found to support the Republican administration, although the Advisory Council's charter statement declared, "We shall not hesitate to agree with the Republican Administration when it is right."[8] The flavor of the DAC's output may be illustrated by the following excerpt from the

[7] Democratic National Committee press release, May 26, 1958.
[8] "The Advisory Council of the Democratic National Committee: Plan of Operation," May 5, 1957, p. 2.

March, 1960, pamphlet of the Advisory Committee on Urban and Suburban Problems:

> This is the eighth and last year of the Eisenhower Administration. We must report that the President and his Administration are either uninformed or unconcerned with the mounting urban and suburban problems around them.
>
> From the lack of sympathy and concern in the White House, it seems to us quite clear that the President and his budgeteers have neither seen nor heard nor felt the plight of the 22 million American slum dwellers. And with 50 million Americans already in the suburbs and 50 million more on the way, it is folly indeed to say that suburban problems are none of the Federal government's concern.[9]

In addition to its relentless criticism of the Eisenhower administration, the Advisory Council's documents were also heavy with specific proposals. The Advisory Council's proposals were directed mainly to national policy; the DAC did little to explore three areas which Butler, in December, 1959, described as proper fields for DAC contributions and outside the scope of federal legislation: *state* legislation, party affairs, and the "development of new ideas and principles" (whatever that may have meant). DAC suggestions inevitably dealt (for those were the interests of the Democratic presidential-wing liberals) with matters in which the Democratic congressional leadership also had a vital stake. Foreign policy was proposed in considerable detail: $1,000,000,000 a year for a five-year contribution to the Development Loan Fund, for example. Domestic proposals were even more clearly and unashamedly put forward: a 5 per-cent annual growth rate for the economy; changes in the Senate rules on limiting debate, liberalization of the rules of the House; increase in the social security tax payments by .5 per cent; increase in the minimum wage to $1.25 an hour; repeal of the Taft-Hartley provisions admitting state right-to-work laws—these and many other concrete policies were urged on the Congress, the Democratic Party, and whoever cared to listen.

It is not at all surprising that the Advisory Council was in disrepute with the Democratic congressional leadership. Nor is it surprising that Butler, after one sharp and public series of disagreements

[9] "The State of Our Cities and Suburbs in a Changing America," March 1960, p. 9.

with Speaker Rayburn and Majority Leader Johnson (exacerbated by Butler's hot-tempered remark on a national television program that the Southerners should accept the majority Democrats' civil rights stands or get out of the party), had to seek a party summit meeting in Rayburn's office to smooth things over—temporarily.

As the preconvention maneuvering intensified during the spring of 1960, the Advisory Council's earlier objectives of liberal image-building and goading of the reluctant Congress were gradually displaced by the preparations for the convention and the campaign to come. The subject matter committees of the Advisory Council turned their attention more and more to the development of materials for making a platform; their reports and statements, along with testimony gathered in nearly a dozen preplatform hearings held around the country by Philip Perlman and Richard Murphy of the DNC staff, were woven into the platform as it was finally drafted under the direction of Chester Bowles. In addition, the committees of the Advisory Council provided a pool of semiorganized leaders for the special campaign committees (of businessmen, labor, farm leaders, and so on) which are thought to be necessary in a full-blown presidential campaign. Many of the members of the Advisory Council's committees were taken into the Kennedy organization, just before, during, or after the Los Angeles convention.

The Democratic Advisory Council died of uselessness at the Democratic National Convention in July of 1960. By long practice party policy during the presidential campaign is what the presidential candidate says it is; limits are placed on the candidate and his organization, of course, but the overriding interest of all party elements is in at least the appearance of harmony, and no agency with as much visibility as the Advisory Council could continue its activities unless it were wholly absorbed into the campaign organization. Elements of the Advisory Council were absorbed into the Kennedy campaign organization, as we have pointed out. In fact, a statement by the Advisory Council's Natural Resources Committee was released after the convention but with Kennedy's personal knowledge; Oregon National Committeeman Davidson, chairman of the National Resources Committee, became adviser to the Kennedy organization.

It is of some little historic interest that the convention at which the Advisory Council died was the convention which formally approved of its life. One of the little-noticed resolutions of the Los Angeles convention, by unanimous voice vote, confirmed and made official the Democratic Advisory Council. The small staff of the Advisory Council was retained until election day. The director, Charles Tyroler II, and the assistant director, Richard J. Wallace, Jr., maintained the suite in which the Advisory Council's offices had been, at 1028 Connecticut Avenue, for some time thereafter as private lobbyists under the rather grand title Counselors on National Problems.

The *de facto* demise of the DAC was noted at the Democratic National Committee meeting on January 21, 1961, and was confirmed at a March 10, 1961, harmony meeting of the DNC chairman and the leaders of the Congressional and the Senatorial Campaign Committee. Chairman Bailey declared that "the Advisory Council had 'served a function' when the party did not control the White House. Now, he asserted, 'policy should be made at the White House and by the leadership of Congress.' "[10]

Any evaluation of the Democratic Advisory Council must note that, for the national liberals who were its founders and driving force, it succeeded far beyond expectations. It constituted a voice of some volume for the presidential wing of the out-party. There was wide media attention to the Advisory Council and its committees because their pronouncements were specialized by subject and committee, supported by persons who were in themselves newsworthy—and because sharp partisan criticism has dramatic value to a press which seeks controversy before responsible commentary.

The old man of *The New York Times* Washington staff, Arthur Krock, somewhat waspishly complained that the DAC gained a

> . . . monopoly of the political publicity market . . . because the national prominence of these citizens effects widespread and generous use by the newspapers of excerpts, and often the full texts, of the long papers issued under their imprimatur.[11]

Earl Mazo called the DAC "the boldest, most imaginative and most controversial political innovation produced by a regular party organization in many years."[12] Mazo's characterization of the DAC as a "super-agency" was well beyond the mark, as was his declaration that "the

[10] John D. Morris, "Democrats End Advisory Council," *New York Times,* March 12, 1961.

[11] *New York Times,* April 14, 1959.

[12] This and the following quotation from Earl Mazo, "Democratic Advisers: 'Shadow Government,' " *New York Herald Tribune,* May 22, 1960.

Council and its committees have become, in effect, America's first 'shadow cabinet.' "

Despite Mazo's exaggeration, it is true that the Advisory Council and its committees served as a vehicle for keeping politically alive and prominent a number of former Truman administration officials and presidential-wing notables, many of whom found responsible positions in the Democratic administration after January 20, 1961. Many of these persons—Acheson, Galbraith, Bowles, Harriman, Governors Williams, Freeman, and Loveless, for example—would no doubt have become part of the Kennedy administration had the Advisory Council never existed, but the existence of such a forum helped maintain their national visibility. It is of some interest that a count in early 1962 showed thirty-four former Advisory Council and committee members to be among the administrative leaders of the New Frontier.

The Advisory Council, during out-party years, was a viable agency for the Democratic Party. The national Democrats, with their base of support in the big cities and heavily populated states, disadvantaged as they are by the structure and rules of the Congress of the United States, will support a body which speaks on issues of social welfare, civil rights, and the positive use of federal power. Money was given generously to the Advisory Council by friends of Stevenson and Finletter and was raised in special events ($100,000 in a single Birthday Dinner for Mrs. Roosevelt in New York in December, 1959). All the financing was done outside the regular channels of DNC fund-raising and was so successful that the Advisory Council from time to time actually helped the Democratic National Committee meet its payroll.

12

The National Committees and Party Government

The quest for responsible government, which permeates the literature of early American political criticism, has become in today's literature the quest for responsible *party* government.[1] The dispute as to the wisdom of permitting or encouraging parties has been swept to the ashbin of history. We are committed to the proposition that political parties are essential to the governance of free societies. The dispute today goes to the question of whether our parties can be permitted to remain overlapping kaleidoscopic amalgams of persons and ideas, diffuse and *ad hoc,* or whether they must be centralized in organization and clearly differentiated in ideas.

One camp insists that we flirt with national survival and damage our potential for achieving the objectives which as a society we pursue through government if we continue to indulge our present chaotic state of political organization. Another argues, somewhat

[1] See Austin Ranney, *The Doctrine of Responsible Party Government, Its Origins and Present State* (Urbana, Ill.: University of Illinois Press, 1954).

225

complacently perhaps, that not many basic issues divide Americans, and it little matters that it frequently is impossible to tell one party from the other. We are told that the loose nature of party organization is in character with the cultural pluralism of the United States and should be valued as such.

In his urbane study of American government and politics, Arthur N. Holcombe employs the following title for a chapter on political parties: "The Unplanned Institution of Organized Partisanship."[2] His point, of course, is that political parties not only were not anticipated by the constitutional framers as essential mechanisms of government in the United States, but that the framers thought they had built into the Constitution positive barriers against them. J. A. Smith, in *The Spirit of American Government,* has pointed out that the government established by the founders was patterned after the British government of the day, which had not yet been introduced to party responsibility and which was characterized by control by property-owning classes and by a positive distrust of party.[3]

Indeed, the very existence of party would endanger the system by resulting in the generation of pressures for expanded suffrage as the parties competed for power at the polls. Madison on faction is representative of the attitude of the framers of the Constitution:

> Among the numerous advantages promised by a well constructed Union, none deserves to be more accurately developed than its tendency to brake and control the violence of faction. The friend of popular governments never finds himself so much alarmed for their character and fate as when he contemplates their propensity to this dangerous vice.
>
> By faction, I understand a number of citizens, whether amounting to a majority or minority of the whole, who are united and actuated by some common impulse of passion, or of interest, adverse to the rights of other citizens, or to the permanent and aggregate interest of the community.[4]

It is said that the federalist system was founded on a quest for union

[2] *Our More Perfect Union* (Cambridge, Mass.: Harvard University Press, 1950), chap. IV.

[3] James A. Smith, *The Spirit of American Government* (New York: Macmillan Co., 1911).

[4] *The Federalist,* No. 10.

which fell short of unity. Tocqueville ascribes the rise of parties in the United States to a cleavage of ideas and interests, the pragmatic resolution of which was accomplished without the development of ideologically doctrinaire parties:

> When the War of Independence was terminated and the foundations of the new government were to be laid down, the Nation was divided between two opinions—two opinions which are as old as the world and which are perpetually to be met with, under different forms and various names, in all free communities, the one tending to limit, the other to extend indefinitely, the power of the people. The conflict between these two opinions never assumed that degree of violence in America which it has frequently displayed elsewhere. Both parties of the Americans were agreed upon the most essential point; and neither of them had to destroy an old Constitution or overthrow the structure of society in order to triumph.[5]

James MacGregor Burns traces from the states rightist Jefferson who purchased Louisiana and from his political protégé and successor, James Madison, two polar extremes in American politics, one identified with strong (presidential) parties, the other with weak (congressional) parties.[6] Ironically, Burns sees in Andrew Jackson the resurgence of presidential control of the party and a reassertion of strong executive leadership. Henry Adams, writing in the *North American Review* in 1869, traced to Jackson's introduction of the spoils system the abdication of the appointing power to the Congress with the resultant loss of the president's capacity to dominate his administration.[7]

This is not the forum for conclusively proving the point, but it is an appropriate place to suggest that, depending on his selectivity of action and utterance for emphasis and his political philosophy, any competent scholar can employ just about any president as an anchorman for a line of development of a strong (presidential) party or a weak (congressional) party. And if one cannot find substantiation in presidential speeches for one position or the other, he can find sub-

[5] Alexis de Tocqueville, *Democracy in America* (New York: A. A. Knopf, 1945), I, 175–176.

[6] *The Deadlock of Democracy* (Englewood Cliffs, N.J.: Prentice-Hall, Inc., 1963).

[7] Henry Adams, "Civil Service Reform," *North American Review*, CIX (1869), 443.

stantiation in presidential action for one result or another. Burns, for example, recognizes Lincoln's ambivalence concerning presidential hegemony and matches his statements as a Whig against his behavior as president. But perhaps the wartime determination to rule without a Congress he was unable to dominate contributed to subsequent congressional domination of Reconstruction policy and the splintering of his party.

American political history and political polemics have contributed more toward exposing the various facets of the problem of party than they have toward dealing effectively with the problem. What should be the power, influence, and role of political parties in our form of society? Who should speak for the party? By what right? Should there be meaningful ideological differences between the two parties, as there have been sectional differences? How and by whom should these be defined? Such is the collective ambivalence of students of politics and history on these questions that we find historians and political scientists defending the blandness of the two parties, while others attempt to polarize them. Hear Allan Nevins on this thesis, writing in 1948:

> The greatest disaster that ever befell the nation in the past resulted from a temporary division of parties along sectional lines. The worst disaster that could possibly happen to it in the near future would be a division along economic and class lines. . . . If we did have a Conservative Party of the propertied and a Radical Party of the unpropertied, we might at last be within sight of the day when the losers in an election would begin throwing up barricades in the streets.[8]

The subtitle to the Nevins article reads, "Our parties are more alike than they are different; this makes for national stability." Nevins pursues his argument further in these words:

> . . . Some critics continually repeat the question: "Why can't we have a Conservative party and a liberal party? Why can't we have parties on economic lines?
>
> Such statements ignore the cardinal utility of our two great parties. They are an amalgam, not a solvent; their

[8] "The Strength of Our Political System," *New York Times Magazine,* July 18, 1948, pp. 5, 31.

fundamental value in the United States is in pulling together an immensely varied mass of social groups, economic
constituencies, racial stocks, and local and sectional interests
for the purpose of governing by consent.

The implication is, of course, that the parties which Madison feared
have, by a supreme irony, served to ameliorate the factionalism
which he thought would be their fatal product. In a way, also, the
Nevins' thesis can be taken as a paraphrasing of Sir Henry Sumner
Maine's view that party is a vestigial remnant of the primitive com-
bativeness of man. "The best historical justification which can be
offered for it is that it has often enabled portions of the nation who
would otherwise be armed enemies, to be only factions."[9]

Political scientists have been the preponderant source of critiques
of the political system, and they have a tendency to measure its
adequacy against a somewhat idealized notion of the parliamentary
system of democracy. There is a tendency on the part of students of
government to seek institutional symmetry as they probe for a logic
in the governmental process. The quest for responsible party government has thus far been largely informed by this preference for institutional neatness.

Some have been sufficiently aware of an instinctive bias in favor
of what they have taken to be the British parliamentary model, and
sufficiently willing to advertise it, as to make open pleas for constitutional reform which would, in effect, introduce fundamental changes
based on the British and Commonwealth systems.[10] Others have called
for tinkering with the machinery of government in an effort to better
rationalize it. Thus, for example, the perennial quest of the late Senator
Kefauver for a question period in the American Congress and the
proposal of J. Steven Horn and others that the cabinet sit in Congress.[11] The main thrust of the reform movement has been directed
at so remodeling and recomposing the two major parties that they
pair off as a liberal and a conservative party, thus offering the electorate a clear-cut choice on the issues and on the candidates.

This was the quest of Paul H. Douglas when he was a University

[9] *Popular Government* (New York: Henry Holt, 1886), p. 101.
[10] See, for example, W. Y. Elliott's *The Need for Constitutional Reform*
(New York: Whittlesey House, 1935), p. 286.
[11] *The Cabinet and the Congress* (New York: Columbia University Press,
1960), p. 310.

of Chicago economics professor.[12] Douglas found that the two major parties of the day purveyed a philosophy of individualism and *laissez faire,* that they propagated the Horatio Alger myth of thrift, intelligence, and perseverance as sufficient to ensure success. They offered, said Douglas, "a strange compound of frontier traditions, the Protestant ethic, and 18th century rationalism." The two national parties were the captives of the same set of business interests. They could not be reformed from within, but must be regarded as one, and fought by a third national party which might be initially built on the non-Communist Socialist parties in those states in which they were strong. But in the United States, since the advent of the Australian ballot in the late nineteenth century, political parties have been the creatures of state law, because the states defined the conditions under which groups could gain designation on publicly printed ballots as parties. And state law consistently has defined the condition of access of new parties to the ballot in highly restrictive terms. Douglas's call for a new party was never muted and never fully realized. Even the Progressive Party, which came close to the claim of national status in 1948, could not gain access to the ballot in Douglas's state of Illinois.[13]

The difficulty of founding new national parties has forced critics of the party system to concentrate on efforts to reform the existing parties. In *The Deadlock of Democracy,* Burns suggests, in effect, that the presidential and congressional parties get together in some kind of conclave and redivide their teams, getting all of the conservatives on one and all the liberals on the other. This kind of prescription is invariably accompanied by a set of recommendations whereby the newly aligned parties can assure stable and responsible party government internally and in controlling the administration when they are in power. The national committees always figure in such recommendations, and the implication is always that the national committees are, or are capable of being, the organizational and power apex of the parties.

A committee of the American Political Science Association took stock of the condition of the American parties in a document published in 1950.[14] Enumerating the inadequacies of the existing party system, the APSA Committee pointed to the independence of state and

---

[12] *The Coming of a New Party* (New York: Whittlesey House, 1932).
[13] See *MacDougall* v. *Green,* 335 U.S. 281 (1948).
[14] *Toward A More Responsible Two-Party System, op. cit.*

national party organizations from each other and their lack of an "appreciable common approach to problems of party policy and strategy." Party leadership, said the committee, is not invested "as a whole in either a single person or a committee. There is at present no central figure or organ which could claim authority to take up party problems, policies and strategy." The national conventions were found "unwieldy, unrepresentative and less than responsible." The national committees lacked influence and were not working bodies. "House and Senate campaign committees do not always have a good working relationship with the national committee." Party platforms were found so badly defined that it was "difficult to determine what the election has decided even in broadest terms." Party membership was so elusive a concept that it hardly merited serious mention, and there was no intraparty effort to develop "a constructive relationship between the party and its members."[15] About the most positive comment the committee could bring itself to make was that "for all practical purposes the major parties monopolize elections" in the United States.

The terms in which one identifies problems are suggestive of appropriate answers to them. Yet the APSA Committee was careful to emphasize that it eschewed the notion of the existence of some prospective panacea to the problems which it defined with respect to American political parties. Its recommendations foresaw no global reform, but a series of incremental changes which might eventually have far-reaching effect. The APSA Committee called for biennial national conventions with more influence over the selection of the national committees. It noted that both national committees had come (that recently!) to appreciate "the need to maintain permanent headquarters, with staff equipped for research and publicity." While calling for a decrease in the maze of party committees which have sprung up for every jurisdiction from which a candidate can seek office, the political scientists proposed to add to the party apparatus a party council of fifty members which "should consider and settle the larger problems of party management, within limits prescribed by the national convention; propose a preliminary draft of the party platform to the national convention; . . . consider and make recommendations to appropriate party organs in respect to congressional candidates," and police state and local party organizations, making recommenda-

[15] *Ibid.*, pp. 3–4.

tions to the national convention and national committee concerning "conspicuous departures from general party decisions."[16] The party council would provide a vehicle for gathering together the congressional, state, and national elements of the party in one periodic conclave.[17] The party council would meet at least quarterly and, in presidential election years, would become a forum for the discussion of presidential candidacies. It might be an adviser to the president or to the leader of the out-party. Perhaps the most important recommendation was that "the national committee reflect the actual strength of the party within the areas they represent."[18]

Prof. Stephen K. Bailey, in *The Condition of our National Political Parties,* provided a more modest and perhaps more far-reaching set of recommendations.[19] He advised creation of permanent advisory councils to the two national committees. Further, Bailey would provide central office facilities for each national party, intermediately between the White House and Capitol Hill, "to serve as symbolic and practical links between the executive and legislative branches of government, as well as between the party and its membership across the country." These would house the national and congressional committees in addition to providing social facilities for a Republican and a Democratic club. In addition to these recommendations, Bailey, like Burns, would provide for mass-based, long-range (at least in part publicly supported) party financing and would, by constitutional amendment, bring the terms of office of president, congressmen, and senators into alignment. Bailey has recommended repeal of the Twenty-second Amendment, as does Burns, the strengthening of leadership in the Congress, and the maintenance of a "roster of talented people for the important executive posts in the national government."

We have earlier paraphrased Burns's suggestion that "the two presidential parties should join forces in Congress and elsewhere just long enough to work out the rules of the game for a fair, orderly, and competitive battle between the two national parties for the decades to come." He, too, calls for congressional reform and for election of the House, Senate and president every four years. He recognizes one of the chief impediments to the rise of a new party, as recommended by Douglas, and would transfer control of national elections to the

16 *Ibid.,* pp. 5–6.
17 *Ibid.,* p. 40.
18 *Ibid.,* p. 39.
19 New York: Fund for the Republic, 1959.

national government. Burns's reference to the national committees is parenthetical, but in the context of an assumption that they will be at the apex of the party organization in something more than an abstractly formal sense. It comes in his recommendation on party finance: "Political money in the national party should be put under the national chairman, who should be held accountable for its use. The national committee should allot money to congressional candidates much more generously than it does now." The out-party, at least, requires "a clearer voice," to be gained by a party conference equipped with money, staff, and organizational effectiveness. The party conference should be held annually, and the in-party might do well to emulate the conference technique. Finally, Burns, like most, calls for a national committee which is "a vigorous, representative body for which the national chairman could speak authoritatively in advancing and defending his party's position on quickly changing events." Recognizing, apparently, the success of Chairman William Miller in denying to Nixon the position of titular head of party, Burns would frankly acknowledge the chairman as spokesman for the out-party.[20]

SOME TENTATIVE RECOMMENDATIONS

What does our study of the national committees suggest concerning the practicality and the prospects of the prescriptions listed above?

First, America is too sprawling, too variegated, too much in conflict with itself, too free, and too ornery to be divisible into two pyramidally organized, ideological political groupings. This is offered as a truism. It may be regrettable. It may be unreasonable and inconsistent with the classification of political behaviors into rationally understandable and predictable sets. It may even be fatally defective to the system. But it is a fact. At least, our political experience and scholarship suggest to us that it is a fact.

But, though we may never have the whole rounded loaf of party government, we might have more than the quarter loaf we now enjoy.

National Committee Membership

We assume that the national committees are and should be the core agencies for whatever system of more responsible national parties may be developed in the United States. We further assume, with the

[20] *Op. cit.,* chap. 14, pp. 323–333.

Political Science Association Committee, that they should be as representative as possible of party power. *We would suggest, then, that most
serious consideration be given to the abolition of the offices of national
committeeman and national committeewoman and that the committees consist of the state chairmen and vice-chairmen of both parties.*

We recognize that we propose here a drastic break with tradition. In some states great opposition would develop to such a proposal,
but we would predict quite ready acceptance in other states. We
recognize, too, that a national committee composed of the chairman
of each state committee and a female vice-chairman of each state
committee would have less stability and greater turnover than the
present committees now have. Decreased stability is a price we would
pay for national committees which would be more representative of
real power in the states, although more mercurial because state party
power is mercurial. And we also believe that a national committee so
constituted, especially if it were further strengthened in ways we
suggest below, would aid stability in state parties, as seniority on the
national committee would bring increased influence there, to be fed
back to the state party.

We would make other suggestions with regard to national committee membership. Regular annual (and possibly semiannual) meetings should be held. No proxies should be allowed; the jobs of state
chairman and vice-chairman should not be lightly regarded or held
by persons unable or unwilling to devote to them a large share of
their time (ideally, full time). The national committees should, as a
matter of policy, pay the expenses of the members at all national
committee meetings unless reimbursement is specifically waived.

National Committee Chairmen

The national chairman of the in-party should continue to be
chosen by the president or by the presidential candidate.

*The national chairman of the out-party should be, if possible,
the titular leader. If the titular leader does not want the office or if
he loses the confidence and vote of the committee, the chairman
should be elected by the committee.* Between the national convention
and the election, during the presidential campaign, the chairman of
the out-party should be the designee of the presidential candidate,
as is currently the practice; but, if the election is lost, the chairman
should resign in favor of the titular leader or person elected by the

committee. *The chairman of the out-party should be a full-time salaried official.* (Whether the in-party chairman is full time and salaried should be at the discretion of the president.)

We well recognize the sweeping nature of our recommendations with regard to the out-party chairmanship. But greater responsibility in our national party system requires, more than anything else, greater unity in the out-party leadership, and the combination of titular leader and national chairman offers the best hope for increased unity. When the titular leader declines the chairmanship (and thereby declines to remain the *de facto,* and in some sense *de jure,* head of the party), a chairman chosen by the collective state chairmen and vice-chairmen may best serve as the chief spokesman for out-party interests.

A Party Council for the Out-Party

The out-party should have a party council, advisory to the national committee and chairman, to interpret the party platform, to recommend a platform to the national convention, and to aid the chairman and committee staff in their publicity and image-making function. The party council should be modeled on the recommendations of the APSA Committee and on such prototypes as the Democratic Advisory Council and the Republican Glenn Frank Committee of 1937–1940; it should be strongly representative of the congressional party, of governors and important local leaders, and of the major auxiliary groups and interest groups allied with the party. Strong as its membership might be in party and public circles, however, it should be solely advisory to the national committee and make only such statements and declarations as the committee (perhaps by extraordinary majorities) endorses.

Financing the National Committees

We support the recommendations of the President's Commission on Campaign Costs as far as these involve the national committees. *Specifically, we support legislation providing a tax credit for small contributions made to the national committees, or to state committees whose chairmen and vice-chairmen are recognized members of the national committees, or to other party committees approved by the national committees.*

The present experiments with small-gift fund-raising at both committees should be continued and intensified; the sustaining-membership programs, especially, are worthy of continued support. Continued reliance must also be made on large gifts and overpriced events, but the broad stability of the party apparatus as well as the gradual development of widespread public support for party financing requires emphasis on programs for recurring small contributions.

Direct federal subsidies to party and campaign costs may ultimately be required, but we would prefer to see all voluntary and indirect encouragements (such as the tax credit proposal) tried first.

National Committee Staffs and Headquarters

Each national committee should have its own building, preferably near the Capitol, which it would share with the Congressional and the Senatorial Campaign Committee. Consideration might be given to a federal one-time appropriation for the construction of such headquarters, but we would also suggest the possibility of private or nonprofit foundation financing of the capital cost of these headquarters.

Each national committee should maintain, in addition to the publicity, political organization, and special group services now offered, increased research and field staffs. There should also be provisions in each party headquarters for programs and meeting rooms for local party visitors and ordinary tourist visitors in Washington.

The above recommendations are baldly stated, for purposes of directness and, to be quite candid, in a spirit of provocation. Our knowledge and our research point us to these suggestions, but we know that others with equal or greater knowledge may find many or all of them unrealistic, naïve, or even dangerous to the body politic. Supporters of the congressional party, or of what Burns calls the Madisonian model, will be especially critical, and to them we owe another word or two.

We concede to a bias for the presidential party. Our bias runs to the presidential party and to the related concepts of party responsibility, because we think the times require greater party democracy, discipline, and responsiveness. But we recognize the traditions and the strengths of federalism, separation of powers, and social pluralism, and we promote no parliamentarianism or logic-chopping rationalism in our political system.

Additionally, we argue the position of the presidential party because our subject is the national party committees which are, in history and in functions, the electoral vehicles of the parties in their concern for the great presidential prize. Parties, we have said earlier and we here repeat, are instruments for winning elections. And we want the parties to compete effectively and responsibly for all elections, in Congress as well as for the presidency.

We do not think the congressional party or the members of Congress would fare too badly were the national committees to be changed as we suggest. Although the number of congressmen and senators now on the national committees (there are not many) might decrease if the committees were composed of state chairmen and vice-chairmen, it does not follow that congressional interests would be less well attended. Quite the contrary might result as the state chairmen were required to think more closely of national politics, institutions, and party questions. By such a change in national committee membership the members of Congress would lose none of their influence with the president and might increase such influence (especially the senators) by their relationships with and through the state party officers.

The congressional leaders and members of the out-party might often, if present trends continue, find one of their Senate numbers as titular leader and national chairman. Given a will to participate and their undoubted advantages in experience and staffing, congressional out-party leaders might have great—even controlling—influence in the party council.

Finally, a regularization and unification of party fund-raising at the national level and the close cooperation of national and congressional committee staffs should strengthen rather than weaken the prospects of effective campaign activity.

We would hope, therefore, that the recommendations we put forward here would be considered by supporters of the congressional party in the same friendly, tentative, and nondoctrinaire spirit in which they are offered.

Index

239